Hope in the Sky

Hope in the Sky

The Hunt for Who I Have Not Yet Become

A MEMOIR

Adel Ben-Harhara

with

Lorna Stuber

Volume Two — Yemen

Copyright © 2022 by Adel's Books Inc.

All rights reserved. No part of this book may be reproduced or transmitted in any form or by any means without written permission from the author.

Scripture quotations are from the *ESV® Bible (The Holy Bible, English Standard Version®)*, Copyright © 2001 by Crossway, a publishing ministry of Good News Publishers. Used by permission. All rights reserved.

Qur'anic quotations are from *The Qur'an: A New Translation by M. A. S. Abdel Haleem*, Copyright ©2005 by Oxford University Press. Used by permission. All rights reserved.

Cover design: Jana Rade

ISBN Print: 978-1-7776000-3-7
ISBN E-book: 978-1-7776000-2-0
ISBN Audiobook: 978-1-7780233-9-2

Disclaimer

Although I have made every effort to ensure that the information in this book was correct at the time of publication, I do not assume and hereby disclaim any liability to any party for any loss, damage, or disruption caused by errors or omissions, whether such errors or omissions result from negligence, accident, or any other cause.

I have tried to recreate events, locales, and conversations from my memories. To protect privacy, in some instances I have changed the names of individuals and places and some identifying characteristics and details such as dates, physical properties, occupations, and places of residence.

This book is not to be used as a religious, historical, geographical, or political reference text. The information, opinions, and details about religion, history, politics, and geography presented in this book are included for the purpose of enhancing my story only, not to teach.

The terms "South Arabian," "Arabian Peninsula," "Arabs," "Arabians," and "Arabic" are strictly referring to Yemenis and the country of Yemen only.

The term "Yemen" refers to the country after the unification of North and South Yemen in 1990.

Dedication

To my daughters, ***Lina*** and ***Summer***, for giving me a reason to live.

To the six mothers who raised me: ***Weinishet, Rukia, Emebet, Maryam, Zainab***, and ***Fatuma***. And the American mother who "adopted" me, ***Norma***.

To the men who assisted me during my time in Yemen: ***Bawazier, Al-Maqaleh, Al-Arasi, M. Hansen, R. Maddy, Al-Razahi, J. Ziegler, J. Rees***, and ***O. Bernard***.

Contents

Foreword	1
Introduction	5
Major Life Events	15
Map	17
Part One	19
I. Promised Land	21
II. Sana'a	26
III. Ta'izz	31
IV. Misfits	36
V. Mocha	42
VI. Hodeidah	47
VII. Opportunity	54
VIII. Muwalladin	58
IX. Al-Arasi	65
X. ID Card	72
XI. Marib	81
XII. My Tribe	88
XIII. Maryam	94
XIV. Sisters	102
XV. Military Service	121
XVI. Cultural Turmoil	125
XVII. Hands Off	133
XVIII. Umrah	141
XIX. Marriage Versus Education	146
XX. The American Dream	154
XXI. Western Education	162
Part Two	175
XXII. Starting Over	177
XXIII. Struggle	184

XXIV.	Coping	192
XXV.	Bookstore	200
XXVI.	Socotra	204
XXVII.	Civil War	209
XXVIII.	Newspaper Columnist	213
XXIX.	Oscar	217
XXX.	Capitalism	227
XXXI.	Arranged Marriage	232
XXXII.	Weddings	242
XXXIII.	Leaving	247

Preview of Volume One	257
Preview of Volume Three	259
Acknowledgments	261
From Lorna (Co-Author)	265
Glossary	268
Appendices	283
Appendix One	284
Appendix Two	290
Appendix Three	293
Appendix Four	294
Appendix Five	299
Bibliography	302
Endnotes	307

Foreword

During 1992, my UK-based company was closing their Houston, Texas office. As the home office in Reading, UK, was preparing to do some work in Yemen, I was offered one of the openings.

Yemen? To be honest, I'd heard of it, but that's it. Where was it?

Considering my impending divorce and the likelihood of needing "financial healing" afterward, the decision was easy. Off to Yemen I went.

The landscape reminded me of an Arizona desert. Or the moon. Barren and dusty. The people were cheerful and friendly, but it was like slipping back in time in some ways. Sometimes I would see men herding their goats through the city streets.

The company had already sent a few expats into Sana'a, the capital city of North Yemen. Most jobs had been filled by a few Brits and a couple of Americans, but primarily by English-speaking Yemenis.

My accommodations were more than adequate: a two-bedroom apartment in a large complex of buildings that also provided housing for a number of employees of yet another large oil company, this one headquartered in the US. All appliances and furniture had been imported from the US, including a TV, which had a satellite connection with several channels, many of which were English. In a way, it was almost like being at home.

Relatively speaking, our office was fairly small, so everyone knew each other. All of my coworkers were friendly, but I was particularly impressed with Adel. He and I bonded for a few good reasons. He was single, so was I. As he had received a lot of advanced education in the US, his English was damn near as good as mine!

To me, Adel was several things: my sort of personal translator, but much more, including my sometimes tour guide. Many days after work, Adel would come to my apartment, where we'd watch US (English-speaking) TV and talk about our families. I had three older boys and a soon-to-be former wife. Adel was quite "electronics smart," which meant he also fixed the things I occasionally screwed up on my TV and/or computer.

Honestly, I felt he was too smart—too talented—to be in his present job. I thought he could do so much better … somewhere else. And we often talked about that—his moving abroad for better opportunities.

We talked about Yemeni society, too. Adel taught me about the tribal structure of Yemen, the corruption in Yemeni society, and cultural aspects that I didn't know much about. He explained why the country is always in the middle of some sort of conflict—because of different tribes fighting with each other for centuries. And I was curious about the Yemeni people's fascination with and use of qat, so I asked him all about that, too.

He wasn't just computer smart; he was knowledgeable and opinionated about the discrimination and corruption in Yemeni culture, too. I thought he should share his knowledge;

I thought the Yemeni people could learn a lot from him! I encouraged him to write articles for the *Yemen Times*. And he did.

Sometimes Adel would accompany me on local sightseeing trips. Adventures. It was good to have him along, not only as an interpreter, but as a "mediator." The Yemenis didn't particularly like Americans in general. Maybe "don't trust" is a better term. Adel would let people know that I was a "nice guy," so I was allowed to take pictures, shake hands, talk to locals, etc.

On some of those trips, I also saw a lot of sad things. Poverty. Illiteracy. People living in basic conditions. The one that shook me the most was people doing electric welding using only sunglasses for shielding their eyes. Blindness was inevitable. I thought about buying many proper welding shields but was forewarned they would probably be sold to buy more essential items ... like food.

Yemen has so many nice things to enjoy such as beaches, unique landscape, culture ... history. Having said that, in the roughly eighteen months I was there, it was not advisable to travel outside of Sana'a. Thus, I heard about more than I was able to see.

In 1994, a civil war broke out in Yemen, and it became necessary for most of us expats to evacuate. After I left, I kept in touch with Adel and continued to encourage him to leave for the West. He had a tough time because of the war and because he didn't completely fit in with the lifestyle and culture. Life was unpredictable in Yemen at that time. Adel was destined for greater things than he could accomplish in Yemen. He needed to leave.

In time, things settled down a bit. Adel married and then they were expecting a child. With some difficulty, he and his wife managed to relocate to Canada. There he has experienced some good times … and, sadly, some bad times too. But I'm glad he left Yemen. I did what I could to support his move because I knew he could have a great life in Canada—a much better life than he would have had in Yemen if he'd stayed. He is smart and hardworking, and he needed to leave. Yemen didn't have opportunities for him to continue his education or to work in jobs that matched his intellect.

And now, all these years later, he's written not just one but three books! This one, Volume Two, is similar in a way to the conversations we used to have and the letters and emails we exchanged after I left Yemen. It talks about the history of Yemen. It explains the reasons for the tribal conflicts that have gone on for centuries. It has some funny stories about his experiences there. And it gives insight into why he had to leave Yemen. In this book, he is honest and straightforward about the problems in Yemen that he and others faced.

He's gone from writing scientific and political articles for the newspaper in Yemen to writing about his life so that the whole world can hear about what he's done. He's doing what I told him he should do: sharing his knowledge about Yemen and telling stories about his life—the good and the bad—with everyone so people can learn from him. He's still my smart little buddy that I used to hang out with in Sana'a.

Damn! I wish he was my neighbor again!

— Oscar Bernard, Louisiana, US

April 2022

Introduction

The lineage of my father, Majid Ahmed Hussein Sheikh Ali Ben-Harhara, stems from a group of sultans from Upper Yafa, one of the most idyllic spots in the Yafa region situated a short distance inland from the southern coast of South Yemen. Yafa is both a tribe name and a geographical area. Yafa was the center of the ancient Himyarite dynasty, which lasted from 110 BC to AD 632. (See Appendix Four for more information on Upper and Lower Yafa.)

The prefixes *Bin, Ibn, Al,* and *Ben* denote *the son of.* Therefore, when referencing members of the Harhara Dynasty, we commonly use Bin/Ben-Harhara, as a family name, which means the person named is the son of Harhara. This is similar to the Western world using last names such as Anderson (son of Ander), Peterson (son of Peter), Van Gough, (*Van* being the Dutch prefix meaning *from* or *of*) etc.

The Harhara Dynasty

Due to tribal conflicts—power struggles over control of land, food, and women—the Yafa region went through power shifts and other changes and was split into Lower and Upper Yafa in the early 1700s. The Yafa tribe in Yemen was traditionally divided into ten branches of sheikhdoms, of which five were in Lower Yafa and five in Upper Yafa. Upper Yafa was ruled by the Harhara Dynasty between 1730 and

1967. The people of Yafa are known for being religious scholars and for bravery and military capabilities.

Several sultans—Kathiri, Mahra, Qu'aiti, Hadhrami, Juban, Hawraal, and Harhara—went on to rule Hadhramaut (Yemen's largest governate) around Mukalla (the current capital city of Hadhramaut) and Al-Shihr, the city of my father's birth. As part of the Qu'aiti Sultanate, my father's great-great-grandfather moved from Yafa to Hadhramaut around 1800.

Sultans and Sheikhs

A *sultan* is a person of moral, religious, or political authority. Sultans traditionally hold positions of power such as rulers, judges, teachers, and tax collectors. The term sultan is a noble title; it was originally used to mean *strength* or *authority* but later evolved to become the noun used to refer to sovereign rulers—men who controlled large sovereign kingdoms in Arabia and therefore did not answer to any higher authority. Its use is "restricted to Muslim countries, where the title carries religious significance, contrasting the more secular *king*, which is used in both Muslim and non-Muslim countries."[1]

A *sheikh* holds a lower position than a sultan, and the term refers more specifically to the leader of a Bedouin tribe or a member of a royal family rather than a political leader in society as a whole. A sheikh may also be a religious (Muslim) man who is well versed in the teachings of Islam. Not every tribe has a sultan, but every tribe does have a sheikh. My family's tribe had both.

Introduction

A sheikh's power is social rather than political. Unlike in Canada or the US, where government officials are held to the same standard as civilians, sheikhs aren't necessarily held accountable for their actions. Civil law is not imposed on them; they are given a pass because of their standing. For example, if a traffic officer pulls over a sheikh who has committed a traffic violation, the officer will likely let the sheikh go.

Shia Versus Sunni

Zaydism is one of the Shia sects of Islam which emerged in the eighth century. Those who follow Zaydi Islam are called Zaydi Shia. About 25 percent of the Muslims in Yemen are Zaydi Shia.[2]

> The origin of Shia-Sunni relations can be traced back to a dispute over the succession to the Islamic Prophet Muhammed [peace be upon him][3] as a caliph[4] of the Islamic community. After the death of the Islamic Prophet Muhammed [pbuh] in 632, a group of Muslims, who would come to be known as the Sunnis, believed that Muhammed's successor should be Abu Bakr, whereas a second group of Muslims, who would come to be known as the Shia, believed that his successor should have been Ali [Bin Abi Tahib]. This dispute spread across various parts of the Muslim world.[5]

Abu Baker was a close friend of the Prophet Muhammed (pbuh) and his father-in-law. He was voted by the *Khalifa*[6] to be the Prophet Muhammed's (pbuh) successor. Ali was the Prophet Muhammed's (pbuh) cousin and almost like a brother. The Khalifa wanted leadership, or the State of Islam, to be led by one of their close associates and kept in the bloodline.

Approximately 90 percent of Muslims worldwide are Sunni. Although the Shia are smaller in number, they have remained strong. The Harhara family, along with other Sunni families/tribe members, have been at war with the Zaydi (Shia) tribe from North Yemen for centuries.

"Although all Muslim groups consider the Qur'an to be divine, Sunni and Shia have different opinions on Hadith."[7]

True to their reputation as brave soldiers, my ancestors often fought for power in South Yemen. Appendix Four depicts the march of Sultan Omar Ben-Saleh Ahmed Harhara to Hadhramaut, where he defeated his opponents and took control over Al-Shihr in the early 1700s.

My Father

Like many Hadhrami youth, my father left his home village (Al-Shihr) at the age of fifteen seeking a better life in Aden (South Yemen), Indonesia, British Somaliland, and Mombasa in Kenya. He served in the British Army and fought in WWII as part of the Abyssinia campaign.

My father ended his military career after WWII and embarked on owning a private business. He was one of the best-known merchants in the 1940s, in Jigjiga, Dire Dawa, and

Introduction

Harar (cities in the eastern region of Ethiopia), before moving to Addis Ababa during the early 1950s. In Jigjiga, Dire Dawa, and Harar, along with his business partner he was an import/export agent of goods and services.

When he moved to Addis Ababa, his primary business was coffee. He was considered one of the richest merchants in Addis Ababa in those days. Back then, the Arabs in Addis Ababa were divided into three groups: small shop owners; rich merchants and conservatives; and rich merchants who mingled with Europeans (Greek and Italian), East Indians living in Ethiopia, and the Ethiopian royal families. He was part of the group of wealthy merchants who mingled with others, particularly Europeans.

*

The Hadhramis (natives of Hadhramaut) are known for their integrity, loyalty, and strong sense of identity. They are also known for being what some would call frugal, and others would describe them as resourceful. Another interesting quality of Hadhramis is that no matter where they migrate to, they will always value and celebrate their origins. Roots and identity play an important part in our lives.

I'm a living example of the teachings that Hadhramis such as Bansser, Bagarsh, and Baobaid tattooed on my brain at a tender age. As explained in Volume One, these were the men/friends of my father who supported me during my childhood in Ethiopia. I lost my dad when I was five and was practically an orphan despite my biological mother being alive still now. These men were worried I would lose my way. If you've read Volume One, you know the rest is history.

About the Title

Hope in the Sky was coined as a reference to the airplane I was in, flying over the Red Sea toward Yemen, when I was sixteen. I was both smelling the sea and feeling the sky during that flight. It was my first time in a plane and my first experience being up in the air at a much higher altitude than I had previously ever imagined. I envisioned the sky as an infinite space of opportunity, an expanse full of possibility, and I pictured my soul and spirit flying through the majestic clouds toward an exciting and rewarding life. Just six years prior, I was a barefoot, homeless boy, and over a single flight, I became an astrophile!

This is it! I now have some control over my life! I'm an Arab, and I should be one good Arab, too, I said to myself. I vowed to learn more of and ultimately master the Arabic language. I always saw Arabic calligraphy as a distinct kind of art, like a drawing or painting. The writing is beautiful and is viewed by Arabs as a superior, more poetic language because of its beauty. I felt it was an honor and privilege to know how to read and write it properly.

At that time, I knew very little about the history of Yemen. But I took great pride in my Arabic language skills and especially my Arab heritage despite largely feeling disconnected to it growing up. My perception of Arabic language and culture was not an exaggeration in my mind by any means. Rather, it was born out of the oral and written history I was taught in my childhood. My Arabic teacher in Ethiopia used to show me a compilation of books listing out all the synonyms of certain words in Arabic. There was a book mentioning seventy synonyms for honey and 400 ways to describe a lion!

Introduction

I'm aware the Arabs, before the advent of Islam, were largely an illiterate society. However, oral poetry was how news was spread and stories were told. Events were commemorated through poetry. Some poets became so powerful that sometimes all it took was a single line of poetry to make a tribe lose its status. And sometimes the opposite happened. Perhaps out of this obsession, Arabs became true masters of language. I was taught that Arabs consider fluency to be the ability to express the maximum meaning in the smallest possible number of words. Arabic is a remarkable medium through which to express oneself, and I wanted badly to be part of that history!

I had learned that Yemenis are from the Arabian desert and are the root of Arab ethnicity. Arabs conquered the Middle East from the Sassanian and Byzantine empires and established a succession of Arab-Islamic Middle Eastern empires from Spain to Central Asia and from the Caucasus to India. The Queen of Sheba has been claimed by both the Ethiopian and the Yemeni people as one of them, and perhaps the dispute will never be resolved, as there is evidence of her presence in both countries.

> The story of the Queen of Sheba appears in religious texts sacred to Jews, Christians, and Muslims. Described in the Bible as simply a queen of the East, modern scholars believe she came from the Kingdom of Axum in Ethiopia, the Kingdom of Saba' in Yemen, or both.[8]

I thought she was both Ethiopian and Yemeni, just like me! Like her, I felt I had a relationship to the land of both countries.

As the airplane cut through the sky, I was busy imagining the emotional reactions of my sisters from my father's side when they would meet me for the first time—jubilation! My older brother,[9] who left Ethiopia in the late 1950s, had attended a prestigious British English school in Addis Ababa, and I was told his English was as good as that of native-speaking people. I was rehashing my English sentences so that I could impress him.

The Qur'an mentions Yemen several times. The sand dunes mentioned in 46:21 are in the region of Al-Ahqaf, in eastern Yemen.[10]

> It mentions ... the tribe of Ad:[11] "He warned his people among the sand dunes—other warners have come and gone both before and after him—'Worship no one but God: I fear for you, that you will be punished on a terrible day.'"[12]

> Also told in 27:15-44 is "the story of Suleiman ..., the Prophetic King of the Israelites, with his conquest of Saba' and the submission of the Queen of Sheba and her people, who worshiped the sun prior to their acceptance of Islam."[13]

The Prophet Muhammed (pbuh) is known to have said, "The best of men are the men of Yemen, belief is Yemeni, and I am Yemeni." His descendants, the Quraysh tribe, "are descendants of a pure Arab tribe from Yemen called the Banu Jurhum tribe. The Banu Jurham tribe emigrated to Mecca around AD 200 ... It is evident through the many Ayahs[14] and Hadiths[15] that the Yemenis have an elevated status in Islam."[16] *I'm Yemeni and I will die Yemeni*, I said to myself!

*

Part One of this volume is about my life those first several years in Yemen: finishing high school, starting my career, finding my ancestral roots, and struggling to fit into North Yemen society. I then followed my dream of obtaining a Western education and moved to the US, but after eight years, I was forced to go back to Yemen. My return to Yemen is presented in Part Two of this book, and the time I spent living and studying in the US is covered in Volume Three of my book series.

As I was traveling on that plane from Ethiopia to North Yemen, I was happy to be reconnecting to my roots and looking forward to uniting with my father's side of my family. Ahead of me were memorable visits to many beautiful Yemen cities and historical sites including Marib (the home of the Queen of Sheba) and Mocha, the origin of Arabica coffee. I was anxious to discover more about my heritage and history. The end of an era and the beginning of a new life cycle!

However, my mid-flight dream and aspiring beliefs about Yemen and being Yemeni crashed and burned shortly after I landed in Yemen! The subtitle, *The Hunt for Who I Have Not Yet Become*, sums up my time in my ancestors' land!

Major Life Events

Volume One

1962	Born in Addis Ababa, Ethiopia.
1964	Separated from my mother and started to live with my stepmother and father.
1967	My father died of cirrhosis.
1967	Began studying Judaism and Islam.
1970	My uncle squandered my father's estate and disappeared. Abandoned. Left for two years without a home or a parent.
1971	Rescued by and lived with my aunt until 1978.
1972	Attended an evangelical bible school until 1974.
1976	Arrested and detained three times throughout 1976 and 1977 for being a member of a communist party (youth branch).
1978	Moved to North Yemen.

Volume Two[1]

1978	Completed high school in Ta'izz, North Yemen, and then lived in Hodeidah, North Yemen.
1981	Moved to Sana'a, North Yemen, and started to work for US Aid Development Agency (USAID).
1981	Made frequent trips to communist South Yemen over the next three years to visit relatives.
1983	Made the Umrah pilgrimage to Mecca, Saudi Arabia.

1984	Moved to the US to study computer science and engineering.
1992	Returned to Yemen (North and South were united by this time).
1994	Survived the Yemen Civil War.
1995	Married a woman from South Yemen.

Volume Three

1985	Married an American woman to obtain US resident status. Shortly after, detained by the Immigration Naturalization Service (INS) and lost US resident and student status. (Marriage was soon annulled.)
1987	Embroiled in a six-year-long legal quagmire in a quest for political asylum in the US.
1996	Moved to Canada.
1996	My first daughter was born.
2003	My second daughter was born.
2006	Earned an MBA.
2010	Ended a fifteen-year long marriage; reunited with biological mother.
2014	Ran my first marathon, in Calgary followed by twenty-one more since then, including four of the six majors: Boston, Berlin, Chicago, and London.
2017	Climbed Mount Kilimanjaro.
2020	Visited the hottest and one of the lowest points on the planet: Danakil Depression, Dallol.
2022	Published my first three books: *To Have Nothing*, *Hope in the Sky*, and *My Silver Lining*.

Map

Map created by Janine Shum (2022). Use by permission.

Part One

I

Promised Land

When we undertake the pilgrimage, it's not just to escape the tyranny at home but also to reach to the depths of our souls. The day arrives when the guilty must return to save those who could not find the courage to leave.

— Orhan Pamuk

On Friday, January 13, 1978, I arrived at the Sana'a International Airport. My flight to Sana'a, the capital of North Yemen, from Addis Ababa, the capital of Ethiopia, was my first time on an airplane, and I vomited during takeoff and landing because of my nerves and from being over-tired. In anticipation of my move from the country of my birth, I hadn't slept much the night before.

I had a window seat and was able to view the landscape of Addis Ababa as we departed and Sana'a when we descended. As a sixteen-year-old boy who had never set foot outside of Nazreth and Addis Ababa, the cities I grew up in, I was amazed to see the differences between the two capital cities and countries. From an aerial view, Addis Ababa looked cleaner, more modern, and more orderly with many house rooftops painted red. Much of the scenery was greener than the dusty looking Sana'a that presented itself to me. Sana'a looked like more of a sandy cemetery surrounded by a few paved roads scattered about.

The flight time was around two-and-a-half hours, and we landed shortly after 2 p.m. All passengers were escorted to the entrance of the airport hall. The airport officials and guards were shouting, and I wasn't sure what the fuss was about. They weren't fighting; rather this was their way of talking: "*Yala! Yala* …!" ("Move on, move on!" or "hurry up!" or "quickly!")

In Ethiopia, I had seen Yemeni Arabs and Muslim Ethiopians chewing qat[1] in their leisure time, but I had never seen anyone chewing it during official business hours while working. The immigration officer who was checking the passports had a mouthful of qat. His cheeks were so full of the stuff he looked like a chipmunk.

He looked at my passport and landing paper. I had filled in the form with my name and relevant information in Arabic, and I had written the flight number, ET 0311, in English.

"Are you Yemeni?" the immigration officer barked at me, scowling, and mumbling through his mouthful of saliva and mashed-up qat leaves.

"Yes, and that is why I am carrying a Yemeni passport," I replied.

People always question me about my ethnicity, as I don't look like an Arab. Nor do I look the way Ethiopians think their fellow Ethiopians are supposed to look. Due to my dark skin color, hardly anyone has ever suspected that I have a drop of Arab blood in me. Most people's reaction to me is as if a German man with blue eyes and blonde hair was carrying a passport from an Asian country with a name that was obviously Asian.

I asked him why he doubted me.

"If you're an Arab and Yemeni, you shouldn't be completing the landing card in two languages! You're an Arab, and all parts of the form must be completed in Arabic!" he shouted.

I said nothing.

I had written only the flight number in English. The rest of the forms were completely filled out in Arabic, but he lost his mind over this single, miniscule detail.

"Do you have a sponsor?" he scowled and growled at me.

"Why?" I challenged him.

"You're a South Yemeni national, and you need a sponsor to enter North Yemen,"[2] he snarled.

"I have relatives waiting for me outside," I told him.

They were not relatives of mine, rather my father's friend, Bawazier.[3]

Bawazier had served in the British Army with my father in both Aden and Mombasa. After WW II, he too became a successful businessman and escaped the communist South Yemen to run an import/export business in North Yemen.

The immigration officer grunted, thrust my passport back at me, and ordered one of the airport security guards to escort me to the gate, where my relatives were waiting. He took the wind out of my sails, and I knew little about what was to come! I dreaded what might happen next.

I was under the impression that I didn't need a visa to enter North Yemen, so I assumed the folks outside, Bawazier and the others with him, knew the procedure and had any necessary sponsorship papers ready.

Bawazier's driver had parked his Mercedes Benz in front of the exit gate, and Bawazier was sitting in the back seat. He rolled down the window to greet me and asked me to enter the vehicle from the other side. I had never been inside a Mercedes Benz with leather seats. While I was amused and distracted, checking out the car, I missed Bawazier's question to me about my flight.

Another man was sitting in front on the passenger side. This man jumped out of the vehicle and handed the airport security officer YR200,[4] the equivalent of about fifty American dollars at the time, and the security guard left. While the man from the passenger seat loaded my luggage into the trunk, I asked him about the paper we were supposed to give to the officials.

"Don't worry about that," he assured me. "They only needed to get some cash for qat," he added as he got back into the vehicle.

That was the end of it. We were off.

I handed Bawazier a couple of handwritten letters that had been given to me by his and my father's mutual friends who resided in Ethiopia. He quickly opened the envelopes from Bansser and Bagarsh and started to read the letters as we drove away from the airport. After he was done reading each one, he folded it and inserted it back into the envelope it came in. He was silent in the moments between finishing one letter and beginning the next.

Once he had gone through all of the correspondence, he glanced at me and said, "The last time I saw you was in 1965, and you were only three years old. You're so tiny. How come you didn't grow tall like your father?"

I didn't respond to his question, but I asked him why these people, North Yemenis, spoke differently than the Yemeni Arabs I was used to.

He said, "They are *Shemalin*."[5] He added, "We speak Yemeni-Hadhrami, but they have their own dialect of Arabic."

"I don't understand a word they are saying," I told him.

"Son, I have been here for several years, and I often don't understand them either," he assured me.

He added, "Yemen has one of the most varied landscapes in the entire Middle East. The scenery is often breathtaking. As a developing country, however, Yemen offers many opportunities and challenges, and the lifestyle can be relaxed. And it's definitely different from East African countries or India or Indonesia, where I have been in the past. Did you know that, as a young man, your father lived in Indonesia, too?" he asked.

"No, I didn't know that," I replied. "Do you live here?"

"No. I live in Hodeidah, a port city on the shore of the Red Sea, about 224 kilometers (139 miles) west from here. That is where my office is. My family resides in Ta'izz, about 260 kilometers (161 miles) south from Sana'a. I came to Sana'a to pick you up and address a couple business matters," he answered.

II

Sana'a

Everyone has something ancestral, even if it is nothing more than a disease.

— Edgar Watson Howe

Sana'a is the oldest city in the Arabian Peninsula and perhaps in the world, too. While the view of the city from the sky more or less looked like a large cemetery in the desert, the reality from the ground was totally different. As we were driven to the city center, I noticed the streets were teeming with people, and perhaps 90 percent of them were men. The men were wearing typical North Yemen garb: a long dress-like caftan with puffed sleeves. A richly decorated dagger was thrust into their wide embroidered belts at the front. Hadhrami don't wear the dagger; maybe it is not part of the culture, or perhaps due to British influence they are not allowed to, but men from North Yemen wear it.

I noticed multiple other details that were new or foreign to me. I didn't see any wooden doors. All doors were made of metal with iron gates. Nearly everyone wore the same type of shoes: brown, leather-looking, slip-on shoes (no laces).

Both women and men wore these shoes, which had a bit of stretch to them. Despite the stretch, many people wore the wrong size because the shoes were rationed by the Russians or some other country supplying goods to Yemen.

Every street had shops. All shops' signs were in Arabic, and a few had both English and Arabic. Those written in English had plenty of typos. Nearly every shop had a Yemeni flag and a picture of the president. And it was hard to tell apart the residential and business areas; shops and homes were all mixed together.

There were also many brand new cars and makes of cars that I didn't see in Addis Ababa. Plenty of taxis were on the streets, and they were covered with dust. But no public transit bus was anywhere to be found.

The house I was taken to was adjacent to a mosque. When the call for prayer was announced around 5:50 p.m., roughly thirty minutes after I arrived from the airport, it made me jump out of my seat. I thought someone was screaming at me through a megaphone a couple inches from my ears. The head of the family I was staying with immediately asked me to clean myself up and join the men for prayer. I hadn't prayed in years and didn't even recall all the Qur'anic citations that are required during a prayer, but I joined in. All I needed to do was say "Allahu Akbar"[1] and follow the rhythm.

On the same day, I wrote a letter to my aunt and uncle in Ethiopia stating I was unable to tell heads from tails when it came to the religion.

*

The family Bawazier took me to stay with upon my arrival had lived in Ethiopia during the 1950s and 1960s. They spoke some Amharic and managed to greet me well. After I spent one night in Sana'a, the same driver took Bawazier and me to the second largest city, Ta'izz.

Bawazier had arranged for me to stay with family members and friends he knew in Ta'izz. When I asked him why I was staying there with them, he said, "Son, the people in Sana'a are a bit primitive, and it will be difficult for you to get used to their way of living. The people of Ta'izz are much easier to get along with, and you should also be able to easily finish your schooling there."

"You guys immigrated to many parts of the world and worked with all sorts of people and communities. How hard would it be to live with North Yemenis from the Sana'a area?" I asked.

He looked into my eyes and said, "The North Yemenis, in particular the people of Sana'a, are different types of creatures. They have been locked down in their own world for centuries, with inadequate understanding of how the rest of the world is operating. That is not to say they are bad people, but they still require ages to catch up with the rest of civil human societies. Tai'zz, Aden, Mocha, and Hodeidah have all been exposed to international travelers, but because Sana'a is in the middle of the rugged mountains, far from the coastal regions, it is more isolated. Therefore, the people in Sana'a have not been exposed to outsiders."

He added, "Sana'a, or a good portion of North Yemen, was locked in time and almost lost at the southern end of Arabian Peninsula. It remains a mystery to many of us. For almost all of the twentieth century, it has remained essentially closed to most outsiders. First, it was locked down and isolated by the Ottoman Turks, and then by a succession of Zaydi imams who created a theocratic state that cut itself off from the world."

He continued, "Only less than two decades ago, in 1962, North Yemen emerged violently into the twentieth century. Just remember, despite all the things you will see here that you may not like or appreciate, this is the land of the Queen of Sheba. It's a nation that proudly traces its civilization back 6,000 years and considers the founder of its capital city, Sana'a, to be Shem, son of Noah. Ancient Yemenis built skyscrapers ten stories high, and Yemen has the Arab world's mightiest dams. Later with the Hadhramaut merchants, Yemen prospered, as they supplied Mediterranean markets with spices, incense, and other treasures from the East."

I said, "That was plenty of history that I was not aware of."

He replied, "I heard, instead of learning your own ancestral history, you have been too busy reading those stupid Marxist books, and you were also jailed. You need to know your history. In time, trade routes shifted, and the glory of the Yemeni rulers waned. All the same, the cities, magnificent terraced mountains fields, gardens, and dynamic villages remain frozen as they were back in the fifteenth century."

That summed up everything I needed to know and shaped my expectations of North Yemen from day one!

He added, "It's better for you to live in Ta'izz because I hardly come to Sana'a, but I drive to Ta'izz from Hodeidah a couple times in a month to be with my family. If you are in Ta'izz, I will be able to check on how you're doing. You're our son. Your father was a dear friend of mine. A very good man. And I hope you turn out to be like him."

In those days, words from an elderly person, in particular from my father's friend, were taken as the gospel. Based on his commentary, I instantly developed a distaste for Sana'a and its people without even knowing them. Perhaps we are all born to love but taught to despise!

Bawazier handed me his office phone numbers and address along with some cash to use as pocket money and told me to phone him if I needed any help or ran into troubles. He also told me he would return to Ta'izz in a couple weeks to see his family and me.

Welcome to the city of culture—Ta'izz!

III

Ta'izz

We went on ... to the town of Ta'izz, the capital of the king of Yemen, and one of the finest and largest towns in that country. Its people are overbearing, insolent, and rude, as is generally the case in towns where kings reside. Ta'izz is made up of three quarters; the first is the residence of the king and his court, the second, called 'Udayna, is the military station, and the third, called Al-Mahálib, is inhabited by the commonalty and contains the principal market.

— Ibn Battúta, *Travels in Asia and Africa*

Ta'izz, the third largest city in Yemen according to 2005 figures, is located in the Yemeni Highlands in southwestern Yemen near the port city of Mocha on the Red Sea. It is the capital of the Ta'izz Governorate, one of the twenty-one governorates that Yemen is divided into.[1] "Ta'izz has a very different feel from other North Yemeni cities and Ta'izians are in general regarded to be more relaxed and laid back by nature"[2] than other North Yemenis. It was long known as the cultural capital of North Yemen; however, because of the ongoing campaign as part of Yemen's recent civil war, it has become a battleground and a war zone and is known these days as the city of snipers.[3]

The people in Ta'izz spoke a different dialect of Arabic than the residents of Sana'a. I didn't understand most of the words spoken in the capital, but I had a much easier time understanding the Arabic spoken in Ta'izz. Many of the male residents of Ta'izz wore trousers rather than caftans. A few spoke some English, and many happened to have previously lived in Aden, South Yemen.

School hadn't started yet when I arrived, but in the first several days while I was out and about on the street exploring and shopping, I was able to make friends with other teenage boys who were living in my area. Some of them had either lived in or been born in Ethiopia. They immediately detected my Arabic accent as being different from that of the locals and were eager to introduce me to other children and teenagers who had come from Ethiopia. Some had come to Yemen a year or two prior to my arrival, but most of them had left Ethiopia much earlier and at a younger age, so they didn't speak Amharic well.

I also interacted with children who had previously lived in Kenya, Tanzania, and Sudan. Among them was a boy named Haron Baharon and his brothers. Coincidently, their uncle was also one of my father's best friends. Their older brother, Hussein Baharon, played soccer in the Yemeni league, as he had done in Ethiopia playing for the Saint George Sports Club team.

Making friends didn't require too much time or effort as we had common backgrounds, so the bonding took place overnight. We spoke in mixed and multiple languages, ventured out to cinemas, and attended a few football (soccer) matches together. A couple of boys told me that they could take me to a zoo to show me a lion that had been given to the King of Yemen by the Ethiopian king, Emperor Haile Selassie.

When schools opened, I went to register so that I could complete my high school education. I had arrived from Ethiopia with a grade ten school certificate, but I was given an evaluation exam to determine where I would fit in the North Yemen schooling system. The exam was in Arabic, and I scored poorly. Yes, I had studied the Arabic language as a child, perhaps up to a grade four level (at most), but the amount of religious material covered on the entrance exams was beyond my comprehension. Even though I scored in the upper 90 percent in English, science, and math, my Arabic language skills were too poor to even grasp the questions on the remaining subjects. As a result, I was told to start at the grade four or five level. I refused!

My other option was to attend a private English school called Mohammed Ali Othman School (MAO). It was one of the best schools in North Yemen. The coeducational MAO was established in 1972 to provide an international education in English for the local community. The MAO followed a British curriculum in the core subjects and the Yemeni Ministry curriculum in religious studies.

This school was an expensive choice for me, as it was an institute the children of rich merchants or government officials attended.

I phoned Bawazier to let him know the outcome of the school evaluation results. He told me that he had kind of suspected I wouldn't do well. "The language will be problematic for you," he warned me, and he requested that I stay put for a couple of days until he got back to me with a solution.

After consulting with the Mekaleh family, Bawazier offered to cover the cost of the private school for me. Mekaleh was a man who was working as a subcontractor providing custom clearance services for Bawazier and other merchants at the Hodeidah port. He didn't know my father, but he too had once lived in Ethiopia, and that was a good enough reason for me to establish a trusted connection with him. Mekaleh had two twin younger brothers, who were the same age as I was and who were attending school in Ta'izz. Mekaleh and Bawazier arranged for me to live with the twin boys. The two men sent the three of us around YR2,000 a month, the equivalent of US$500, to cover living expenses. In return, I would help the twins with English, science, and math lessons. Since they had grown up in Yemen, the twins' academic skills weren't as developed as mine. On the other hand, since they only spoke Arabic, the living arrangement would help my Arabic language skills quickly improve.

In addition, I was to assist Bawazier's family in Ta'izz. Bawazier had four daughters who lived in the city with their mother. He arranged that I provide the women help, as needed, after my school day was over. In Yemen, women from a typical well-to-do family didn't go grocery shopping. Instead, a servant or a trusted family member like a brother, husband, or uncle performed those duties. My job was to swing by their house, take their orders, pick up the necessary items, and deliver the groceries to their house. This was done on a daily basis during the months when Bawazier was away from the city on business trips. Unlike when I was initially living with my aunt in Addis Ababa, I had agreed to this arrangement, and my helping out was more of a courtesy than a forced duty. On occasions when Bawazier was around, my help wasn't needed.

The routine was set every day. The Mekaleh twins and I got up early in the morning and fetched breakfast (mainly eggs and beans) and tea, which was mixed with evaporated milk. After school, we stopped at a Yemeni-Vietnamese restaurant for something to eat. We called it a Vietnamese restaurant even though the food wasn't authentic. As is the case in Asian restaurants in Canada, the US, or elsewhere, the food served in the restaurant wasn't necessarily the same as what people cooked and ate at home in those cultures, but we enjoyed going there for a few reasons. The restaurant was cleaner and the meals were fancier than what we could get at a typical North Yemeni restaurant. The way the Vietnamese people cooked their food was different, so we enjoyed trying something more exotic. For example, the chicken was fried, compared to how North Yemeni people ate chicken, which was more often in a stew with bread. We felt like nobility eating something we would not get at home. The other reason we enjoyed going there was purely carnal. The girls working in the Vietnamese restaurant didn't cover their hair like Yemeni girls did, so we boys enjoyed going there to look at them.

IV

Misfits

Everything in the universe has a purpose. There are no misfits, there are no freaks, there are no accidents. There are only things we don't understand.

— Marlo Morgan

During the Vietnam War, and particularly after the fall of Saigon in 1975, thousands of Yemeni-Vietnamese migrated to North Yemen. Many were of Yemeni ancestry or were wives of Vietnamese men who could trace their origins back several generations to North Yemen. Initially, nearly all of them settled primarily in Ta'izz, as it was the only city that had direct flights to Vietnam.

There were, however, multiple cultural conflicts between the locals and the Yemeni-Vietnamese. For starters, the Yemeni-Vietnamese weren't nearly as conservative in their Muslim practices as those native to Sana'a and Ta'izz at that time. The women didn't cover themselves completely as North Yemeni women did, and their clothing was more modern. As a result, North Yemeni men perceived them as being more "available" than the local women.

They also lived in clusters in the cities they had relocated to. The small communities they formed within cities only served to further segregate them from the rest of the population thereby increasing the chasm between the two cultures.

When I was taking an evaluation exam for school, there were many Yemeni-Vietnamese children lined up with me in the hallway to take the same exams. I ended up befriending a couple of them. At that time, many of the Vietnamese children who were attending Arabic school left one by one because they didn't have the language skills needed to understand the teachers.

Jamal was one of my Yemeni-Vietnamese friends. His mother spoke French and had found a job in a local branch of a French bank despite her lack of Arabic. With the money she earned, she was able to send her two children to the same private school in Ta'izz that I was attending. There, Jamal and his sister learned Arabic and English. Each child's tuition was more than US$1,200 a year, but a rich Yemeni merchant, who gave scholarships to help members of the Yemeni-Vietnamese community, paid all but US$100 per child for Jamal's and his sister's tuitions.

Jamal's father said of his days living in Vietnam that he became frightened when the Vietnamese communist authorities began a review of citizens' identity papers to trace their past because he had previously been an agent of the French intelligence service. I drew parallels between his father's situation and my past in Ethiopia. It reminded me of the harassment, imprisonments, and executions I witnessed in Ethiopia while I was a member of the Marxist party youth branch. In fact, the struggles and overall situation of most of the Yemeni-Vietnamese immigrants resonated with me deeply. And in a sense, those of us who came from East Africa were much closer to the Yemeni traditions and customs than the Yemeni-Vietnamese were.

Jamal and I joked and laughed about North Yemenis' primitive lifestyles and ways of thinking. Often, we wondered how they managed to leave their respective villages, travel abroad, and assimilate into other societies because they were so disconnected to the rest of the world intellectually and culturally. He told me how his grandfather, who had left North Yemeni in the 1950s, used to tell him stories about North Yemen. Jamal was just now realizing how his grandfather had lied to him and his father about how green, prosperous, and beautiful North Yemen was. When Jamal came to North Yemen and saw the cities and countryside, the reality did not at all fit the image he had had. The people were unpleasant, racist, and dishonest. Sometimes we were ashamed to call ourselves North Yemenis.

He and I talked a lot about the Vietnam War, the revolution in Ethiopia, and our childhood days. We both came from countries where communism had ravaged the equilibrium of society. Neither of us had ever imagined or dreamed of coming to North Yemen; the socialist governments in the countries of our births forced us to do so.

There were some differences in our views, though. I was partially sympathetic with Marxist ideas, but he wasn't. I told him that when I was fifteen, Ho Chi Minh was my hero just like Che Guevara was. Although Jamal admired some of Ho Chi Minh's achievements, he was not fond of the leader or his policies. On the other hand, Jamal didn't think the Americans were taking the right approach in Vietnam, either.

I wanted to go to the UK or US to earn a higher education, but Jamal did not. He wanted to return to Vietnam or anywhere else in Southeast Asia. Despite being half Yemeni, he looked Vietnamese, and he saw no future for himself in North Yemen. He had no intention of attempting to assimilate into North Yemeni society.

The other significant difference between my friend and me was that I grew up without a father or a mother, but he had both his parents and a younger sister. I was often invited to their house for meals. His mother spoke no Arabic at all, but she was a good cook and a gracious host, and they always had a nice variety of food. Jamal's younger sister, Jamila, was around twelve when their family moved to North Yemen. She had been attending school, but soon, by age thirteen, she had to quit and stay home. She was simply unable to cope with the harassment she was receiving from school kids and the teacher—typical schoolyard taunting such as having her hair pulled, being poked or pushed around, receiving racial insults and goading such as, "How come you don't know Arabic?" I was the only non-Vietnamese person to ever visit their house.

There was a rumor in the city at that time that the Yemeni-Vietnamese ate dogs. I didn't dare pose this question to Jamal, but I thought of asking Jamila. Since she was younger, I thought she might tell me the truth. I asked her if the rumor was true.

She paused for a moment and said, "Yes, we do eat dog." She immediately added, "I also heard Ethiopians eat humans."

I shouted, "No!" smacking my forehead with my palm and vigorously shaking my head. I pressed her to tell me where she had heard such a horrible story. "Just in the way you assumed we eat dogs, I made up a story about you, too. What made you think we eat dogs?" she asked.

"I heard it from different people."

"That is not true," she told me.

With that brief exchange, this young girl taught me a vital lesson about not making assumptions or believing rumors or stereotypes without verification.

*

On weekends, Jamal, and I would travel to the city of Ibb, about sixty-five kilometers (forty miles) east of Ta'izz. Ibb was developed during the Ottoman Empire, and it remains one of the most important cities in the country.[1] The Mekaleh boys I lived with were from the Ibb area, and they encouraged us to visit Ibb and the surrounding areas.

> Ibb has been occupied since ancient times, and due to its strategical importance, the Ottomans used it as an administrative center. It thrived as a market town and the Ottomans established the Wednesday market in Ibb. At times in its history, many people have migrated to Ibb from areas of North Yemen that had been experiencing drought to find work in farming. [2]

Ibb is one of the most scenic places in North Yemen and perhaps in both South and North Yemen combined. It is surrounded by picturesque mountains and is known as the green city. When I first visited, I was fortunate that we had gone during one of the greenest periods of the year, which comes after the land is blessed with abundant rains. Both Jamal and I felt nostalgic about Vietnam and Ethiopia, as Ibb reminded us of the lush landscapes we missed. Our weekends always started with a cup of coffee on the rooftop of the hotel where we were staying, talking, reminiscing about our homelands, and breathing in the fresh wind blowing from the mountains.[3] We enjoyed our visits to Ibb as it was beautiful, and the local people were polite.

After high school, once I moved to Hodeidah and then to the capital city Sana'a, I unfortunately lost touch with Jamal and his family.

V

Mocha

First you buy me a mocha. Then you let me help you hide a body. Now you take me to a biker clubhouse. Best. Day. Ever.

— Kelley Armstrong, Canadian writer, 1968

From 1978 to 1980, between the ages of sixteen and eighteen, while I was in high school and still living in Ta'izz, I was able to travel many times and spend a considerable amount of time visiting the port city Mocha. Bawazier's office was in Hodeidah, and Mocha was not far from there (less than 200 kilometers or 120 miles), so I was able to visit easily, and it was particularly enjoyable during the winters when the temperature cooled off. Mocha was a place where I felt safe.

The time I spent in Mocha was when I started to examine, reflect on, and ask about my childhood. It was when I was transitioning from boyhood to adulthood. It was when I had to calmly think about many aspects in my life—where I had come from and where I was going. And it was also when I was happy for the first time in my life!

Mocha, or in Arabic, *Al-Mukha*, is on the Red Sea coast of Yemen. Until the nineteenth century, when Aden and Hodeidah gained greater significance, Mocha was the main port for North Yemen, relying heavily on the coffee bean trade. I have always been amazed at how many people in the world think that Mocha is only coffee rather than a place. There seems to be a lack of awareness of the link between this port city and the coffee itself.

As a young boy, I had read about Mocha in my school textbooks and always wanted to visit it. There was also some personal connection for me, as I had once heard a story about my father briefly being incarcerated in this city in the 1930s. I don't recall much of the story, but I understand he was helping the British gather intelligence, possibly against the Germans, so the North Yemen king or the Turks detained him for a time.

Mocha, as its name suggests, was best known between the fifteenth and eighteenth centuries as the major marketplace for coffee (Arabica). Up until the early nineteenth century, the British, Dutch, and French maintained factories there due to the thriving coffee industry.[1] Still now, mocha beans are desirable because of their distinctive earthy, chocolaty flavors, even after other coffee beans have become popular and well-known. The beans themselves are not grown in Mocha, but they are transported to its port from coffee plantations in the interior mountain regions and then shipped abroad.[2] "Mocha's coffee legacy is reflected in the name of the mocha latte and the Moka pot coffee maker."[3]

Those days, the city's economy was based on fishing and tourism, as it was no longer used as a major trading port.[4] Later, I concluded that the reason some North Yemenis hung around in the area was that there was access to alcohol because the area was known for transporting liquors to Saudi Arabia. Because Mocha was one of the main international ports for trade, smugglers would bring alcohol from Europe, India, or elsewhere, into North Yemen. My friends and I stumbled upon shops involved in bootlegging the alcohol, selling it to cities in the interior of North Yemen and to Saudi Arabia.

No special experiences or events happened in Mocha. Rather, it was a destination for a bunch of teenagers who decided to drive somewhere relaxing and spend time doing nothing. Perhaps it was the happiest and most peaceful period of my time in North Yemen. We all felt free and able to just be. We spent most of our days swimming, playing soccer, collecting seashells, and running around.

One early evening, an older teenager who was about nineteen, swam from one end of the Red Sea to the other, about one kilometer (0.6 miles). Upon exiting the water and coming onto the shore, he looked at me and told me to walk one kilometer to bring his T-shirt and his change of clothing. Apparently, he was too tired and lazy to go and get it himself. I refused his request. He tried to intimidate me by raising his voice and ordering me again to get his clothing for him. Again, I refused, and I didn't even show him the slightest respect; I wasn't looking at his face when he spoke to me. He was furious that such a skinny boy would refuse to adhere to his order.

He then grabbed me by my hair and dragged me to the sea. I struggled to free myself, but he overpowered me. He pushed my head deep into the water.

Why is he targeting me?

I felt helpless, terrified, confused ….

I'm going to die! I'm going to die! Is this what death is like? I thought. *I can't breathe ….*

I thrashed about until I became unconscious. At that point, he left me to die face down.

I wasn't moving. My friends, who were not too far from us and who didn't know what had triggered the fight, rushed to rescue me. I don't recall beyond the moment I started to swallow the salty sea water while he was pushing my head down. My friends managed to get the water out of my system, but I was sick and had to miss school for a couple of weeks. For two weeks I couldn't eat; anything I tried to eat came back up immediately. I was passing out, getting headaches, and experiencing a combination of physical and mental pain. I had recurring nightmares, and the more school I missed, the more I worried about getting behind in my studies.

The older boy who did this to me just disappeared. I could have died and no one would have known who he was.

Even though the incident never stopped me from heading to the sea, I never swam again. In fact, to this day, I can only shower. I get panicked if I try to take a bath or if I'm in any other situation where the water reaches as high as my chest and neck. I do cautiously enter shallow water, but if the water reaches my chest or neck, it feels like someone is trying to choke me. My daughters, at times, have tried to drag me into deeper water and always laugh at me when I spring out of a swimming pool or jacuzzi; they don't realize how traumatized I still am from that incident.

My love for the image of the ocean, sea, and water in general, though, was formed long before this incident, during the time I spent at Mocha. In spite of this event, I always felt free, happy, and limitless when I ran around on the banks of the Red Sea. When I go to Hawaii, Aden, Al-Shihr, or any city with access to the ocean, huge lakes, or the sea, I get lost in watching the waves.

As teenagers in Mocha, we rented boats and sailed, and we often joined the local fishermen to fish. Perhaps I enjoyed those experiences even more than I enjoy hiking in Alberta these days. That period of my life holds special memories without any significant event … simply, the happiest moments of my life in North Yemen were in the Mocha and Hodeidah areas. The city of Ibb was green and reminded us of the places we grew up, but Mocha gave us a different dimension and perhaps hope.

VI

Hodeidah

By doing, you become employable. It doesn't matter what the job is; by working, you learn new things, meet new people, and are exposed to new ideas.

— Kate Reardon

I completed high school in spring 1980 and wrote the General Certificate of Education (GCE) exam[1] in the same year. Perhaps due to the British colonial influence, the school system throughout all of Yemen was based on the British system at that time. The true measure of completing high school was to take the standard GCE exam.

After high school, during the summer of 1980, I moved to Hodeidah and started to work at Bawazier's import/export business. I was hired to assist two men, an Indian named Ingy and an Egyptian named Al-Shenawi. Ingy oversaw the communication aspects of the business, handling all telegrams, telexes, commercial letters, and relationships with the banks. Bawazier imported goods from Asia and East Africa. At the office, Ingy typed up letters to export agents in

East Asia and Africa to request samples and pricing. He sent telex messages just like we do in the modern days of faxes and emails. Al-Shenawi was an accountant who kept the books and handled all financial transactions from his desk. He never left the office. During this period, I took bookkeeping and accounting courses from the UK via correspondence.

*

Hodeidah sits on the banks of the Red Sea and has been an important port city for centuries. It gained importance as a center for trade when the Ottomans took control over North Yemen in the 1520s. It was turned over to the North Yemeni imam family in 1849 after being controlled by Turkish troops in the 1830s. The handover made it officially a part of North Yemen.[2]

Over the centuries, Hodeidah gained its significance, eventually replacing Mocha as North Yemen's main seaport.[3] It remains the main port for the majority of North Yemen's commercial imports and its exports of coffee, cotton, dates, and hides.[4] Much of the city was destroyed by a fire in January 1961, and it was quickly rebuilt with help from the former Soviet Union. "A highway to Sana'a, the capital, was completed in 1961. The city was also the site of a Soviet naval base in the 1970s and 1980s."[5]

*

Bawazier was clear with his instructions to me. I was to shadow these two individuals—the Indian and Egyptian men—and learn everything I could from them. My impression of Al-Shenawi was of someone who was preoccupied with his appearance, particularly his clothing, and his role in the office. He liked to be called the office manager, and he loved history. Whenever he spoke, he mentioned the history of Egypt and the Egyptian contribution to the Arab world in general and specifically North Yemen. He always said, "Egypt is a mother of the world," or in Arabic, *Misr Umm Al-Dunya*. Unlike Ingy, Al-Shenawi was always eager to teach me anything I asked about. Most of our conversations focused on the history of Arab civilization. He was passionate about the 1973 Egypt Israeli war,[6] as he had served in the military. Because of him, I started to listen to and grew to love Arabic and Egyptian songs. Among the singers we continually listened to in the office were Umm Kulthum, Abdel Halim Hafez, Farid Al-Atrash, and Warda Al-Jazairia. I was interested in Abdel Halim Hafez's songs more so than the rest, though. His songs were sad, personal, melancholy, and meaningful. I found his melodies calming and soothing.

I knew a thing or two about Gamal Abdel Nasser, the president of Egypt from 1954 to 1970, and I grew to respect and admire him more because of the conversations I had with Al-Shenawi and the literature I read.

Ingy was all about saving money. He couldn't care less about wearing shirts that were purchased decades ago, as long as they were washed and ironed—he always wore perfectly ironed shirts. He was also protective of and very insecure about his job and was never willing to share with me his job skills or tricks as he felt I was a threat. His command of English was superior, and he believed the British Empire was the best. Al-Shenawi and Ingy continually argued about the British colony, which Al-Shenawi hated.

During the workdays, Saturday to Thursday, Ingy took me to the bank to deposit cash and checks from the previous day's transactions. Before dashing out to the bank, he meticulously sorted the currency notes in the order of 100s, 50s, 20s, 10s, 5s, and 1s. Then he counted each note and wrote down how many bills there were, along with the total value, and wrapped them up with rubber bands. Next, he sorted the checks by the banks' names. There were three banks: French, British, and National. Checks had to be deposited to whichever bank had issued the check. He put paper currency and checks into a briefcase and walked to the banks. All three banks were within two kilometers (1.2 miles) of Bawazier's office. It was an easy walk except during the summer season, when the temperature often rose to 48 degrees Celsius (118 degrees Fahrenheit).

In those days, the bank employees were men from India who had come from Aden after the British left. There were also a few Yemeni-Ethiopian and Yemeni-Vietnamese staff, along with a handful of Egyptian and Jordanian men. Ingy often took time to have tea and chat with some of these bank employees when there was a need to issue a letter for credit (L/C). The L/C was a document confirming that the bank was holding the funds needed for purchasing the items Bawazier ordered, such as ghee, beans, and other goods. During those days, company owners deposited the funds into the bank, the bank held the funds, and the L/C confirmed that the funds were available for the seller. The exporter needed to see a copy of the L/C to be sure the buyer had the funds for the purchase.

Between the stops at three banks and Ingy's time for socializing, nearly half of the day was gone by the time we returned to the office. When I asked Bawazier why he never commissioned Al-Shenawi to deal with bank matters, he responded, "Don't ever mix the bookkeeping with the cashiering tasks. When the numbers don't balance, either the employees fix the books, or they fiddle with the cash ... neither is a good measure or outcome." *Business Management 101*, I noted to myself.

Within a couple of months, dealing with banks became my primary responsibility. After Ingy started to give me handwritten notes, I would type up business correspondence. Often, I had to type identical letters for multiple companies, only changing the company names. I wasn't the greatest typist, and Ingy used to get mad at me for making so many typos on the letters, as I kept using up the typewriter ribbon. Typewriter ribbons back then were as valuable as modern-day printer ink cartridges, and it was onerous to get replacements since Amazon Prime wasn't delivering packages in Yemen at that time! (It still isn't.)

It was during this time, the summer of 1980, I taught myself how to drive a car, and my self-directed lessons were pure trial and error. As many people know, automatic transmissions are common in Canada and the US, but vehicles in most of the rest of the world use manual transmissions. As is typical for anyone learning to drive a stick shift, I had a lot of jolting experiences—grinding the gears, stalling, etc. When I began driving to the grocery store and other places for errands, the car would come out of gear, or I sometimes drove into a wall. Most of the time, I simply took a long time to get from place to place because I could get the car into first gear, but I couldn't shift up. Fortunately, at that time there wasn't much other traffic on the road because most people didn't own cars, so I didn't get yelled at!

The entire time I lived in North Yemen, the only cities where I didn't feel discriminated against were Mocha and

Hodeidah. Aside from those who came from the interior lands of North Yemen and resided in the city, the native local people from Hodeidah have darker skin. They are hardworking and humble. I was never reminded of being dark because I didn't stand out. And I tried to be a hard worker.

*

One evening in late December 1980, at the end of the working day, between six and nine p.m., Bawazier drove me to the banks of the Red Sea, which were about 500 meters (546 yards) from the house we lived in and told me that he had a big plan for me. Impetuously, I asked, "What is that?"

"I'm thinking of letting go of the Indian and the Egyptian staff members, and I would like you to take over the entire management of my office administration. I will hire locals to assist you in various aspects of the work. You have turned eighteen. In fact, you will be nineteen next month, and I'm also thinking you would marry one of my daughters. There is an old Hadhrami saying, 'Gain a son without losing your daughter.' *Taksib waladan dun 'an tafqid abnatak.*' I have no sons, and I don't want to lose my daughters to a stranger. I would like you to remain with me."

I went silent.

He looked at me and asked me why I wasn't responding.

I drew in a deep breath.

"I promised myself and Bansser that I would go to England or the US. In fact, I came to North Yemen only as a transition and to obtain a North Yemen passport, then to reconnect with my brother, who was living in Jeddah, Saudi

Arabia, but he passed away last year. He left behind a thirty-year old widow and four daughters. My plan is to be in the lives of those nieces as a role model throughout their lives, if I can. In addition, I plan to locate my family in Hadhramaut and stay in touch with my sisters. But I'm not interested in staying in North Yemen at all. A marriage is not something on my radar at this moment in my life. I do really appreciate the notion and the trust, but I'm afraid my head is in a different space."

He gave me a disappointed look, and as we drove back home, he asked me to think about it.

He added, "Don't be stubborn like your father. He never listened to anyone in his life."

The topic never came up again.

VII

Opportunity

If somebody offers you an amazing opportunity but you are not sure you can do it, say yes – then learn how to do it later.

— Richard Branson

The combined two years I spent between Hodeidah and Ta'izz gave me enough of a sense of each city to realize that those were not places I wanted to remain. Despite my apprehension to deal with the people of Sana'a, I wanted to move to the capital city, assuming better opportunities existed for me there. I was also aware that Sana'a had a large contingent of *Muwalladin,* Yemenis who were born in Ethiopia. The loose English equivalent of Muwalladin would be *mulatto*—a term used to label those of us who were mixed race (now considered outdated and derogatory by many). Ethiopian-Yemeni youth in the late 1960s, 1970s, and early 1980s tended to be focused on education and were therefore leaving North Yemen for the US, UK, and even the former Soviet Union. Connecting with them would give me a greater understanding of my options for departing North Yemen. In addition, it had been more than two years since I had spoken the Amharic language or eaten an Ethiopian dish. I made up my mind to move to Sana'a as soon as I could.

*

The basic definition of the term *Muwallad* refers to someone who is of mixed race, specifically a person who has one parent of Arab descent and one non-Arab parent.[1] The true meaning, though, is much more varied and

> is shaped by context and perspective; however, the usage—extended to those of Yemeni and Ethiopian parents—reflects contemporary practice in Ethiopia. Overwhelmingly, the Muwalladin trace Yemeni descent through paternal lines.[2]

According to this definition, my identity could arguably be labeled as more similar to Jamal's mixed Yemeni and Vietnamese heritage than to anyone who is fully Ethiopian or who has a Yemeni mother and a Saudi father, for example. Arab women don't typically migrate. Therefore, mixed-raced children are typically born to non-Yemeni mothers in Sudan, Kenya, Tanzania, Somalia, Ethiopia, or other nearby countries.

*

In February 1981, while I was still residing at Bawazier's house, I sat down with him in his home and told him that I had decided to move to Sana'a, giving him sufficient notice so that he could find an alternative to cover the work I was performing at his office. Initially, when I asked to meet with him, he said "I thought you came to speak to me about the conversation we had on the beach," his proposal from a couple months prior. Without my saying so, however, he knew that my marrying his daughter and staying with him in the city of Hodeidah was out of the discussion.

After I told him of my plans, he silently rose and walked to his home office, where he kept the cash vault. Moments later, he came back with a bundle of money—YR24,000—the equivalent of US$6,500 using the exchange rate at the time. That was a huge amount of money and perhaps equal to the yearly salary of a teacher in Yemen in those days.

"What is this for?" I asked him, surprised and puzzled.

He responded, "Your wage for the past several months. I kept it for you."

I was stunned. I had been under the impression that I was working for him for free to learn the mechanics of office business and perhaps in exchange for the room and board he provided me and the school fees he had paid.

With that gesture, he reminded me of typical Hadhrami discipline, loyalty, generosity, and trustworthiness. I got up from my seat and kissed him on his forehead as a token of respect and gratitude. I had never encountered a Hadhrami person who told me lies, cheated me, or pointed me in the wrong direction. Still, I hadn't been entirely open to trusting him. My natural inclination was to be suspicious, as I had been used, abused, and taken advantage of in the past, even by members of my own family. Primarily because of how I was treated as a child in Ethiopia, my trust level for adults was low. Therefore, it had never occurred to me that Bawazier wasn't taking advantage of me, as well. At that moment, I felt guilty about all the erroneous thoughts I had had about him, and he made me feel proud to be part of the Hadhrami bloodline.

There is a saying among Hadhramis, "You can't trust a man with your wife, but you can trust him with your money." This moment humbled me, and I began to gain a deeper understanding of tribal loyalty and integrity.

VIII

Muwalladin

Our true nationality is mankind.

— H.G. Wells

A month later, I bought a small brown carpet bag, packed a few items that were important to me (my school certificate, a small accounting textbook, a typing textbook, photos, and of course, clothing), and took a taxi to Sana'a. The distance between Hodeidah and Sana'a is 224 kilometers (139 miles), and the trip took almost eight hours. Compared to Hodeidah, Sana'a was a dusty, crowded city. I felt cold, as the average temperature in Hodeidah at that time of year was 36 degrees Celsius (97 degrees Fahrenheit), and it was about 10 degrees Celsius (50 Fahrenheit) when I arrived in Sana'a.

Even though both cities are in the same country, they seemed like parts of two different nations. The darker-skinned people of Hodeidah were politer and calmer. The people in Sana'a spoke faster, were semi-frenzied in their manners, and projected a somewhat superior attitude. I felt as if I were a farm boy from Idaho landing in the busy, hurried, noisy streets of New York City for the first time.

In Yemen, windows in homes are built with iron bars, similar to what you see in jails. By nature, Yemenis don't steal, and robberies are not common. At least, theft isn't as pronounced as it is in other parts of the world. The protection put around the houses, including iron gates, is to protect the female residents. Significant effort is put into keeping women out of sight of men and, in particular, sexual predators. For a single man to rent a unit in an apartment complex is considered calling for trouble. Women or girls could potentially meet the bachelor, and the single man could end up enticing the women to have sexual affairs. Therefore, most landlords prefer to keep single men from renting apartment units. As a result of the hesitancy to rent to bachelors, it took me more than a week to find a place to rent.

While I was looking for housing, I also made it a goal to find someone who had been born in Ethiopia and was able to lead me to an Ethiopian restaurant, if there were any. I missed Ethiopian food so much. On the streets, I ask any random person if they knew of any Ethiopian restaurants. People tended to avoid responding with, "I don't know." Because they wanted to be helpful and didn't want to admit their lack of knowledge, they would give me directions, often steering me wrong, even if they had no clue what they were talking about. I finally did find one restaurant. The owners were the Banajah family in partnership with an Ethiopian lady. The Ethiopian lady was living in North Yemen as she was married to a Yemeni man.

At that restaurant, while waiting for the food to be served, I saw a lighter-skinned young man waiting for his meal. He was the only other customer in the restaurant. I initially thought he was Egyptian, but he was much smaller in his stature. Most Egyptians are wide-boned and bulky, and he wasn't. I also thought he could be Jordanian or Lebanese.

The ladies didn't come out of the kitchen or the cooking area to serve the food. Rather, once the order was ready, they handed the plate through a window or an opening in the wall that separated the seating area from the kitchen.

When his name was called to receive his meal, the light-skinned man spoke in Amharic with the lady behind the counter. I found that remarkable. Since hearing a British man speaking Amharic at an evangelical church in Addis Ababa, Ethiopia, I had never heard of a person who didn't resemble anything close to an Ethiopian speaking the Amharic language. Shortly after that man received his food, my name was called, too.

After I picked up my meal, I didn't return to my table. Instead, I approached this young man and asked him if I could share his table. He didn't mind, and we started talking in Amharic. Amharic after two-plus years! I was stumbling to utter words a bit, but it quickly became natural to me.

"Hi, my name is Adel. I just arrived from Hodeidah a couple of days ago. What is your name?" I asked.

"I'm Al-Arasi."

"I heard you speaking Amharic, and I was kind of taken by surprise, as I didn't expect you would. Due to your skin color, your clothing, and physical build, I didn't think you were a Yemeni let alone someone who could speak Amharic."

"I get that often," he told me. "Both my parents are Yemenis. I was born and grew up in Addis Ababa, though. I came to North Yemen a little over five years ago, in 1976."

I told him that I had come to Yemen three years earlier and had been in the city of Ta'izz, where I finished my high school. I informed him that I had spent a considerable amount of time in Hodeidah, too.

"I'm staying in a hotel and looking for a place to stay. I'm finding it difficult to find an apartment for a single man."

I then asked him, "You speak good Amharic. Where and how did you study it, and what do you do for a living?"

He said, "I work at the international airport. I'm a person who processes passengers before they board the airplane. I like the job. It gives me an opportunity to study. If we are lucky, we have two flights in a day, but I also work some night shifts. It pays well, and I get free flights."

I asked what he was studying at university.

"English literature," he said.

He then asked me what city I was born in and where I grew up. He was surprised that I had managed to obtain a high school education, as most Muwalladin didn't have the opportunity to do so. He was impressed when I told him about my love for reading.

"I just didn't feel lonely when I read books during my boyhood days," I told him.

He agreed.

He told me he wanted to be a writer, perhaps of short stories. I confided to him that I had never developed any interest in writing. The only thing I wrote was my journal, which I had kept up from the time I was eleven.

He asked, "What types of books do you like to read?"

I listed them all—the fiction and non-fiction books I had read.

He said, "Yes, I've read all of them with the exception of a few of the Marxist books you mentioned."

After the meal was done, we spent several hours chatting over tea at the restaurant. In fact, I didn't realize at the time that we were there talking about everything for at least five hours.

When I met him, Al-Arasi was a second-year university student majoring in English literature at Sana'a University. He was about six years older than I was. He spoke eloquently in Amharic, Arabic, and English, and he instantly became my hero, as he was a well-read individual with an intellectual presence. The round-shaped glasses he wore made him look like John Lennon. He spoke softly and orderly, using high-level and intellectual vocabulary, and he projected a scholarly posture and demeanor. Al-Arasi didn't study Marxism as much as I did, nor was he imprisoned in Ethiopia, as he didn't care much about communism during those days, but he had a different dimension than many people: he was a literary student and was well-read.

I gravitated toward him, and I was captivated by his mannerisms. When I told him that I hadn't been getting my hands on enough books to read during the past two years, he offered to show me where the British Council was located, as they had books I could borrow from their library. When I confided in him my challenges in finding a place to rent, he quickly suggested, "I have a one-bedroom apartment. You can move in with me for now, and we can search for a two-bedroom apartment. We can share the expenses. Would you be interested?"

I have always been attracted to radical minds. Without hesitation, I responded, "Yes!"

We agreed to meet again the following day.

The owners of the restaurant where I met Al-Arasi, the Banajah, were a Hadhrami family who also lived in Ethiopia. After I briefly exchanged family news and history with the owner on that initial visit, she invited me to their home to meet the rest of the family, which consisted of her three sisters and their mother. Their father had long since passed away in Ethiopia. The owner of the restaurant and one of her sisters were married; the other two daughters were not. All four daughters, the two husbands, and the mother were living under the same roof. The mother was Ethiopian from the Wollo area of northern Ethiopia, a place where people of different ethnic groups, beliefs, and cultures still coexist peacefully. In Wollo, one can find a Muslim mother and a Christian father or siblings in the same household.[1]

When I visited their home, the mother asked me several questions—mostly about my childhood, my mother, how long I had been in Yemen, what I was doing, and whether I had family in Yemen. I didn't know it at the time, but this was basically like a job interview. She was carefully examining my behavior and attitude, sizing me up as a potential son-in-law for her two unmarried daughters. It was not common to invite a teenage boy to a house where a few single girls lived, but they had done so because we had a common background. From a religious and cultural perspective, to invite a young single man to a household with single women was (and still is) unacceptable and inappropriate. I took being allowed to mingle in their house as a token of trust, and I made sure I didn't step outside my bounds.

It didn't take much for the mother to figure out how innocent and gullible I was. Therefore, she began to invite me to have lunch with the family once a week on Fridays. (The Qur'an invokes the importance of Friday as a sacred day of worship in a chapter called "Al-Jumu'ah," which is also the word for *Friday* in Arabic. Muslims believe Friday was chosen by God as a day of worship. It is the day, as designated by God, when every believer is to pray in congregation. According to Islam, it is the day Adam, the first human, was created, and it is also the day when Adam was removed from paradise.[2])

The two married Banajah girls were married to sons of the Bazara and Baharon families. But that still left two for me. It was quickly revealed that Baharon was one of the men whom I had met in Ta'izz almost three years prior. His uncle had been a good friend of my father. Baharon's uncle was the man who had fallen in love with a woman from the Ethiopian royal family. When she told him that his nose was fuddled, he went on to get surgery on his nose, but he died during or shortly after the operation. This was the friend whose death had impacted my father deeply shortly before he also died. The Bazara family had also been acquaintances of my father. Two more pieces for me of the puzzle of my father's life.

Fortunately, there was never any great pressure for me to marry one of the daughters, and in the end, I developed a strong and wonderful relationship with the family.

From that point on, I also stayed close to the Baharon family, who knew me better than anyone else in the area did and who had known my late father. The connection I felt with the Baharon family was something I held on to, wanting familiarity and seeking a deeper connection to my father and his history.

IX

Al-Arasi

You can tell he's your real friend when he acts like your brother. I discovered the brother I never had when I met my best friend.

— Unknown

Between March 1981 and July 1984, I continued to live with Al-Arasi. He played a significant role in my life during those years. Not only was he six years my senior and more mature, but he also had plenty of adult life experiences in both Yemen and Ethiopia. He was a writer and a poet, and he introduced me to many types of literature I hadn't yet read, such as Albert Camus, Fyodor Dostoevsky, Leo Tolstoy, Maxim Gorky, Charles Dickens, Jane Austen, Mark Twain, and Ernst Hemingway. He was an intelligent man who served as a positive role model, and I had great respect for him.

Prior to coming to North Yemen, other than the oral story I was taught as a child in Ethiopia, *The Arabian Nights: One Thousand and One Nights* (in Arabic: *Alf Laylah wa-Laylah*),[1] I was never exposed to Arab literature. Discovering the existence of Arab writers and literature was eye-opening. Among the books Al-Arasi led me to read were those by Naguib Mahfouz, Khalil Gibran, Taha Hussein, Abbas Mahmoud Al-Aqqad, and Nawal El-Saadawi.

Al-Arasi was about 5'6" tall with a receding hairline. He always pulled his hair over from the side to cover the balding areas. He didn't chew qat and mingled with only a select few. Unlike many Yemenis and Muwalladins, Al-Arasi regulated his habits and was extremely regimental in his daily life. He never liked or wanted to drive a car, which made no sense to me. There were a few other aspects of him that piqued my curiosity.

The first was his relationship, or the lack thereof, with his immediate relatives. I came to be aware of the existence of his brothers, sister, and parents.

His father lived in Asmara, Eritrea, and had served in the Italian Army. Al-Arasi was the second of nine children. His mother was born in Asmara to a Yemeni family. I met his father once, and within a few months of my meeting him, his leg was amputated due to his being diabetic, and he died. Al-Arasi had two sisters and six brothers. He was close to one of his sisters, but sadly she, too, died in a car accident a couple of years after their father passed away. Al-Arasi only spoke about his father, not the rest of his family, and he hung a picture of his father above the bookshelves.

When I learned about the death of his sister, I tried to console him, as he was deeply saddened. I didn't know what to do, so I decided to tell some mutual friends about her death in order to allow them to express their condolences. When people came to our place to pay respect, he sent them away and for the first time, exchanged harsh words with me. He made it clear that I shouldn't be telling anyone about the death of his sister, and he didn't want anyone to come to our place to pay their respects.

While I was puzzled about that matter, several months later he came to learn that I had met his mother. There weren't a lot of Muwalladin in the city, and we were visibly recognizable to one another, so when we Muwalladin crossed paths in the markets, at weddings, or elsewhere, we would engage in small talk. I had met his mother in passing, and coincidentally, she also worked in the hospital where my sister was a patient, so I talked to her there, as well.

When I mentioned to Al-Arasi that I had met his mother, he sat me down to tell me to stay clear of her, as he didn't have a good relationship with her. That conversation baffled me further. As tight family relationships are the case in many cultures, including Yemeni or Ethiopian, it was inconceivable to me for a person to say, "I don't like my mother and I have no communication with her," but those were his words. Every now and then, I encountered his mother by chance. Most interactions with her occurred when my own sister was in the hospital. Al-Arasi's mother was working there in the women's wing. She always asked me, "How are you able to live with my son? I think of him as being a beast and devil."

Her comment and his indifference toward his family perplexed me. I would not think of my mother or son (if I had one) the way they thought of each other regardless of my upbringing. To me, a mother and child ought to respect and love one another despite any differences they may have.

On the other hand, Al-Arasi was the kindest person I knew. Whenever I got sick, he was there for me. Anytime I had personal issues, he was the one I turned to for guidance and consolation. I saw him helping many people who needed financial or other types of assistance. Yet, he never provided anything to his immediate family.

*

Al-Arasi was the most sexualized human I have ever known. When he read a book that had intimate details, he marked the section and re-read it a few more times. I had never been interested in literature or writing. (I have always loved reading, but I prefer biographies and books about war and history, politics, philosophy etc. over poetry and stories. Al-Arasi was more into wordsmithing and enjoyed poetry and such.) Every now and then, he tended to discuss with me books he was reading and on occasion, I read a few of them. I kept noticing the bookmarks and highlights on intimate encounters and acts. The pattern caught my attention and I had to ask him about it. He told me, "The best part of any book is the intimacy, the sex!" When my mind was busy juggling my priorities, sex was the last thing on my mind.

In North Yemen during the early 1980s, it was almost impossible and also forbidden to have any type of relationship with a woman outside of one's family let alone have sex outside of marriage. Not to mention the associated punishments! (For example, those who were found to have committed adultery could be beaten on the streets; women were buried up to their head and people would throw stones at her until she died.) Al-Arasi didn't seem to be concerned of any potential repercussions for his sexual encounters with various women.

On a number of occasions while I was living with him, authorities and/or influential parents of various girls and women came searching for him. Often, that exposed me to unnecessary harassment. Even being a third party to his misdeeds, I was often accused of being his collaborator. That was not the type of attention I was looking for in the country where I was trying to find peace and harmony.

On one weekend in 1982, while I was lying in bed and reading, I heard a women's voice. I concluded Al-Arasi must have a female companion in our unit. I continued to read. About thirty minutes later, I thought I heard a knock on the door of our apartment. I waited a bit to hear if it repeated, as I often opened the door to find that the knock was on the door of the unit across from ours. Yes, I heard it again, and I jumped out of my bed to see who was at our door.

When I opened the door, I saw one of the ladies I had seen in our apartment in the past—one of Al-Arasi's girlfriends. I said to her, "Did you manage to leave the apartment? I didn't hear the door being opened." I added, "I was up while you guys were giggling."

She gave me a confused look and said, "No!" And she asked, "Is Al-Arasi in? And are you going to invite me in me or not?"

I froze. I immediately realized the existence of another woman in our apartment, in Al-Arasi's room. My mouth and throat quickly dried up. While trying to breathe, I quickly replied, saying, "No Al-Arasi isn't home."

She said, "How come? He told me today's his day off work. Can I come in?"

I told her no, and I tried to convince her that he had left earlier, so there was no point for her to be alone with me. Moreover, I told her, "I am not sure when he will be back."

She really wanted to come in, and I insisted she go away. She kind of suspected something was wrong in the way I was rattled. At the same time, I worried that she would storm over to his bedroom and find another woman in his bed. My imagination went wild with the potential unintended outcome. Thankfully, I finally convinced her he wasn't around, and she left.

As much as I admired and respected him for all his other excellent human attributes, I started to worry about him harming himself and others. I started to worry about my sister, Muna, and my cousin, Ferdows, visiting our apartment, fearing that he might make sexual advances toward them. Keeping my sisters and cousin away from our apartment came across to them that I didn't want them to be near me; they didn't know the reason I stopped inviting them over.

Almost forty years after I lost touch with Al-Arasi, working on my book project and reading many of my journal entries from the 1980s prompted me to ask about his whereabouts. I discovered that he died unexpectedly on June 4, 2016, in a remote town named Buta Jera, Ethiopia. Ethiopian writer and poet Abera Lemma managed the burial services for Al-Arasi. Lemma went on to set up a photograph gallery and library as a living memorial for Al-Arasi.

According to the medical report, the cause of his death was deemed to be from hepatitis B virus. Al-Arasi was buried at the St. Joseph Cemetery in Addis Ababa, as if he were a Christian. Some mutual Arab and Muslim friends are still talking about him being buried in a Christian cemetery instead of an Islamic one, which reminded me of my father's story when he died in 1967. What Arabs don't understand are the circumstances at the time of Al-Arasi's death. Without Abera Lemma, Al-Arasi's daughter, and the supportive community, his body would have been put in the municipal landfill, as he had no one else who would take responsibility for him after his death. Moreover, the people near him at the time of his death had no knowledge of or connection to the Islamic community, so they couldn't have provided him an Islamic burial service. And knowing him as I did, I assume that if Al-Arasi had the chance to choose where to be buried, he would have said, "Put me in the Christian cemetery."

From conversations and email communication I've had with people associated with him, I gathered that in Ethiopia Al-Arasi was arguably one of the most prominent literary critics of Ethiopian writers. Some of these people showed me some of his writings. Al-Arasi provided writers and writing communities with comparison, analysis, interpretation, and evaluation of works of literature. His literary criticisms and opinions were highly valued, as they were supported by evidence relating to theme, style, setting, or historical or political context.

X

ID Card

There were so many different ways in which you were required to provide absolute proof of your identity these days that life could easily become extremely tiresome just from that factor alone, never mind the deeper existential problems of trying to function as a coherent consciousness in an epistemologically ambiguous physical universe.

— Douglas Adams

Most Yemeni children born outside Yemen are not treated as equals or as complete, competent people in North Yemen. Preference is given to those whose fathers from the Shia (Zaydi) tribe descend from well-connected tribal families. During the late 1970s and early 1980s, job opportunities in regular newspaper, TV, and radio announcements clearly stated that to apply for any type of government job, one must be Yemeni from both sides, as well as be born in North Yemen. This was an open and blunt way of instructing all Yemenis born outside the country and with non-Yemeni mothers not to apply for any government jobs. There was no shame about it, and it was a commonly acceptable standard practice to blatantly discriminate in this way.

The same notion applied to scholarships to travel abroad to most Western countries, primarily the US and UK, for higher education. The education in North Yemen was substandard, and there weren't enough programs like engineering or medicine during those years. One had to leave the country to obtain a useful education. As a result of the discrimination, every person who happened to be born with lighter skin and was able to speak in a North Yemeni dialect and accent changed their documentation to indicate a birthplace in North Yemen with the intention of qualifying for prospective work and going abroad for education. At that time, no one wanted to admit to being born outside of North Yemen, including communist South Yemen.

In North Yemen, obtaining a Yemeni ID card was harder than getting a university degree. Without a North Yemeni ID card though, one could not get a passport or driver's license, find a job, open a bank account, or enlist in military services. To get an ID card, most children had to obtain testimony from relatives and a local sheikh.

The entire process of obtaining a North Yemeni ID card took six to eighteen months. The speed of obtaining the card was based on how much money one could spend in the form of bribes, as well as the applicant's patience and persistence in enduring the long process and dealing with the multiple people involved in the approval process, including the federal investigation bureau.

Several steps were involved in acquiring a Yemeni ID, which I, and so many other Muwalladin, had to go through.

The process was different and more complicated for those of us from South Yemen than it was for Northerners.

Step One

To begin the process, an application had to be written by a court clerk requesting that an ID card be issued. The clerk had no stationary office or formal working hours. One had to chase down and find the clerk in his home and/or places where he chewed qat (which was subject to change on a daily basis). He may have been found on a bench in front of the courthouse or in taxi stations, where he worked part time. It was like a competition on "The Amazing Race" TV show! You found the clerk; you won the prize. And the prize was the opportunity to fill out government paperwork.

The clerk kept the official letterhead paper and stamp in a small pouch. Applications were not accepted without those. Wherever you found the clerk, you would find his office and office supplies, including the letterhead and stamp. Despite his receiving wages from the government, he ensured he collected additional bribes ranging between US$200 and $250 per application. He often split it with the judge approving the paper. In the 1980s, US$250 was a lot of money—the equivalent of the monthly wage of a civil servant, teacher, etc.

Once the application form was accepted and stamped, the applicant took the paper to their home village to obtain an additional confirmation letter confirming that they were North Yemeni and stating that they belonged to a specific tribe and family name. Depending on the family, in most cases, the villagers asked for a reward of some sort to confirm the identity of the child or children. Nearly all the children who were born outside North Yemen had to give up all inheritance or property rights from their father's side in exchange for their uncle's acknowledgment of them as members of the family. In some cases, a female seeking this verification from a relative may have been forced to marry her uncle's son with the intent that the rest of the family obtain a North Yemen ID card.

In my case, Bawazier and Basherahil vouched for me, so I was fortunate as they had no ulterior motive nor did they expect anything in return for supporting me in my application.

Step Two

Then the application and the confirmation letter were brought forward to a responsible person—a local community leader (Sheikh Al-Hara, as it's called). The intent of this step was to establish that the applicant was a known resident and had a physical address. As with the hunt for the court clerk, locating this individual could be a daunting task, as this person also didn't have a fixed office. His office could very well have been the same bench that the clerk had been sitting on when you found him!

Once the community leader's (sheikh's) location had been scouted out, the applicant had to corner him and convince him to provide the necessary confirmation. This may have required waiting patiently by gate of his home, stalking him, and nabbing him to make the necessary connection.

He, too, collected some cash for writing a certificate letter stating that the applicant was known to him including the duration of the relationship and the applicant's address. Often the sheikh *didn't* know the applicant though; he simply gathered all information required from the applicant to complete the paperwork.

Individuals like him routinely asked the applicants what they did for a living. He was not needing this information for the letter, nor was he making small talk thinking he had made a new friend. No. The intent was to size up the amount of money he could extort from the applicant. I would often say I was a student so that the expected bribe would be low. However, I gave twice as much he asked for. That way, when I returned in two years' time to renew my ID card, he would remember me and the process would hopefully be smoother.

Step Three

After obtaining the above two letters for the original application, the next step was to go to the local police station to get a clearance letter. Naturally, the local police station had no records of any crimes. Why would they? The police station was not where you went to obtain assistance from the police; it was where most officers and friends sat around to socialize and chew qat. A very smelly and crowded place. Police officers obtained lists of people who were detained for a couple days for minor disputes, had defaulted on rental payments, or were unable to pay back amounts they had borrowed. An applicant, among others who were there to get clearance letters, took a seat in the room and waited. And waited.

The system was first-come, first-served. The applicant who arrived at the station first, normally around noon or shortly thereafter, had the chance to speak to the officer in charge once the officer was good and ready to extract himself from his qat-chewing buddies. When that person was done, the next person took their place to address their matters. On any given day, there would be up fifty individuals sitting in line. Knowing the waiting took between five to six hours, everyone brought their own qat and sat there, joining in the munching and mingling.

The procedures were interrupted three times for prayers between 1 p.m. and 8 p.m., which, coincidentally, happened to be the hours that the police station was open. The three interruptions were at the prayer hours *Asr* at 3 p.m., *Maghrib* at 6:11 p.m., and *Isha* at 7:41 p.m. If the police station was located near a mosque, everyone went there to pray; if not, all would stand up and perform the prayers in the station. I normally don't pray, but when processing paperwork, I begrudgingly did pray with everyone so that I wouldn't upset anyone by refraining.

When my turn came, the officer examined all the paperwork I brought to him, asked a few questions, collected his bribe, and wrote a note on top the application form confirming that I had no criminal record without knowing whether I had one or not. I could have been Yemen's Ted Bundy, and he would have approved my paperwork with the right amount of a bribe.

He signed and stamped the papers.

Step Four

Finally, we are at the last step in this process! The final task was to visit Yemen's internal security division.

> Yemen's primary and most feared internal
> security and intelligence-gathering force
> [emphasis added] is the Political Security
> Organization (PSO), led by military
> officers; it reports directly to the president
> and operates its own detention centers. ...
> The Central Security Organization, which
> is part of the Ministry of Interior,
> maintains a paramilitary force, and has its
> own extrajudicial detention facilities. Also
> attached to the Ministry of Interior is the
> Criminal Investigative Department (CID)
> of the police, which conducts most
> criminal investigations and arrests. ...
> According to the US Department of State,
> members of the PSO and Ministry of
> Interior police forces have committed
> serious human rights violations, including
> physical abuse and lengthy detentions
> without formal charges.1

(Ministry of Interior, Criminal Investigative Department, Political Security Organization ... it all sounds a little too Orwellian.)

Those whose origins were in South Yemen, such as myself, were expected to present all the paperwork to the internal security division. The division had its own form applicants had to complete. The form contained no fewer than one hundred detailed and personal questions and a section for the applicant to write up an autobiography. (In hindsight, after all the work I had to put into that form and all the work I put into this three-volume memoir, I should have just kept those forms, changed a few words, and published them as my life story!) If any discrepancies were found between a previous and current application, the applicant was detained and tortured—as if the whole application for the North Yemeni ID card wasn't unpleasant enough.

The applicant was often asked to show up at this office at midnight. Perfectly logical. During my first visit to this facility, I collected the application and told the agent that I had a severe stomach pain and had to depart immediately. I left the building with a blank application that he didn't notice I took with me. The following day, I completed the application form and kept a couple photocopies before returning to the facility. Upon arrival at the site, I copied all of my information onto a new application form and handed it in. I did the same on all future visits so that I could stay consistent in my stories and be able to avoid any differences in my application. With that, I hardly was questioned, detained, or tortured like others before me were.

Getting clearance from this security regiment was the most difficult step—some applications could be sitting in someone's file drawer for months, or the original application could get lost altogether. When that happened, the applicant had to start from the first step above.

Abuses of the System

From some of my friends and relatives, I had learned of many individuals who were beaten and detained and received other harsh treatments during the process of obtaining their IDs. I also became aware that some girls were sexually assaulted in exchange for getting an ID for herself and the rest of her family. Some of the security officers didn't stop there; they continued to demand sexual favors of some of the girls on a regular basis even after their paperwork was processed and the ID was approved. Most vulnerable women accepted such treatment out of fear, wanting protection, or simply as a way of survival in a society that had no respect for women. I also know some individuals who were forced to surrender wedding rings to those corrupt officials in order to get signed paperwork released.

When the officials involved in the above listed steps discovered that the process was being used as a revenue stream, they began to add expiration dates on those IDs so that every couple of years, we had to go back through the process from the beginning to renew our IDs. It was a great source of money-making and an avenue through which many Yemenis born outside of Yemen received the most abuses.

On the upside, in the 1970s and 1980s, most Yemenis didn't know how to read and write the Arabic language let alone foreign languages such as English and French. Banks, airlines, embassies, non-governmental organizations, etc., required a lot of staff members in order to conduct business. No one other than a Yemeni who was born outside Yemen was able to fulfill such demand, as most of us came to the country better equipped to fill these gaps. During those two decades, 90 percent of the private sector positions were dominated by those who were born outside of Yemen, and those were the people who were earning handsome salaries. If one could put up with cultural and social discrimination, it was a prosperous era for most of us.

XI

Marib

Now when the Queen of Sheba heard of the fame of Solomon concerning the name of the Lord, she came to test him with hard questions.

— 1 Kings 10:1

I wasn't familiar with Sana'a when I first moved there, so in addition to showing me around, Al-Arasi took me to the US Aid Development Agency (USAID Yemen) to apply for a job. He encouraged me to apply for entrance at Sana'a University and assisted me in enrolling in the Faculty of Science. In spring 1981, I started to work for USAID as a bookkeeper, earning about US$1,800 a month. That was around US$21,000 tax free per year—almost the same as the average college graduate income in the US at that time.

Such earning power providing me the means to purchase a brand new car, rent an apartment in an upscale neighborhood, wear fancy and expensive clothing, equip my place with modern furniture, and focus more on non-immediate needs. I no longer had to worry about food, clothing, or shelter, which was the significant challenge during my childhood. Every time any American—an embassy worker or one of the USAID staff—went home on vacation, I asked them to bring a couple of books back for me to read. By the time I left USAID in 1984, my wage had doubled to US$3,500 per month, which was considered a handsome income. Therefore, life was good in Yemen, at least economically. Not so, socially.

While living in Sana'a, I was able to roam around the country to visit places I didn't have the means to get to in the past. I traveled to Marib and other locations within North Yemen. Marib was the capital of the ancient kingdom of Saba', which "some scholars believe to be the [land of the] ancient [Queen of] Sheba of biblical fame."[1] According to the Jewish and Arabic teachers I had while I was growing up, the Queen of Sheba was a legendary figure for her cleverness, intelligence, and wisdom. She was presented to me as a potential equal to Solomon, the tenth century BC king of Israel who was generally upheld as the wisest figure in Jewish history. (See Appendix Five for more information on Marib and the Queen of Sheba.)

Marib is in the Sarawat Mountains, about 170 kilometers (105 miles) east of Sana'a. Most of the Americans I worked with through USAID and the US embassy made frequent trips to the city of Marib with their families. I was often invited to go with them, primarily to help them translate when communicating with the locals.

It appeared that the Americans knew a lot more about the people and the site long before arriving at Marib, but they wanted to see it for themselves and interact with the locals. What they didn't know, though, were the intricate details of Yemeni culture and which questions were appropriate to ask when they wanted to learn more. The Americans often asked about topics that are offensive to Yemeni locals such as, "How many wives do you have?" and "How much do you pay for a wife?" I didn't translate those questions for the locals because I knew how they would react; Yemenis didn't want to talk about these topics. But the sensitive questions went both ways, with locals wanting me to ask the Americans questions such as, "Why do you not cover your wife's legs and face?" or "Why is your daughter not married?" I censored these questions, too, so as to keep the peace.

Some Yemeni were suspicious of Americans and thought all of them were spies. There was a misconception that all white people, and in particular all Americans, supported Israel. Because of the deep tribal system in North Yemeni society, the locals assumed that all white people were from the same tribe—if you were a white person, either you must be Jewish or a Jewish sympathizer.

With both sides asking a lot of inappropriate questions and putting me in the middle as translator, sometimes I felt very uncomfortable. Moreover, I wasn't a tourist guide; I, too, just wanted to visit and enjoy my trips to Marib rather than feeling like I was working as an unofficial (unpaid) translator.

In all, the Yemenis were hospitable, and the Americans were considerate. There was a lot of genuine mutual respect. The awkward questions came from a place of wanting greater understanding of the other culture. The locals tried to be good hosts. Yemenis are known for generosity even though they have nothing. They always portrayed smiles and happiness when they saw the Americans.

*

USAID, funded by the US government, established its presence in Sana'a in 1975 and focused its efforts in the 1970s on providing food, water, roads, and agricultural development. Funding to North Yemen increased fourfold in the 1980s and expanded to include assistance for education, health, and clean water.

During the late-1970s, USAID Yemen and the government of North Yemen jointly sponsored a technical assistance and training project designed to improve the capacity of the Yemen Arab Republic Government (YARG) to plan and monitor a national agriculture development program supportive of private sector production and marketing. Phase I of the project had a bilateral-aid funding grant of US$34,494,000 (fiscal years 1978 to 1988). The US government and Wang Computers supplied the project with a large number of computers; many were used for word processing and some for data entry and tabulation.

Through my duties at work, dealing with financial books and related matters, I came to know more about US government operations than most North Yemenis. A good portion of the local staff were drivers. Likewise, when I worked for an oil company, during the early 1990s, the locals were hired for working on the rigs; office admin work was done by foreigners. As a result, the North Yemeni employees rarely or never had the opportunity to learn about the financial aspects of the organizations they worked for, which only served to perpetuate the problem of keeping the local population in the dark regarding white-collar work details and more current worldly affairs.

*

When I was working for USAID Yemen as a bookkeeper and cashier, my manager, Richard Maddy, chose me to be the resident computer expert and had me shadowing an American expat named James Ziegler. I was able to master operating computers, writing up computer programming codes, and training other local staff. I was, and still am forty years later, filled with pride at my achievements; learning these skills was a significant accomplishment given that I was a product of a primitive, developing country with little exposure to modern technology up to that point. By mid-1982, I had gained confidence in my increasing work skills and ability to collaborate with Americans, and I began investigating and contacting American universities to pursue my higher education.

Richard was convinced that I had to travel to the US to obtain further education in computers in order to assist Yemen in future expansion of technology in the country. However, there were huge hurdles to deal with in North Yemen's archaic cultural, legal, and political systems. I was a person of color, born in Africa to an Ethiopian mother. I was not from North Yemen. Rather, my roots were from the Hadhramaut area of communist South Yemen. Moreover, I had no tribal supporters to advocate on my behalf at any level of the social or bureaucratic systems.

During the first two years of my stay in North Yemen, I hadn't been able to connect with my biological relatives who were living in South Yemen, Saudi Arabia, Kuwait, and the United Arab Emirates (UAE). My desire to connect with my family was necessitated due to several physiological and survival needs. North Yemen, and in fact all of the Gulf states, are tribal. Society, and the identity, safety, and well-being of a person is closely intertwined with the tribe one belongs to. No one cares how well educated and well-mannered a person is. The first question everyone asks is what tribe you belong to; they need to know where you fit before they form any kind of social or personal connection with you. When one of my sisters moved to Kuwait, people she met reacted to her instantly, recognizing that Sheikh Ali-Harhara is a well-known and respected name in the Arab world. (She continues to refer to herself with the full surname of Sheikh Ali-Harhara, whereas I have only ever used Ben-Harhara as my last name, dropping "Sheikh" from my name, as my father also did. With the inclusion of "Sheikh" comes the expectation that she must present herself as someone from the upper echelon.)

These tribal groupings share a mentality. They band people together and establish rules, which creates a sense of safety and belonging. Tribal connections align people with the goal of fighting a common enemy or working together to achieve meaningful accomplishments. In business, tribes are often social groups linked by a leader, and they share a common purpose, goal, culture, or organizational boundary.

While growing up in Ethiopia, I had morphed from an abandoned and lost child to a quasi-Marxist teenager. And now I was thrust into adopting the identity of a tribal Yemeni young man, but I had no direct tribal connections. I felt as though I didn't exist. I was nothing, because I had no identity without my tribe. I needed to start identifying myself not as an individual but as an ethnic person within a tribe, carrying my family name.

From the literature I had read, the Harhara tribe members were reputed to be brave warriors, religious scholars, and sultans. I was none of that. In fact, I was constantly being taunted by ordinary North Yemeni traffic police or civil security agents attempting to extract money from me or abuse me with racial insults simply because I stood out due to my darker complexion. I was trapped in a daily tug of war, seeking my identity and looking to find my ancestral foundation while still being kept at arm's length by general society—one that I genetically belonged in.

And so, in 1982, my attention shifted from survival and settling mode in North Yemen to finding and visiting my paternal relatives, who were living in the cities of Aden and Hadhramaut in South Yemen; Abu Dhabi, UAE; and Jeddah, Saudi Arabia.

XII

My Tribe

A people without the knowledge of their past history, origin, and culture is like a tree without roots.

— Marcus Garvey

To verify my origin and obtain a North Yemeni ID card, I had always relied on my father's Hadhrami friends, who happened to be advancing in their ages with failing health conditions. I foresaw most of them not living beyond another five to ten years. I began to wonder, *What will happen if they all die? Who will vouch for me to say, "He's our son, and he is a Yemeni boy"?* Because of my appearance, I could easily be confused with many Somali and Ethiopian refugees living in North Yemen. That's one of the reasons I needed to find and reconnect with my sisters, uncles, cousins, and other extended family on my father's side.

Origins

My ancestors on my father's side came from Yafa, "the seat of the ancient Himyarite dynasty, which lasted from 110 BC to AD 632, when it was fully integrated into the Rashidun Caliphate."[1] The Yafa tribe is one of the biggest tribes that descended from the ancient Himyarites and "was traditionally divided into ten branches or sheikhdoms of which five are in Lower Yafa and the other five are in Upper Yafa."[2] Members of the Yafa tribe moved and settled in some parts of Hadhramaut, a region in South Arabia which presently includes eastern Yemen and parts of western Oman and southern Saudi Arabia.[3] They assimilated and became part of the Hadhrami culture and social fabric during the past 300 years.

The Harhara family were both sheikhs[4] and sultans[5] of Upper Yafa from 1730 to 1967. Some countries that are ruled by a sheikh are not necessarily referred to as sheikhdoms. They may be a kingdom, emirate, or simply a state. Rulers of these countries do not hold the title sheikh; rather, they will hold a different royal title such as king or emir.[6] "A sheikhdom is a geographical area, or a society ruled by a tribal leader called sheikh. Sheikhdoms exist exclusively within Arab countries, particularly in the Arabian Peninsula (Gulf countries)."[7]

I had read and heard so much about Hadhramaut and badly wanted to visit that area. Yemen was still divided into two countries when I lived in North Yemen, and the division was not only geographical but also ideological. The North looked more like the Taliban-ruled areas of Afghanistan (simple and underdeveloped), and the South looked like the rest of the Gulf nations or perhaps India but was communist.

The two countries were at war when I was living in Ta'izz in between 1978 and 1979.

As it used to be with East and West Germany, North and South Korea, and North and South Vietnam, crossing borders between the two countries of Yemen was challenging. South Yemenis were concerned about the type of people who would enter the country. They were primarily apprehensive about watching for Islamic agents or recruiters from Saudi Arabia, and the North Yemen government was worried about the infiltration of South Yemen communists. Subsequently, my plan to visit my family, who were living in the communist South Yemen presented some difficulties.

I decided to take the chance and fly to the South Yemen city of Aden to meet my father's old friend Obeid Ben-Shahna and inquire as to how I would be able to connect with my siblings who lived in Aden and other cities in South Yemen. Before heading to Aden, I obtained letters from my father's friends, Bansser, Bawazier, and Basharahil to legitimize me as a true son of my father (Majid).

On my first trip to find my family, I flew from Sana'a to Aden. Within a day, I was able to locate Fawzia, one of my sisters. She was living in the Mensura neighborhood of Aden with her mother (Maryam) and son (Ben-Braik).

I have four sisters on my father's side, and long before flying to South Yemen, I wasn't even sure if any of my sisters knew about my existence. When I traveled to Aden, I carried several pictures of my father as well as my Yemeni ID card and my passport stating my full name. But none of that was necessary to prove my identity to my sisters I met on that trip. They even knew my childhood nickname given to me by my father: Add (عدل).

Aden

Aden was one of the most important ports and transshipment points on the route between India and Britain. While under the British colony, up to 650 ships a month docked in the harbor, making Aden the second largest port in the world after Liverpool. In contrast to medieval Sana'a, Aden has, despite all the effects of socialism, remained an essential cosmopolitan city to both Yemen countries.

My nephew, Ben-Braik (Fawzia's son), took the responsibility of showing me around on my first visit to Aden. He was a few years younger than I was but competent and proud of his knowledge of the socialist South Yemen. Every day, we left the house to visit sites including the Military Museum in Tawahi (a district of Aden), which contained impressive artifacts of ancient Arab culture. I was astonished to visit the Park of Tanks, where the water tanks used to store the rain which periodically falls on Aden have been used since ancient times.

One of the interesting aspects of that visit to Aden was when Ben-Braik took me to the house of Arthur Rimbaud, the French poet, which was located near the main post office. My nephew thought that I was a well-read person and found it odd that I didn't know about Rimbaud, who first arrived in Aden in 1880, having turned his back on literature as the tender age of nineteen. Apparently, Rimbaud also lived in Ethiopia and taught the Ethiopian King Haile Selassie while living in Harar.[8]

On that and all of my subsequent trips to Aden, I continued to explore other areas of the city including the Gold Mohur Bay, with its excellent swimming. I enjoy the ocean, and this was another excellent picture-taking session. I'm embarrassed to show those pictures, as one can count my ribs because I was so skinny. The bay got its name from the Mohur, a former gold coin of India and Persia. My nephew warned me not to go into waters due to the presence of sharks—I noticed a steel net to protect the beach from the predatory sharks.

I was able to visit Christian churches in Aden in 1982. Until that trip, I hadn't seen any Christian churches since leaving Ethiopia. (The North Yemenis were not tolerant of this type of diversity.)

Crater is the oldest district in Aden and was where my cousins lived. Its official name is Seera, and it is called Crater because it is located in the crater of an ancient volcano. The bay of the crater with the outlaying peninsula of Seera was, until the middle of the nineteenth century, the city's original harbor.

In all my visits to South Yemen, my nephew took me to watch movies and enjoy disco bars. When I was in Ethiopia, I was too young venture out to coffee shops or bars. In North Yemen, there were no bars and few decent movies theaters to go to. Being in Aden and seeing boys and girls attend school, go to movies, and dance in bars together was a brand new experience. I didn't think such co-mingling existed; I certainly didn't expect to see it in Arab culture. Noticing how timid I was in those places and situations, my nephew told me, "This is South Yemen; it is a free country! Enjoy it!"

My nephew and I were teens, but he ordered local beer and found me odd for not drinking any. He was drinking Aden's Seera Beer. I asked him if the beer was imported or brewed in Aden. He said, "Yes, of course proudly brewed in Aden!"

Aden was the only city in Arabia that held to its tradition of producing beers since its colonial days while all around, Islamic pressure mounted against the consumption of alcohol. In the Arab world's most leftist state, South Yemen, not all were ashamed of their country's secular ways. I was proud of my South Yemeni heritage just because they had the freedom to choose whether to drink beer or not—and I chose not to!

After the 1994 civil war, when the Northerners took over South Yemen by force, the tribe leaders from North Yemen removed the beer from the storage and burned the beer factory to the ground. (They also turned the local churches into storage buildings.) Ironically, while liquor was banned in North Yemen, you could go into people's houses and find complete bars. This was one of the hypocritical aspects of life that I continually witnessed, which made me wonder how long such acts would carry on.

XIII

Maryam

Little souls find their way to you, whether they're from your womb or someone else's.

— Sheryl Crow

The day I met my stepmother Maryam (Fawzia's mother and Ben-Braik's grandmother), I spent the entire night talking with her. My stepmother had spent a little over five years in Ethiopia, and even though had she left Ethiopia over twenty-five years earlier, she managed to recall a few Amharic words and sentences. She was the most beautiful woman I had ever seen.

Much of my conversation with Maryam was focused on my father. She seemed to know other aspects of my father that Bansser[1] didn't know. She shared with me about my father's childhood days, his conflicts with his older brother, his military service, injuries he received during his military service, his habits of throwing a house party every week, his infatuation with cars and guns, his womanizing, his addiction to alcohol—and how much she loved him.

I kept probing her about how she met my father. She told me she was a married woman when they met. Her husband was out of the country at the time, and my father was in the city to visit his mother.[2]

"His mother introduced me to him. Then, I started exchanging letters with him through his wife, Zeinab, who was my cousin. Zeinab didn't know how to read and write. At the time, my brother was sick, and your father pretended to send information on recovery remedies. His mother and his wife kept us in communication. That is how things started."

"I got pregnant while my husband was still away. Your father bribed and threatened every authority and judge in the town to grant me a divorce from my husband so I could marry him. Your sister was born only a few months after my marriage to your father. It was the biggest story in the village, and my daughter and I were cut off from the entire family chain. Your father then thought it would be best if I left my hometown and headed to another country, so that's why we went to Addis Ababa, Ethiopia."

Maryam was five months pregnant when she divorced her husband and married my father.

The interesting part of the story was that my grandmother (my father's mother) was the matchmaker. Moreover, Zeinab, his wife, was carrying love letters between her husband (my father) and her cousin Maryam, his lover at the time. Because Zeinab didn't know how to read and write, she had no clue what was transpiring.

My grandmother was accessory to the whole scandal. My father was his mother's third and youngest child, and she loved him more than she loved her other two children. Either she, like Zeinab, didn't know the content of the letters, or, because she loved him so much, she simply went along with the affair as a willing participant.

Zeinab had two daughters (Hind and Sheikha) and a son (Hussein), and Maryam had only a girl (Fawzia). As a result of such a mixed family and the shame due to the love affair, not only did the cousins, Zeinab and Maryam, stop talking to each other, but my sisters from the two mothers also never talked to each other. Over the past forty years, I did try, albeit unsuccessfully, to bring my sisters together. Because of the rift, I had to have two wedding receptions so that each sister could attend my wedding separately.

This situation always reminded me of what Bansser used to say: *Arabs have a long memory like elephants, but the sad part is that they never forgive or forget let alone learn.*

Maryam had vivid and fond memories of Addis Ababa, including the streets she lived on, people she met, and the names of her maids. While living in Addis Ababa, she found the weather conditions to be a challenge, as Addis Ababa is at in a higher altitude, so it's colder than what she was accustomed to. She also struggled with the language.

She asked me about many of the Hadhrami families she knew and socialized with back then: Baharon, Al-Bar, Baobaid, Bansser, Bagarsh, Basherahil, Ben-Salim, etc. In particular, she asked about Bansser's well-being, as he had been hugely supportive of her as he had been with me. She told me once that while she was living in Ethiopia during the early 1950s she had a miscarriage of twin boys at five months. Apparently, my father was nowhere to be found at the time, and Bansser took her to hospital and stayed beside her. She said she would never forget his kindness and that "Majid owes

Bansser a lot!" I gave her all the updates and the news about those families—as much as I remembered or knew.

She asked me if my mother ever drove a car, and I told her no. "Your father had many lady friends, and one of them used to come and wait for him near our house. The maids used to tell me she parked her car outside and waited for him to leave the house so that they could meet. We constantly fought about his womanizer attitudes and drinking habits. He took me out of my culture and tried to make me look and act like a Western woman. He took me to the Ras Hotel[3] for dancing now and then. He even asked me to attend the Armenian Church services, which I refused to do."

She begged for forgiveness from God and continued to tell me some of the intimate stories about my father.

I asked her the types of music he listened to and the materials he read.

"He used to get newspapers and magazines from Egypt and Lebanon, including the Egyptian paper *Al-Ahram* [Arabic: الأهرام; *The Pyramids*]. He often listened to Egyptian singers, primarily Uum Kulthum.[4] He had the best handwriting in both English and Arabic. He brushed his teeth twice a day," and she pointed out that I had inherited his teeth. "He had the most beautiful smile, too," she reminisced.

She confirmed what most people remembered about him. He never wore the same shirt the entire day; he would change mid-day every day so as to always appear clean and well-dressed. He smoked a pipe, and all in all, he was a happy man!

"He was the type of person who could joke and speak his mind. He loved camping and outdoor life. He could kill an animal and build a fire to cook dinner. Most of his friends' wives feared him, as he told them straight to their faces whether the meals they cooked were delicious or not. His approval of anything was so important to those around him. Many in the community looked to hire maids who worked in our house because everyone knew they were well-trained and knew how to take care of a house. He just didn't live his life like any typical Arab family."

There was something that I was curious about. Majid is not a typical Yemeni name for those born prior to the 1980s and is perhaps more modern. Moreover, his brother's names were Ali, Saleh, and Yahya—typical Yemeni names—and perhaps half of the population of Yemen had these names. I asked why and how he had such a different and modern name in comparison.

"Your grandfather, a very well-known merchant in Mukalla, had a business partner from Oman named Majid. One evening when the Omani merchant arrived at the port of Mukalla to meet your grandfather, your grandmother was expected to have a child, and the Omani man told your grandfather to name the child Majid if it turned out to be a boy. Your father was a baby boy, so your grandfather named him Majid as his business partner had requested."

She told me many personal attributes that I wouldn't have otherwise known about my father.

"Most women ask why I was married to a dark-skinned man. I told them his heart was as clean as milk or clear like clean river water. He never took anyone's money, abused anyone, or lied about anything."

Most of all, she loved him because of his antics. She told me they used to go to Sodore, a resort area in Ethiopia, as a family, and the King of Ethiopia also ventured to the same resort area.

"Your father swam like a fish. He would dive deep into the water and disappear for a long time. Sometimes, King Haile Selassie used to amazingly wait for him to see which side of the water he would come out of and smile. Your father was an entertainer, to say the least."

She asked about my father's wealth in Ethiopia, as she was surprised no one knew what happened to it. I told her I knew nothing about it, and I had grown up poor. She was unable to fathom that he had lost all his money. I told her that he may have perhaps entered into bad business arrangements and lost money. (I only began to learn the truth about what happened to my father's wealth in 2010.) And I informed her that he had accidently killed one of his friends and had to pay a huge amount of compensation.

I stayed at my sister's house for two weeks, and the entire time, Maryam and I talked about my father and my childhood, as well as Maryam's life with her daughter after returning to South Yemen from Addis Ababa.

"Do you know a man named Bekele Mola?" Maryam asked me one day.

"Yes, I have heard of this name."

"He was a good friend of your father's. In fact, he borrowed a lot of money from your father to build his hotel chains across Ethiopia. He used to hang a picture of our family in his living room."

Years later, when I contacted my relatives in Ethiopia, I asked my biological mother and Bansser about Bekele Mola. They told me the story was true; Bekele Mola didn't deny borrowing money from my father, but after my father died, he had requested they bring the paper he signed and present it to him as proof he needed to pay back the money he had borrowed. The family who took over my father's house refused to hand over any such papers.[5]

In 2020, I asked around about the whereabouts and business dealings of this man and found one of Bekele Mola's sons. I mentioned to him the story my stepmother had told me and requested if he would locate the pictures of my father at his family's house. He stated he had some pictures, and he would look for them. He recently texted me to tell me he had found nothing.

*

It was rare and certainly frowned upon at that time for Yemeni women to smoke, but my father offered Maryam a cigarette one day, and she accepted. As a result of offering her cigarettes one by one, she became addicted and ended up being a lifelong smoker. Because of his influence, she also experimented with dancing. Going dancing in public with him was also scandalous; at that time and in that culture, for a woman to dance in public wearing a skirt, as she was doing, was on par with being a stripper.

He also removed her veil, but he didn't stop there. Because she was so beautiful, he took a photo of her without her veil and sent the photo to his friends, bragging about what a beautiful wife he had.

All of these actions, punctuated by the fact that she got pregnant by my father while she was still married to another man, made her an unrighteous woman. Despite her own improprieties, however, his womanizing and alcohol abuse were ultimately too much for her. When he went away on business trips and was likely cavorting with other women, she would pour his alcohol down the toilet. My father's antics eventually drove her to leave him and return to South Yemen with the help of my father's friend Bagarsh.[6]

XIV

Sisters

Being a family means you are a part of something very wonderful. It means you will love and be loved for the rest of your life.

— Lisa Weed

Fawzia

One of my two surviving sisters from my father's side is Fawzia. I'm not sure if my father thought of it that way, but her name—which means victorious— is an appropriate one given the circumstances of how my father married her mother (Maryam) and how Fawzia came to this world and survived.

A child born out of wedlock is disqualified from inheriting from their deceased father under Islamic law. If my father hadn't married Maryam as quickly as he did, not only would both Maryam and Fawzia have been dealing with the social taboos, but they would also have been prohibited from receiving any inheritance. Fawzia would have been in the same predicament as I was in when our father died.

Fawzia is a quiet person and always keeps her feelings and opinions to herself. I don't know the reasons for it, but her silence speaks volumes without saying a word. Her choice to remain silent means, "It's best not to talk about it ["it" being anything difficult or painful, including our father's death]. There's nothing to talk about." Instead of discussing issues, she chooses to push them all aside and forget about them. She doesn't brag about the Harhara family name the way my other sisters do, and she doesn't want to talk about our father's faults, etc.

While staying at Fawzia's house in Aden, I always laughed and engaged in lengthy conversation with her son and mother. Her son found me to be an interesting person, as I wasn't praying, yet I didn't drink alcohol or chew qat. He drank alcohol, but I didn't, and that was amusing to him. He was born and raised in a socialist/communist environment, and he was fascinated by my lifestyle. He saw me doing various things that Islam teaches us not to do, but at the same time, I follow some Islamic teachings. To him, I was neither a strict Muslim nor a communist. He saw me enjoying a leisurely, relatively free life in North Yemen and dreaming of going to the US. *Bourgeoisie* was the word he used to describe me, and he often told me, "No matter how poor you were as a child, you're still bourgeoisie." He was about seventeen, only a year or two younger than me, when he first said this to me. Apparently, it was his way of saying that I was a Muslim in camouflage—a mix of sorts, observing rituals or the faith of Judaism or Christianity or another religion publicly while also embracing some Islamic practices.

While I was working on the manuscript for this book, he and I had several lengthy conversations recalling incidents from the early 1980s. He ended up a victim of COVID-19 in

December 2021 and died before having the opportunity to see the draft version of this book. Fawzia's silence is compounded with the grief over the death of her only son. As with everything, she doesn't talk about his death. I can't see her grief, but I know she's grieving. She will never say "I'm hurt. He's the only son I have, and I miss him." She doesn't vocalize her grief, and she doesn't cry; she remains silent.

Since she is a divorcee and now her son has passed away, she has no financial support. Therefore, I passed on to her every inheritance that came my way. As I explained in detail in Volume One, I received no inheritance when my father died. Nor did my mother or any of my stepmothers. However, for roughly 400 years, my family owned an estate in Al-Shihr, Hadhramaut, and in 2019, the family decided to sell it. Most members of my family didn't want to sell it because it's part of our family legacy, but the reality is, there was no good reason to keep it. There are between 150 and 200 grandchildren. Only a fraction of us earn money outside of Yemen, and none of us could afford to buy the estate individually, so we sold it. In doing so, we were forced to embrace the shame that goes with not being able to retain it. Because of the culture, there is a stigma that "we aren't man enough to hold on to the inheritance."

The estate was sold, and as per Islamic inheritance tradition, the money was divided between the boys only. My belief is that a man shouldn't be taking from women; I felt my sisters were entitled to as much of the inheritance as I was. Since I live in Canada and make a good living, I gave all my share equally to all of my sisters, which is not common practice. Hind was dead, so I gave her share to her daughter.

Hind

My oldest sister's name was *Hind*, which means *India*. Everyone called her *Mujudah*, though, because in the local Hadhrami culture, if the oldest child is a girl, a slight change is made to her father's name and his altered name is given to her. For example, if her father's name is Ali, she will be called Aliya or Alaya. In Hind's case, because our father's name was Majid, she was called Mujudah.

In 1982, with my nephew Ben-Braik, I flew from Aden to the seaport city of Mukalla, where we took a taxi to the city of Al-Shihr, about forty kilometers (twenty-five miles) from the Mukalla airport. The news of my visit was delivered to Hind ahead of my arrival, so she had two weeks to get ready for my stay. When I arrived, I saw the house was cleaned and painted, and all people in the village had been notified of my pending visit. Food and music were organized. The reception was beyond my expectations or wildest dreams.

In the Hadhrami culture, a boy is gold. I was the only son of Majid left who would carry the family name, so I was the only person who would support my sisters. And she made sure the whole community knew that Majid's son was in town.

During my visit, I didn't so much as have time to fart because people were constantly streaming in to visit. I had thought I was visiting my sister, but it seemed as though the whole country came to say hello. I had to keep clean, be well-dressed, sit decently, and talk properly. I was expected to portray a sultanic presence, behave respectfully, and keep up the family image and status. What a contrast to the humble background I grew up in! I was never trained to present myself in the manner that a sheikh or sultan was expected to act. It was all so overwhelming and was my first solid glimpse at how important my family is in that area.

Every day was like a holiday with a great feast. The surplus and variety of food my sister provided for all the visitors made the days look like a mini wedding or a large Christmas party. There were endless candies, jellies, homemade (not imported) sweets, fish, and lamb. The lamb was slaughtered, marinated, and then cooked in the ground against and beneath hot rocks.

She made sure that the most important and influential people paid a visit while I was there, as I was the patriarch of the family. Visitors didn't bring anything; they just came with their children to visit because my sister, as the host, had to provide drinks and food. Most people tried not to come at mealtime, but regardless of the time of day, my sister still provided tea, coffee, and dates. Some specially-chosen people were invited for dinner, and dinners typically had around eighteen people. In subsequent years, knowing the expenses for my sister, I brought with me lots of money to pay for these celebrations. I knew the expectations—that she would generously host people. She never let me pay for anything, but before I left after each visit, I would hide the cash under the pillow or somewhere else so she would find it after I was gone.

Arabs are the most generous people; hospitality in the Middle East is boundless. In Hadhramaut, after hosting you—when you leave and say goodbye—they ask for forgiveness for anything they may have missed. When I left my sister's home after my first visit, I found this gesture to be such a humbling, generous way of showing respect.

*

Hind told me, "Except for your height, everything about you is our dad's: your feet, your hands, the shape of your mouth and your nose." She added, "None of us possesses his smile but you. The moment you smiled, I saw my dad. You have his smile and his perfectly aligned teeth. Your mom must be short."

My oldest sister was the funniest of all my sisters. Image was so important to her. She wanted me to look and act rich and project prestige.

"You're the son of Harhara[1] from the Yafa Dynasty!" she used to say. The way I dressed and the quality of my outfit had to be meticulous, and she fussed over me as if I were her child.

My sister's expectations presented an added dimension that I wasn't prepared for. I hardly prayed or fasted. My schooling in the Islamic religion was so weak, I hadn't even memorized most of the Qur'an verses. I was a lost boy who had barely survived being a homeless orphan.

But she never wanted me to say I had been a poor boy. She told me, "No one should know that you were once poor!" I told her that was the truth—I had been poor.

"Yes," she said, "I am not asking you to lie, but you shouldn't be talking about your past misfortunes today. You will be measured by your current standing."

She made sure I pretended to be a well-to-do man so that people assumed I had our father's money.

"He was a sophisticated man, so please don't let him down by mentioning any of the challenges you have faced. Life challenges and prisons are meant for real men and are to be endured in silence unless you want to consider yourself a woman. If you are a man, don't complain. If you complain people will think of you as a woman," meaning I would be viewed as being weak. (In Arab society, if one spent time in prison, he is considered to be a real man—a man of bravery and strength. The expression she and others would use was, "Prison was built for man," meaning girls were never jailed. Only tough guys were imprisoned.) Her determination and obsession with image both frightened me and impressed me.

She quickly asked how much I made and who I worked for, and she wanted to know the level of education I had achieved. She started to tell all the visitors who came to pay their respects that I worked with Americans and earned about US$3,500 a month, a huge amount of money for a high school graduate in South Yemen at a time when the average monthly salary was US$135 to $150. She told them that I spoke English, Arabic, and Amharic. In Hadhramaut, no one pretended to like the former Soviet Union, and she made a point of telling everyone that her brother was associated with the Americans, not the poor Russians. She was embellishing everything, and I started to worry.

Later, I discovered she was building my image so that any family would eagerly accept any marriage proposal if I happened to make one. In addition, it was important for her to keep our family's image and reputation intact. She continually emphasized to me that our family and father had been well-respected. When he had gone around to visit people, the neighborhood children used to line up outside the houses to collect his empty cigarette packages. Our father was civilized and from the upper class, and the cigarettes he smoked were from England. And even when no girls were sent to school, our father sent her to Mukalla to attend school.

Her obsession with our family image was not limited to my visit; it was how she lived her life, presenting herself as an honorable member of my father's lineage, but my visit gave her more reason to project this image, as I was the surviving male and therefore the new head of the family.

I met all my cousins and other distant relatives during that and subsequent visits. I roamed around the city and made trips to historical sites like Tarim, Shibam, and Seiyun. Tarim is a historic town known as the theological, juridical, and academic center of the Hadhramaut Valley.[2] Tarim "is estimated to contain the highest concentration of descendants of the Islamic Prophet Muhammed [pbuh] anywhere in the world."[3] Shibam is a small, walled city of around 7,000; it's known as the Manhattan of the desert because of its ancient mud brick high-rise buildings dating back to the sixteenth century. Some of them are as high as eleven stories tall. It was designated as a United Nations Educational, Scientific and Cultural Organization (UNESCO) World Heritage site in 1982.[4] And Seiyun, in the middle of the Hadhramaut Valley, is the largest city in the area. The city was apparently a resting point for travelers historically. One of the prominent places for travelers to stop was a cafe run by a woman named Seiyun, so the area was named in her honor.[5] Visiting such sites impressed upon me the historical significance of these cities, and I felt the presence of my family's dynasty in this area.

My visits were always overwhelming because of my humble and difficult upbringing. I didn't grow up with my sisters, but they treated me as if I were the most important person to them, thus requiring me to quickly make a huge mental adjustment. I didn't like North Yemenis, but I quickly grew to love South Yemenis and in particular, my family. I want to keep my identity as a South Yemeni because of my sisters, still today. Nothing holds me to the country as strongly as my sisters do. As much as I was mistreated in the North, they compensated for that with their treatment of me. They helped me realize I'm not inferior. They removed the whole complex I had developed as a child.

Once I apologized for not speaking in a local dialect and Hadhrami accent, as I was born in Ethiopia. The local (South Yemeni) folks who were there listening to me were disappointed that I put myself down. They said my Arabic was excellent enough to be understood, and most importantly, "You are here searching for your roots within your family. That is all it counts. You're our son—no more and no less."

Hearing my sisters say to me, "You are our brother. You are the son of our father," made me a complete human. Their treatment of me was in stark contrast to the abuse I took as a child from my mother's older brother simply because my father was an Arab. My uncle had always made me feel inferior. My sisters, however, rewarded me with more than what I had lost in my first eighteen years. Meeting my family was meeting the other half of me.

After I had been in Yemen for two years, I began to focus on forming and building strong connections with my sisters. Every year I lived in North Yemen after first meeting my oldest sister, I took forty-five-days in the form of paid and unpaid vacation time to visit her. Sadly, she passed away in 1998 due to complications from diabetes.

After such trips, all my identity crises were put to bed. I puffed my chest with much confidence. As I was leaving on one occasion, one of my cousins gave me a few books to read about the history of the Harhara family, dating back several centuries. I proudly possess these books still today. One of the books includes a family tree that was kept current for the last 300 years. Seeing my name tattooed in the family tree was better than earning my high school diploma!

Sheikha

The only sister I knew from pictures and phone calls but had never met waited over thirty years to see me in person. That is because, when I lived in North Yemen, most Yemenis were prohibited from entering the UAE; it was very difficult to get a visa, so I couldn't travel to the UAE until I had my Canadian passport.

Her name was Sheikha, and she was a mother of five children. Sheikha means a leader or scholar. Despite being the third child of the family, she was the one who looked after everyone, including her older sister and the children of her late brother's daughters living in Jeddah, Saudi Arabia. Besides being a kind-hearted person, after she migrated to rich Gulf states (Kuwait and the UAE) with her husband, she was in such a financial position that she was able to send remittance, medicine, clothing, and gifts on a regular basis back to relatives in Yemen.

When I arrived at her house on December 13, 2003 (coincidentally, the same day that Saddam Hussein was captured!), I was greeted by scores of her children and grandchildren, mostly girls. The previous exchange of letters and pictures had given me an opportunity to recognize some of the children, so I was able to call some of them by their names. After a long flight from Canada, I was exhausted, but seeing the family gave me an instant boost, so I kept talking and telling stories.

Shortly after I got to the house, my sister came into the room to greet me. I gave her a long hug. I willed myself not to cry, even though I wanted to. She did cry a bit. I kept smiling and said to myself, *Finally, I have managed to meet the last sibling—the only of Majid's daughters I have not met until now.* It was a mix of emotions—of victory and reunion.

Sheikha spoke softly, unlike our older sister, and she didn't joke much. She was a measured and observant person. There is one consistent pattern amongst my sisters though; they all are proper and dignified. They seem to possess an invisible presence of power and other attributes one would expect to see from royal family members, dignitaries, or other persons of high status. They instantly project respect. There is something about them that makes others recognize them as leaders or persons of authority. They all suffer from diabetes and just like my father, they are temperamental—often demanding and quick to anger when things don't go their way, never taking no for an answer. They absolutely despise those who lie and cheat and those who are lazy, unclean, or untidy.

Even though my niece Wejdan looked after my needs during this visit, my sister gave orders to the maids to make sure that I had eaten and that my sleeping area was ready. She had five maids and ensured that I was completely taken care of and all proper protocols were followed. Throughout my stay, she also made sure my clothes were laundered and perfectly ironed. The night I arrived and before heading to her room, she promised to have breakfast with me the next morning.

To my surprise, the first person who came to my room the next morning with two hard-boiled eggs, three dates, and a cup of coffee was my sister. (That has been my preferred breakfast since the 1980s.) At that moment, tears came to my eyes. Her actions were consistent with the pattern and manner I had been treated by all my sisters in Aden, Hadhramaut, and Sana'a. Despite it being early in the morning, she was properly dressed and groomed. She sat next to me and started to ask about my flight. She then asked about my wife—primarily where and how I had met her.

She seemed to really like my daughters and mentioned that my oldest was well-mannered and calm. She commented about my youngest daughter: "I love her smiles!" she said.

In typical fashion of my other sisters, she made sure I was well-prepared to meet other relatives. Impression was important to her, as well. She specifically prepared me to be ready to meet her oldest son, Waleed. In the Hadhrami culture, sons are treated differently than daughters. Boys get the best of everything—meals, clothing, etc., and they receive the majority of the family inheritance. Boys are sent to school both locally and abroad. Also, boys are expected to take care of the entire family's financial needs. She brought me up to speed on her children's spouses and their attributes.

Once I had met her children over the next several days, her focus turned to my childhood, as well as catching up with news about Hadhramaut. Unlike my other sisters, Sheikha didn't ask about my father's wealth. Even though she had left home during the late 1960s, she was up to speed with what had happened back home in Hadhramaut during the past forty years.

Unlike my initial trip to Hadhramaut and Aden, when I hardly knew anybody, this time I was able to speak with Sheikha about cousins, shops, relatives—including those living in Saudi Arabia and Kuwait—and other family matters. We had multiple reference points and people to talk about. She could ask me about relatives in Yemen as I had lived there for several years in the 1980s and 1990s and she had left in 1970, eight years before I first moved there. I needed to catch up with news about back home, as I, too, had been away for almost ten years, and since she had impeccable memories of the past, she was able to get me up to speed. She was a giver; she seemed preoccupied with the welfare of others. I told her everyone must be responsible for their own affairs, as it would be impossible for her to help everyone.

In the middle of one of our conversations, she paused and said to me, "Thank you very much for assisting my sister Mujudah [Hind] when her leg was amputated a decade ago."

I told her, "I did nothing special. She is our sister, and I must do what I can."

*

During the winter of 1993, while heading to attend a wedding ceremony, my oldest sister, Hind, stepped on a nail as she passed by a house under construction. Due to the extreme heat, people in the region wear slim sandals, which provide little protection, so the nail impaled her foot. Even though she was hurt and bleeding, she ignored the injury and headed to the party.

The following day, when the foot was swollen and painful, she went to seek medical assistance. The doctor who examined the injury put my sister on heavy painkillers. Further, he cut the injured leg to clean and drain the blood. He didn't know that my sister was a diabetic who was taking insulin injections to control her blood sugar levels. With her high blood sugar level, the temperature above thirty degrees, and downplaying the extent of injury, the leg was unable to heal. Blood flow to the extremities is generally diminished in people with diabetes, which means that the tissue in these areas is unable to heal quickly. As a result, infection can develop more easily. She unknowingly developed wet gangrene as a result of the foot injury. This condition spread so rapidly that she started to see obvious changes in the skin of the affected area in just a few minutes. She didn't know those were symptoms of gas gangrene, and therefore, she didn't go to the emergency room immediately. Also working against her was the fact that the health care system was ill-prepared to assist as they didn't have good treatments or well-trained professionals.

By the time she contacted me a few months later, she had been told that they had no choice but to cut her foot below the talus (ankle bone). The notion of losing her foot was unbearable to her. She phoned me crying, begging me to help her save her foot. Her daughter's wedding was on the horizon, and she was devastated at the thought of being seen at the wedding without her foot.

I purchased an airline ticket for her and had her fly her from Hadhramaut to Sana'a, where I was living at that time. When it came to medical treatment, the whole country of Yemen had nothing to offer, but I thought I might be able to get a couple expert opinions on her condition. She was immediately admitted to the Kuwait Hospital emergency room in Sana'a. (Every hospital in Yemen was funded by Kuwaitis, so the hospitals were named after them.)

With the help of a friend, I was able to speak to Dr. Ameen Al-Gunaid, the director of the hospital, to explore the options, including perhaps sending her to Amman, Jordan. Dr. Al-Gunaid was direct and clear in his message: There was no hope of saving her leg regardless of what country I sent her to. In fact, since the amputation had already been delayed for more than a month, instead of amputating her foot below the ankle, they had to cut below her knee to have any chance of her leg healing. He added, if they waited any longer, the infection would spread more and perhaps the entire leg would have to go.

It was clear to me we were running out of time. However, breaking these facts and the next steps to my sister was the most difficult task I had to face in my life. Dr. Gunaid had to tell her while I was standing beside him in the hospital room. While crying, she gave me a look that I am unable to forget; that look made me feel like I was watching my sister fall off a cliff with my having no ability to assist her.

The doctors took blood samples, as they needed to have plans in case of loss of blood during amputation, and it turned out my sister and I didn't share the same blood type. I was desperate. A friend of mine named Amin Bahamam, who happened to have the same blood type, donated his blood so they could proceed with the operation. With a stricter diet and all measures in place, the procedure was successful. My sister was able to stand on her artificial leg at both my and her daughter's weddings.

*

The more I spoke about Hind, the more Sheikha cried about her dead sister, so I stopped talking about her. In Al-Shihr, the village where my sisters were born and my father had spent his youth, folks spoke highly about Zeinab, my first stepmother and my father's first wife, as a kind and caring person. She was quiet and spoke more with her eyes than with words. I saw Sheikha as a kind caregiver for all like her mother, Zeinab, was. While our oldest sister was in the hospital recovering from her amputation, Sheikha was on call to be sure her sister was okay. Now, she couldn't help but cry.

I spent the entire two weeks of my vacation getting to know my niece Wejdan's family and my sister's other children and grandchildren. Sheikha passed away in 2012 due to complications from diabetes.

Muna

My fourth sister, Muna, and I are much closer than I am to my other sisters due to our proximity in age and our birthplaces. I am four years older than she is. She is the youngest of our father's children. Muna in Arabic means "little noble and solitary one." In some Arab literature, Muna is defined as "unreachable wishes." Reflecting on all my sisters' names, my father picked names that were secular rather than religious in their connotation.

Muna and I were both born in Ethiopia, and we both lived in North Yemen, so we can relate to one another well. She was living in Sana'a until the Yemen Civil War forced her to return to Ethiopia in 2016. Of all of my sisters, she is also the only one that I have fought with and reconciled with many times. She is a kind-hearted person and would go to the moon to get me anything I asked for. Muna praises me in public, but she's also the first one to provide me the harshest criticism in private.

Although she didn't go far with her education, she was a pillar in assisting her younger siblings from her mother's side with completing their education as well as maintaining a good standard of living. Despite, or perhaps because of, her lack of formal education, she is a strong proponent of education. When my daughters and I make long-distance phone calls to her to ask how she is doing, she always inquires on how my daughters are doing in their respective schools. When my girls were in grade school, she encouraged them to aim for high school. Once they completed high school, she talked to them about university programs. When my oldest daughter completed her undergraduate degree, Muna demanded to know when my daughter would start a master's program. She consistently raises the bar and wants to see them be successful. She tells them, "You're learning for me and for yourself. You have opportunities that I don't have, and you should make the best of the prospects you have in Canada, as free women."

Whenever I'm in Sana'a, she oversees my affairs. Among most people there, I'm known for being Muna's brother, as if I don't have a name of my own. Like my other three sisters, she is too consumed with family status and my image. Due to having lived so long in North America, I tend to be open and forward. Often, I joke around or frequently mention how poor I was during my childhood. That is a no-no in her books. She doesn't want anyone to know the vulnerable side of me.

She repeatedly tells me, "Around here, people don't respect you when you tell them you had misfortunes in the past." I am supposed to be the golden boy from the Harhara family.

As I have spent two thirds of my life in Canada and the US, my Amharic language skills are gradually fading away, and often my Arabic comes across with English sentence structure rather than Arabic. She prefers that she talk on my behalf so that we make a good impression rather than allowing me to proceed in my clumsy way of talking. She tells me, "You don't know how to talk!"

Her mother was a Yemeni woman who hardly spoke much Amharic. I grew up with an Ethiopian family from an Amhara ethnic background, so I had a greater advantage of learning the local language, but it turned out she is better at speaking Amharic than me … perhaps my attention to language was diverted more to Arabic and English.

Whenever I visit her, she has a list of relatives I should visit. In most cases, her list contains relatives whose family members passed away several years ago, and my visit is a token of expressing condolences. Even if I don't know or no longer remember those folks, it doesn't matter. It's important to her and it must be done.

Despite the health and financial challenges she has faced, she has never asked me for one cent. She remains a dignified and proud woman. Initially, she never appreciated my effort to find my father's military records or pictures; she thought it was a waste of time. Even writing a book was an unimportant matter to invest my time in, as far as she was concerned. She never wants to look back. Her focus is only the future.

After much discussion, and my assurance that I would present a full and fair depiction of our family and not necessarily focus on the negative or on any scandal, she finally agreed with and approved of my intent to write my autobiography.

"As long as you mention some positive details among the bad, I guess it's OK," she relented.

XV

Military Service

I told her I knew when I was going to die because my birth certificate had an expiration date on it.

— Steven Wright

During the early 1980s, North Yemen required military service of men who had completed high school or a university degree. In particular, military service was mandatory for men who wanted to travel to Saudi Arabia to work as temporary workers. The Saudi Arabia government subsidized the entire military defense system in North Yemen; at the same time, the USSR subsidized the military in South Yemen, as neither country had the resources to fund their own defense systems. Every able-bodied North Yemeni man who went to renew a driver's license or an ID card was asked to provide evidence of military service, with the exception of men who were the only son in their family. (Women were able to drive, but they weren't required to do military service.)

In 1982, I was unable to renew my driver's license due to the absence of a civic military service certificate. I approached the Ministry of Defense to state that I was originally from South Yemen, born in Ethiopia to an Ethiopian mother, and I was the only surviving male within my family. My intent was to obtain a military service exemption paper. The person in charge requested that I draft an application letter and submit it to the appropriate authorities, which I did. I was hoping the decision would be made quickly so that I could resume normal life. Instead, I was ordered to enlist in the military branch for training while my case was being investigated and the outcome was being determined. The order meant I had to take an unpaid leave from my job, forcing me to live on a military income of US$175 a month.

During the initial screening and the interview process of me and the youths who had enlisted with me, the authorities discovered that I was able to read and write in Arabic and English. They were also impressed by my beautiful handwriting. Apparently, there was a demand within Immigration and Citizen Services for individuals who could write names and related information in English.

Immediately, I was told that after four weeks of military training (basic physical training, mastering how to set up a tent and a wear a uniform, learning how to line up and march, etc.), I was to report to the immigration office. Report I did, and I was assigned my duties: every morning, I was handed between 125 and 150 citizens' passports to translate from Arabic to English.

In those days, North Yemeni passports included one's first name, last name, father's name, birthplace and date, blood type, profession, marital status, and the list of countries where the North Yemeni passport could be used as a travel document.

I quickly noticed that in the Arabic version of all passports, every person's birth date was January 1, every person's blood type was O, and everyone was a laborer by profession. After translating nearly forty passports to English, I approached the officer in charge to uncover if what I witnessed was a mistake or ... was I missing something? What was going on here? Something strange ....

He responded to me, "Hey, Philosopher, we have no time to go through the citizens' applications. Just copy all relevant information to the passports. Nearly all of the applicants don't know their birth date, nor do they know their blood types. Ninety percent of the Yemenis are migrant workers heading to Saudi Arabia to work as daily laborers. Just translate the passports as they are, and I don't want to hear any more questions!"

I went silent and returned to my desk to continue translating.

A couple of weeks later, during a coffee break, I asked one of the military officers who was filling the passports in Arabic why he consistently chose applicants' blood type to be only O. He said, "As you know, the letter O is an identical character to the number 5 [٥] in the Arabic numeric system. I don't know any other blood types, and I don't know how to write the English letters for any of them, so I opted for O."

It made complete sense to me.

After four months of this type of military service in the North Yemeni army, I was discharged with an exemption because I was the only surviving male of my family. During those four months, I translated around 4,000 passports. Officially, those 4,000 individuals were all born on January 1.

All had the blood type O, and they were all laborers by profession.

And once again, I was the outcast, because despite being born two months prematurely, my birthdate is January 6. The other officers wanted to make my birthdate on my passport January 1, but I insisted on keeping my actual birthdate (January 6) on my passport, and my manager supported me. I was glad to have connections and know the right people so as to keep it as it was!

XVI

Cultural Turmoil

Don't let anyone tell you that you are half anything.

— Dean Atta

In the 1970s and 1980s, North Yemen was a melting pot of foreign advisors and workers, some of whom were traditional enemies with each other: North Koreans and South Koreans, Communist Chinese and Nationalist Chinese from Taiwan. There were also US Peace Corps volunteers and Saudi Arabians, both bearing huge gifts: the Americans supplied weapons, cars, and other equipment, and the Saudis paid for these supplies. Yemen also attracted Italian mechanics, Dutch doctors, Pakistani pilots, Filipino waiters, and Egyptian teachers.

The international aid projects often cut sharply across national and ideological lines. The airport, for example, was started by the Soviet Union in the early 1970s and completed by West Germany in the mid-1970s. It was then expanded by China in the early 1980s.

North Yemen's three main paved roads were also built by different groups. The road from Sana'a to Ta'izz was paved by Americans and West Germans, the one from Ta'izz to Hodeidah by Russians, and the one from Hodeidah to Sana'a by the Chinese.

Most of the teachers, doctors, and civil servants at that time were Egyptians whose presence totaled 25,000. The Sheraton Hotel, completed in 1980, was staffed largely by Filipinos, who came on two-year contracts. The best restaurant in the capital was owned by Lebanese.

During the 1960s and 1970s, with no oil and an illiteracy rate of 80 percent, many of the North Yemeni men became almost as accustomed to carrying rifles as they were to be wearing the traditional *jambiya,* or large curved dagger which is worn on the side by most men in the country. The jambiya has traditionally been a symbol of male honor and status in North Yemen. The steel blade is kept in a sheath made of wood, which is covered by cloth or wood. The decoration on the sheath represents status: the more ornate, the higher the status. The handle is the most important part of the jambiya. It used to be made from rhinoceros horn, but with recent policies banning poaching, the handles are now made from bull horn and other animal bone.[1] Like a jambiya, the gun symbolized manhood and virility while serving as a means of protection in a society that was ready for battle. Every man had a gun, and every man was a potential killer—that's what it means to be a *kabeeliy* (tribesman)—a man who's prepared to go to war with little or short notice.

At the same time, South Yemen was calling for the liberation of Yemenis from backward tribalism. Within South Yemen, there was a split between Mao and Russian models of socialist groups. The Maoist group's conciliatory overtures

Cultural Turmoil

toward North Yemen provoked trepidation among the pro-Soviet faction, resulting in further killings in South Yemen.

In June 1978, six months after I arrived in North Yemen, the pro-Saudi Arabia leader of North Yemen was killed by a briefcase bomb, delivered to Sana'a by the South Yemen leaders. Two months later, a mid-ranking army commander named Ali Abdallah Saleh came to power. The rumors were that Saleh had built a military power base through a controlling stake in the army's trade in bootleg alcohol. The interesting part was that within forty-eight hours, the presidents of both North and South Yemen had been eliminated as Salim Rubai Ali, the head of state in South Yemen, was executed on June 26, 1978 after attempting to seize power against other top coalition officials.[2]

Fundamental ideological differences between North and South Yemen were fueled by the fact that both states were embracing their neighbor's exiled opposition movements. In 1979, war broke out between the two countries, and the South took several towns beyond the border, bringing them under control within a matter of months. At the same time, the US promised to deliver US$300 million in support to North Yemen. American aircrafts were soon shuttling in and out of North Yemen, bringing tanks and anti-tank missiles. The American involvement also included the arrival of several hundred US military trainers to North Yemen.

*

Starting in the mid-1970s, invisible tensions were building between the local Indigenous citizens and so-called imported Yemenis—Muwalladin, as they called us. The source of the conflict was fourfold: economic, political, cultural/social, and historical.

Economically, the Muwalladin were earning a middle-class income through employment because of the aforementioned advantages due to our language skills and so on. We were able to quickly purchase and drive brand new cars, frequently travel, and easily build or rent houses considered lavish by the country's standards. We held positions as district managers and branch managers in most industries while most locals were left as spectators of the Muwalladin's successes in their homeland.

Moreover, during the 1960s and early 1970s, when North Yemen engaged in a war between Saudi-backed Royalists and Republicans supported by Egyptian President Jamal Nasser, nearly all Muwalladin oversaw operations of the military equipment as they were able to read the instructions. Yemeni individuals who were born outside Yemen were amongst civilian and military aircraft pilots, also. This is not because the Egyptians who trained them favored them over locals. It was simply because the locals didn't have the educational background to take on such roles.

Politically, as the Zaydi tribe members imposed their influence on the North Yemen political systems, they systematically removed those Muwalladin from their posts and, in some cases, eliminated them. The conflict was a result of a power struggle based on jealousy and a combination of fear and pure hatred toward those born overseas.

When I was in North Yemen during the late 1970s, Saudi-sponsored Islam become a weapon against leftist and subversive Arab nationalist ideologies that threatened the region. The Zaydi and Hashid tribes were playing a more prominent role in government and national politics.

It was also a time when the South and North Yemen countries were at odds, and the death of Al-Hamdi, former president of North Yemen, was still fresh in the mind of many North Yemenis. Colonel Ibrahim Al-Hamdi was a progressive leader who had the support of many people. However, his attempt to diminish the influence of tribal ways of thinking resulted in many prominent people resenting him. In addition, Al-Hamdi ignored the imperious effect of the Saudis and attempted to normalize dealings with communist South Yemen by having talks with their leaders. Shortly after his presidency ended, he and his brother were assassinated prior to having unity talks in Aden. Obviously, the Saudis feared the creeping influence of socialism in the region, and the public widely believed the rumors of the Saudi's involvement in the killing of the Yemeni leaders. Overwhelmingly, the majority of Muwalladin loved and supported Al-Hamdi.

Culturally and socially, Yemenis who had lived in East Africa, Vietnam, and other places had a much more worldly outlook. Due to exposure to more refined and modern standards of living abroad, Muwalladin dressed in Western styles and appeared cleaner than the locals. Often, the women didn't cover their faces or hair. In some cases, Muwalladin were known for gathering in social circles for partying, which is a transgression according to Islam and is therefore prohibited in North Yemeni customs.

The generation who came to Yemen in the late 70s and early 80s—those who were a few years older than me—were exposed to Marxist-Leninist views, and a good portion of them (including me) were never seen during the Friday mosque prayers. Also, the ceremonies for everyone born in

Ethiopia who got married during those decades were conducted according to Ethiopian customs, which included men and women dancing together. That was unheard of in North Yemen.

The historical aspect of the conflict was just an excuse to justify the above two issues—economics and culture— when the actual inability to reconcile or accept the influx of newcomers led to a backward lockdown of the country for many centuries. The resentment of local North Yemeni folks was wrapped up in historical pretext, primarily due to the rule of the Ethiopian King Abraha and the destruction imposed on the Yemeni people in the fifth century when Christianity was introduced, and the Jews of Yemen were persecuted. The result of his actions is centuries of deep-rooted hatred.

*

In the period between AD 500 and 520, a Jewish Himyarite ruler of North Yemen named Dhu Nuwas embarked on a military offence against the Aksumite Christians in Ethiopia and local Christian Arabs.[3] Many members of the Himyarite Christian group were massacred.

> Abraha Al-Ashram was an Aksumite army general, then the viceroy of southern Arabia for the Kingdom of Aksum who later declared himself an independent King of Himyar. Abraha ruled much of present-day Arabia and Yemen from at least AD 531-547 to 555-570.[4]

Al-Ashram led his army of 100,000 men with hundreds of elephants to successfully crush all resistance of the North

Yemeni army and then, following the suicide of Dhu Nuwas, seized power and established himself at Sana'a. In addition, Al-Ashram built the Al-Qalis[5] Church with the intent that all pilgrims direct themselves to his new cathedral, thereby bringing more profit to the area.

> The Al-Qalis Church, Sana'a, was a Miaphysite church constructed sometime between AD 527 and the late 560s [just outside] the city of Sana'a. The church's lavish decorations made it an important place of pilgrimage in competition with *Kaaba* [the building at the center of Mecca] in Mecca.[6]

Because Al-Ahsram had built a cathedral to rival the Kaaba at Mecca and specifically came with his forces of elephants to destroy the Kaaba, the local North Yemenis painted a damning picture of *all* these newcomers taking over, as Al-Ashram did, thereby tainting their reputation.

The death of Al-Hamdi and the influence of Zaydi tribal personalities in the government circles appeared to be the beginning of discrimination and prejudices against those who were born outside Yemen. In an attempt to modernize Yemen and establish civil institutions, Al-Hamdi issued free airline tickets to airlift and return Yemenis born abroad to their native land (North Yemen). He knew the benefits of highly skilled individuals' contributions toward a better North Yemen. Most Muwalladin benefited from opportunities and flocked to North Yemen. Nearly all of them joined the work force, including the military. Those in the military held high-ranking posts. Many of the Muwalladin fought alongside the Republicans to defeat the Saudi-backed Royalists, which resulted in increased hatred from the Royalists. However, the Muwalladin were gradually removed or systematically jailed. I also heard of a few being killed due to power struggles.

Systematic isolation, persecution, discrimination, and prejudice lingered in North Yemen for decades as a result. I, too, was a recipient of a great deal of the aftereffects.

What was the direct impact on me? Constant harassment and humiliation, making it difficult to live. I can speculate that it was similar to how Black Americans were treated in the South during the 1950s. I suffered from a primitive way of life and from the rotten, corrupted system. I was denied any kind of scholarship or job working for any government entities. I had to constantly fight to get a driver's license or ID card, and I was harshly interrogated every time I intended to travel to South Yemen to visit my sisters.

I was in the mix of all of this, and exodus from North Yemen became more imperative than ever before!

XVII

Hands Off

Hand off my ass or I'll rip off your balls.

— Katie McGarry

I have a perpetually bad habit of tailgating the vehicle in front of me. All of the car accidents I have been in involved me rear-ending the person ahead of me.

One day in 1982, I was driving in the streets of Sana'a and trying to swap a music cassette tape in the car while following another car at high speed. From the license plate, I could tell that the Gary Volvo was a diplomatic car, but I wasn't aware of who the driver was.

For some reason, the Volvo stopped suddenly, and I ended up smashing into the back of it. The other driver and I both stepped out of our vehicles to inspect the extent of the damage. At the same time, a military truck with several soldiers loaded on the back stopped behind us. The driver of the military truck and an officer got out of the truck to talk to us. The officer noticed the man in the Volvo wasn't Yemeni and inquired as to which country the diplomat was representing in North Yemen.

The other driver introduced himself as the ambassador of Iraq. The officer immediately saluted and apologized to the ambassador. He then turned to me and asked for my ID. When he glanced at my ID, he noticed that I was born in Ethiopia and shouted at me, "*Ya habeshi! Ya Muwallad,*" meaning, "Hey, you, the Ethiopian born and imported Yemeni!" He continued screaming at me, "You have caused some issue here. Who taught you how to drive, anyway? Where is your driver license?" I handed my license to him, and he kept both it and my ID card.

The officer told the ambassador that he would follow up with him at the embassy office to further discuss how the vehicle would be repaired. He also assured the Iraqi man that I would be kept in jail until the situation was sorted out. The ambassador was perplexed but didn't say anything.

The officer then turned to me and ordered me to hop into the back of the military truck with the remaining twenty-plus soldiers. Instead of quelling the problem, the officer ordered me to the traffic detention center. He also instructed one of the soldiers to drive my car to the nearest police station where it was to be impounded until the accident was resolved. When we arrived at the jail, the officer departed with my driver's license and ID.

I spent the night of December 13, 1982, in jail. I vividly recall that date because it was the day North Yemen experienced an earthquake with a magnitude of 6.2 Mw[1], more than six meters in depth.[2]

I was wide awake all night wondering how I was going to pay for the damaged cars—mine and the ambassador's.[3] In addition, I didn't even know the name of the officer who had taken my driver's license and ID. If I couldn't locate him, I had no idea how long it would take me to obtain replacements of those vital documents.

Around seventeen men were in the holding cell with me. All of them were jailed for traffic violations and accidents. Some had killed pedestrians; others were long-distance taxi drivers who had been involved in fatal traffic accidents. Some were there at no fault of their own. Rather, they happened to have had a traffic collision with a powerful tribe leader or another influential person. Every time there was a situation like this, the driver who happened to be a poor Yemeni guy was deemed to be at fault and put in jail.

The following day at about 4 p.m., a little more than thirty hours into my incarceration and while the other men in the room were chewing qat and yapping, I fell asleep.

Within forty minutes or so, I felt my body moving. I thought I was dreaming or reliving the earthquake from the day before. But I then felt someone trying to pull down my pants, and I felt a hand touching my buttocks. I violently jumped out of my sleep and stood up. One of the men who was lying next to where I had been sleeping was both astonished by the speed of my awakening and frightened at what I would do.

I immediately realized what he was trying to do to me. I have no idea where I got the power or the ability to turn into a violent animal. I said to myself, *I'm either gonna' become a solid dude, or I'm gonna' be this guy's little bitch.* I grabbed his *al-asba* (Yemeni-Hadhrami word for head covering or Arab turban, also called *emama* in Yemeni-Hadhrami or *mashada* in Arabic), put it over his neck, and tried to kill him. The other men in the room quickly grabbed me and tried to get me off of him. It took five men to separate us. While he was struggling to get me off of him, I took a bite out of his ear, which prompted a lot of bleeding and screaming. The guards added to the struggle by rushing in and separating the two of us.

One of the guards exclaimed, "This *habeshi* is an animal!"[4] (He was referring to me.) The other guard asked who knew what had triggered the fight, and one of the other prisoners stated, "I would do the same if a dog like this one was trying to mess with my butt. I would kill him." I felt good that most of the men and the guards sided with me by praising my reaction and condemning the man who had tried to assault me. I learned the best thing to do is stand up for myself at all times.

*

I'm not sure what prompted the Iraqi ambassador to inquire about me, but after I had been detained for about a week, he showed up at the traffic holding cell where I was being kept. Not only was I confused and surprised by his visit, but the guards and my cellmates also were. No one received any visitors, so his appearance was of great interest to everyone.

The place I was held was a typical North Yemeni two-bedroom house made of stone with a flat roof, chain fence, big driveway, and metal gate. The gate was chained with a lock, and one or two guards sat outside with rifles, making sure we didn't escape. The washroom was like an outhouse, with running water including a shower. We spent much of our days outside in the yard sitting on the cobblestones in the sunshine, and we went inside the house in the evening to sleep, so everyone was outside and saw the ambassador when he drove up and approached the house. He was bigger, taller, and lighter-skinned than the average Yemeni, and he had a driver, so those who were in the jail with me knew he was someone of importance.

When he arrived, I was escorted to the door (gate) of the traffic holding cell. The ambassador remembered my name and asked me, "How are you, Adel?" He also asked if I was Sudanese, as the name Adel wasn't a common name in North Yemen. I told him that I was Yemeni from the South. He even became interested to hear my father's name, too.

"Both your name and your father's name, Majid, are common names in Iraq," he informed me.

He went on to ask if I had had any visitors and if I had been eating and looked after by my family while I had been in jail. I told him that all was fine with me. He promised me he would be back, and he left. I returned to the holding cell.

The men in my cell started to inquire about his visit and what we talked about. In the meantime, they turned to the man who had tried to mount me, telling him, "You're messing around with the wrong boy."

Most of the men in our cell had been there for about eight weeks without hearing of their case being investigated or addressed. To have the attention of the ambassador within less than a week was unprecedented, and they all thought I would be released quickly.

While everyone was providing their analysis of my case and the probable outcome, I waited. In about an hour or so, the ambassador returned and requested that I see him again. This time, he said, "I just spoke to the head of the Traffic

Department, the person in charge of this jail cell, about the case. I informed him that I am no longer interested in pressing charges, as I will be fixing my car. I also requested they release you immediately."

With my heart pounding fast, I asked him, "What did he say?"

He responded, "He initially didn't agree, as he felt you needed to be punished." He also said, "He probably needs some money paid to him and the staff to release you and your car. Do you have money?"

"I can manage," I assured him.

Just before departing the vicinity, the ambassador asked me, "What kind of people are these? We don't even put our animals in these types of conditions. This is an appalling place to be locked up." He handed me his business card and suggested I could visit him at his office if I chose to do so.

After bribing the officers and paying a fine, I was released free and clear with my badly dented car. I was also able to collect my ID and driver's license after providing additional bribes. I didn't mind paying the bribes, as it would have cost me twice as much money and taken a lot of time and effort to obtain new documents.

I can only speculate on why the ambassador helped me: I believe he did not like the way I was being treated, and he particularly thought the conditions of the jail were not fit for humans. He saw me as helpless in dealing with an officer who just immediately treated me as though I were a criminal. He brought his own humanity to the situation. Although I thought of visiting the Iraqi ambassador to again thank him and perhaps ask him about obtaining a scholarship, as two of my friends had gone to Baghdad to earn engineering and medical degrees, I decided to drop the notion and continue to focus on migrating to the US. In the 1960s, 70s, and 80s, Iraq was recognized as having the best universities in the Middle East and so I briefly considered pursuing my education there. However, Bansser had encouraged me to go to the US or UK, and knowing my father was a British citizen, I felt pulled to those places.

*

About two or three weeks after being released, I started to see that food supplies that had been sent to North Yemen by many international donors were being sold in local grocery stores. Yes, I could say a portion of the aid that was supposed to be delivered to the victims of the earthquake didn't benefit those in need; rather, it was sold underground by corrupt officials. I quickly realized that despite being citizens of an Arabic and Islamic country, praying several times a day, and fasting, Yemenis were as corrupt as any group of people we speak ill about. I was disheartened by such actions.

Lo and behold, when I returned to Yemen from the US in 1993, the food and other support that the World Food Programme (WFP) was sending to help the Somali refugees in North Yemen was also being openly traded in local markets. I began to realize that international aid such as oil, milk, vaccines, and other medicines sent to developing countries don't necessarily reach the intended recipients. People take these products from the ports and sell them. Through what I witnessed, not only did I become suspicious of individual adults, I also developed skepticism toward any aid organizations or governments providing aid to developing countries. Many NGOs are purposely misleading the public, soliciting donations and aid but then redirecting the resources.

From my first-hand experience, it seems that most social assistance money never reaches the intended destination; instead of being used for social development and the construction of roads, hospitals, and schools, the money moves from one pocket to another or is entirely swallowed by corrupt local officials. Even though imperialism ended many years ago, the developing countries are still indirectly operating under the rule of former new colonies. Decades ago, European countries took over developing countries to obtain raw materials and ruled by force. These days, the approach is different but the outcome is the same. Rather than ruling by force, Western countries provide loans, knowing that the vast majority of the money will end up in the hands of corrupt individuals. When the borrowing country cannot pay back the loan, the West then takes the raw materials as a form of payment. It's a modern form of colonialism, equally as cruel and self-serving as what was done in previous decades.

XVIII

Umrah

The Prophet Muhammed (pbuh) said "Whoever performs Hajj with any obscenity shall return (from Hajj) like a newborn baby."

— Al Bukhari

Hussein, my older half brother, was the second of Majid's children. Born in Hadhramaut, he spent a good portion of his youth between Aden and Addis Ababa. He didn't go to Arabic school, and his first language was English. That wasn't a surprise to me as our father wanted his children to grow up with Western styles and standards. Our father took Hussein to Addis Ababa in 1948, when Hussein was a seven-year-old, and registered him at the Sanford International School Kebena.

The Sanford International School Kebena was established in the early 1940s when Mrs. Christine Sandford, the wife of Colonel Sandford, head of the British Military Mission to Ethiopia during World War II, wanted to open an English-speaking school for her children.

> Colonel Sanford, along with Cunningham and Wingate, led the British contingent that was dispatched by the British government to help Emperor Haile Selassie I and the Ethiopian army reclaim the country from five years of Italian occupation under Mussolini's government.[1]

The school was initially called the Sandford English Community School. It quickly expanded, and as a result of an agreement with the imperial government, elite Ethiopians including the royal and other leading families were allowed to enroll their children in the school, as well. The school's role has been unique in Ethiopia and in Africa since it was established. "It was one of the first international schools in Africa for both nationals and expatriates learning on an equal basis"[2] and continues to be today.

Hussein later moved to a secondary boarding school. Without a mother around and with no support system on the home front, he enjoyed partying, drinking, and frequenting bars and nightclub. His grades were not impressive, and he constantly had issues with our father. According to my father's and Hussein's friends, the situation was tense between the two of them, and in 1959 when Hussein was nineteen, he left Ethiopia for Yemen. Perhaps Hussein's leaving Ethiopia for Aden was the best outcome for all parties.

After spending several years in Aden working for Besse Company, and after Yemen gained its independence from the British, Hussein packed up again and left for Jeddah, Saudi Arabia in 1969. He was married to a Hadhrami woman and had four daughters before he passed away in 1979 at the age of thirty-eight. The plan was that once I landed in North Yemen and changed my passport, I would be heading to Jeddah to meet him. However, he passed away a year after I arrived in North Yemen and before I was able to visit and meet him.

With his death, I became the only surviving son of Majid. The expectation was that I pay a visit to those four girls Hussein had left behind. My visit wasn't to provide any financial support or rescue them from anything, but to be a token uncle. In 1983, after exchanging a few phone calls and letters with the family there, I planned my trip to Jeddah, Saudi Arabia.

My journey to Jeddah was my first major flight outside North Yemen, and Saudia, known then as Saudi Arabian Airlines, was the biggest airline I was on during the early 1980s. Hussein's oldest daughter, Arawa, who was thirteen at the time, and her uncle (her mother's brother) came to the airport to pick me up. They lived in an area called *Bab Mecca*. It reminded me of the *Bab Al-Yemen* area of Sana'a. There were modern buildings, as well as mud houses, and lots of Hadhramis.

Jeddah is Islam's holiest city. *Bab Mecca*, the arched gate marking the entrance to the city of Mecca, is the most important gate historically for Jeddah as it is the official boundary between the *haram* (sacred area where non-Muslims are not permitted) and the rest of the city. Billions of pilgrims have passed under this gate in the past fourteen centuries as they have made their pilgrimages to Mecca, the birthplace of the Prophet Muhammed (pbuh).

Hussein's children were Arawa, Ebtsam (ten), Amani (nine), and Amira (seven). They were thrilled to see me. Apart from the oldest, the children didn't have any recollection of their father. I tried to prompt their mother to share stories with me about her late husband, but she either knew little about him or chose not to speak much about him. She told me he traveled a lot for work and mentioned he had spent considerable time in Beirut, Lebanon.

After a couple of days in Jeddah, my family asked me to get ready for a trip to Mecca for *Umrah*, the Islamic pilgrimage. Unlike the *Hajj* pilgrimage, which is scheduled on a specific date each year and which every Muslim (both men and women) is required to do once in their lifetime, the Umrah pilgrimage to Mecca can be undertaken at any time of the year. Although I had studied the Qur'an at a young age and lived in North Yemen for several years by that point, I never went for prayer regularly or practiced Islam, as was expected of me. By the time I visited Jeddah, I had completely forgotten the protocols for reaching a state of purification achieved by completing cleansing rituals, wearing the prescribed attire, and abstaining from certain actions. Arawa took on the responsibility of giving me a refresher course on all aspects of the protocols. She said to me, which I will always remember vividly, "Uncle, your knowledge of religion is very pathetic." I laughed.

Umrah requires Muslims to perform two key rituals: *Tawaf* and *Sa'i*. Tawaf is a counterclockwise, circular procession around the Kaaba, which must be completed seven times. It is recommended to do the first three circuits at a hurried pace, followed by four rounds at a more leisurely pace. Tawaf is followed by Sa'i, a walk back and forth between Safa and Marwa[3] in the Great Mosque of Mecca, a walk that commemorates Hagar's search for water for her son and for God's mercy in answering prayers. Pilgrims conclude the pilgrimage with *Halq*, a partial or complete shortening of the hair. The Kaaba is a place where men and women are treated equally except at prayer time, when men are in the front of the prayer area and women are in the back.

Umrah is sometimes considered the lesser pilgrimage in that it is not compulsory but still highly recommended. It is generally possible to complete Umrah in a few hours in comparison to Hajj, which may take a few days. Umrah is also not meant to be interpreted as a substitute for Hajj. However, both are demonstrations of the solidarity of the Muslim people and their devotion to Allah. I managed to do all of what was required for Umrah so as to please the family.

*

The highlight of my trip was getting to know Hussein's daughters. My nieces had a lot of fun with my appearance; they enjoyed dressing me like a lady and putting makeup on me. Due to the color of my skin, they thought it would be funny to try to make me look like a Somali or Ethiopian housemaid.

After visiting more family members and my brother's friends and spending lots of fun time with my nieces, I returned to North Yemen, ending my two-week visit.

XIX

Marriage Versus Education

Let there be spaces in your togetherness, And let the winds of the heavens dance between you. Love one another but make not a bond of love: Let it be rather a moving sea between the shores of your souls.

— Kahlil Gibran

My oldest sister, Hind, made it her goal to find the most beautiful girl for me to marry and form a suitable family. In Arab culture, marriages are often arranged between parents—no shame or guilt about it—but since I had no parents, my sister took on this role. It is said that the love for a child is born the moment the child enters the world. Marriage is assumed to be similar, as you grow to love your life partner from the day you get married.

At the time, in my mind, nothing was nobler than marrying a beautiful girl selected by my sister. It meant bonding with my family and cementing my status within my father's side of the family. I had left Ethiopia at a young age. I had zero plans to return to Ethiopia or marry an Ethiopian girl. Due to my awareness of and exposure to hidden intolerance of Christian Amharas[1] toward Muslims or Arabs, the notion of marrying an Ethiopian girl didn't cross my mind.

The girl my family selected for me was also a friend of my niece's (Hind's daughter) and was from Hadhramaut. My niece managed to secretly bring my future wife's picture for me to see. Indeed, the girl was beautiful and reminded me of my stepmother Maryam. Why do we pick partners who resemble our parents?

At the time, I was living in North Yemen (pro-West), and she was living in South Yemen (pro-Soviet Union). Going back and forth between the two countries was complicated and at times almost impossible. Through my niece, I secretly managed to exchange letters with the girl, and our love intensified day by day. I started ordering wedding gifts—gold and clothing from Gulf countries. We talked a lot about our future lives, our children, education, and the two Yemen countries. I wasn't interested in living in communist South Yemen, and she didn't want to leave her family and her country. Despite these hurdles, though, we were optimistic things would work out between us.

After consultation with members of the families on both sides, it was agreed the marriage would take place on March 26, 1984. Both families embarked on renovating their respective houses as well as making the necessary arrangements.

*

Before Islam came to South Arabia in the seventh century BC, a variety of marriage practices existed, the most common and recognized being

> marriage by agreement, marriage by
> capture, marriage by mahr, marriage by
> inheritance, and "mot'a" or temporary
> marriage. In Mesopotamia, marriages were
> generally monogamous, except among
> royalty, who would have harems consisting
> of wives and concubines. The Sasanian
> society followed Zoroastrianism, which
> viewed women to be possessions in
> marriage, although consent was required in
> both marriage and divorce.[2]

Because of the attitudes toward women at that time, women had little to no say over any decisions to do with the marriage. They were not given a choice as to who to marry, nor were they allowed to divorce their husbands. More of these rights were granted to women when Islam came to the region. They were allowed to negotiate the terms of their marriage contract and could also request a divorce.

Today, consent by both the bride and groom is required in Yemeni-Hadhrami marriages. The bride's *wali* (custodian, guardian, protector, etc., usually her father or, in the absence of a father, another significant male relative) is also required to consent to the union. The marriage is arranged but not forced. Whether it be verbal or in writing, a formal, binding contract is necessary to validate an Islamic marriage, and the contract outlines both the bride's and groom's rights and responsibilities.[3]

Once an agreement has been reached, plans for a wedding can be made. The marriage ceremony is performed publicly and preferably by a religious leader or at least someone knowledgeable in religious practices. Following the ceremony, a reception is held according to the couple's or local customs. The reception could last anywhere between a couple of hours to several days.

The Qur'an tells believers that even if they are poor, they should marry to protect themselves from immorality and asserts that marriage is a legitimate way to satisfy one's sexual desire.[4] Islam recognizes the value of sex and companionship and advocates marriage as the foundation for families and channeling the fulfillment of such a base need.

According to Islam, the husband is financially responsible for supporting his wife or wives and children including, at the minimum, providing a home, food, and clothing. In return, it is the wife's duty to protect the husband's possessions and be judicious in how earnings are spent:

> Husbands should take good care of their wives, with [the bounties] God has given to some more than others and with what they spend out of their own money. Righteous wives are devout and guard what God would have them guard in their husbands' absence.[5]

With this responsibility in mind, part of the agreement or marriage contract is the expectation that the husband (his family—usually his father, but in my case, because my father was deceased, the responsibility was on me) provide to his wife a *mahr*, which is set aside for her exclusive use. The word dowry is often used to explain mahr, but a mahr is different from a marriage dowry in that it is required in a Muslim marriage, and the mahr may consist of money, but it does not have to. It could also consist of gold, furnishings for the house, land, or other goods that may be useful to the bride.

Culturally, we don't say that the mahr goes to the bride; it goes from the groom's family to the bride's family, but the mahr is for the bride to use.

There is a minimum but no maximum to the amount that the mahr is worth. The minimum equates to the amount that would allow the woman to support herself if her husband dies or if they divorce.

If agreed upon by both parties, the mahr may also be paid in parts. A *mu'qadam* is a portion of the mahr paid to the bride at the time the marriage contract is signed. A later portion called a *mu'akhaar* (meaning *delayed*) is paid at an agreed-upon date during the marriage. Regardless of when the mahr is paid, the full amount is to be paid unless the wife waives her right to it: "Give women their bridal gift upon marriage, though if they are happy to give up some of it for you, you may enjoy it with a clear conscience."[6]

*

In Arab culture, and according to the words of the Prophet Mohammed (pbuh), there is a belief and saying that "half of your faith and religion is marriage *(elzawaj nisf aldiyn)*," meaning one must be married to be a complete person. In other words, half of a successful person's achievement in life will be their marriage. In Arabia, marriage is a legal contract between a man and a woman.

The Prophet Muhammed (pbuh) said, "When a man marries, he has fulfilled half of the deen; so let him fear Allah regarding the remaining half."[7] Marriage is said to help in fulfilling one desires in a halal[8] way, the message being that a companion will undoubtedly encourage you to live better in life and help you in raising a family. If a man has the means to marry and has no fear of mistreating his wife or of committing unlawful acts if he does marry, then marriage is preferred.

The Qur'an emphasizes that women are entitled to not only financial but also emotional support and that men cannot take back any of the mahr unless his wife is found guilty of sexual impropriety:

> You who believe, it is not lawful for you to inherit women against their will, nor should you treat your wives harshly, hoping to take back some of the bride-gift you gave them, unless they are guilty of something clearly outrageous. Live with them in accordance with what is fair and kind: if you dislike them, it may well be that you dislike something in which God has put much good.[9]

If partial payment of the mahr was postponed, some husbands might pressure their wives to forfeit what he still owes or return what he gave her before he agrees to a divorce, but to do so is not allowed in Islam. Additionally, the husband does not have the right to keep the rest of the mahr if he has been abusive or neglectful to his wife.

The Qur'an also instructs that if the husband is neglecting his family, women are entitled to seek a divorce: "If a wife fears high-handedness or alienation from her husband, neither of them will be blamed if they come to a peaceful settlement, for peace is best."[10]

> If you [believers] fear that a couple my
> break up, appoint one arbiter from his
> family and one from hers. Then, if the
> couple want to put things right, God will
> bring about a reconciliation between them.
> He is all knowing, all aware.[11]

In Yemen, most marriages are arranged by the bride's and groom's families. The groom's female relatives suggest potential brides to the man and his father, who then decide together on the most suitable bride based on compatibility and social standing. Before the marriage contract is drawn up, the woman's father asks the potential bride for her input and takes into account her wishes. In Arab tradition, the ideal match is between cousins when the daughter of the groom's uncle (father's brother) is the bride. Other endogamous[12] matches are encouraged as well.[13]

According to *shari'a* law,[14] a man may marry up to four wives as long as he treats them all as equals. However, the rate of polygamy in Yemen is low. Half of the adult population is married, and four percent is widowed. Only one percent of the population is divorced.[15] Divorce in Islam can take a variety of forms, some executed by a husband personally and some by a religious court on behalf of a plaintiff wife who is successful in her legal divorce petition for valid cause. Both men and women can request a divorce; divorce and remarriage are not frowned upon.

If the husband initiates the divorce, the ex-wife keeps her mahr. She is permitted to remarry after four months and ten days, and her ex-husband is required to support her during that period. If the woman does not remarry, children up to seven years old remain with her.[16]

Marriage is something that I highly value as a noble state of adulthood. Family is the most important aspect of Yemeni and Ethiopian lives. It forms the basis of people's support networks, with relatives often being mutually reliant on one another to meet everyday challenges.

Because I grew up without a mother and father, I wanted my children to have both parents around them, helping them grow. In addition, from the perspective of social standing, a married man has a higher stature and greater respect than a single man.

I was a single man living in a society that had no space for single men. I was never invited to social gatherings, and I always had difficulty finding a place to live. Due to the religious and cultural restrictions, I was at the point in life where I needed to marry. In Yemen, marriage is one of the most important aspects of a person's life once they reach the age of eighteen. The common view is that once a girl becomes an adult, her place is in her father's home, her husband's home, or the grave. Boys, upon reaching adulthood, have no status, no manhood unless they are married. Without a spouse, you are not a complete person. It was time for me to be a whole person.

However, there was a conflict within me.

XX

The American Dream

Those who pursue the American dream believe that no matter how much they accomplish, there is always something better to strive for.

— F. Scott Fitzgerald

I met Mark Hansen in 1982. He originally came to North Yemen to teach English as a second language (ESL) at the Yemen-American Language Institute (YALI). YALI was founded by the United States Embassy in Sana'a in 1975. It was and still is supported by a range of public and private sponsors and several bilateral and multilateral development sponsors. YALI also works to promote cultural understanding through its information programs and cultural activities. The locals and staff from other developing countries who worked at USAID, the US Embassy, and other US-affiliated NGOs were sent to take English language courses. I was part of the crew who was selected and regularly sent to take English language training at YALI.

I caught the attention of Mark because of both my appearance and my schoolwork. Due to my dark skin, he assumed that I wasn't a Yemeni. Moreover, in comparison to his other Yemeni students, I was the only one who was able to correctly pronounce the letters P and V. Most of the Arabic speaking population pronounce Ps like Bs, and Vs like Fs. For example, *Pepsi* sounds like *Bebsi*, or the word *video* sounds like *fideo*. Ditto for *ch*; Arabic speakers tend to mistake the *ch* sound for *sh*, which means the word *check* will sound like *sheck*.

The courses were given after working hours in the evenings. Most students used to come to class after qat-chewing session and in some cases, some arrived at the class still chewing qat. Nearly two thirds of them smoked. I didn't go for smoke breaks, nor did I chew qat. I piqued Mark's interest because I was different.

One evening, Mark asked me where I was from. I told him, "I'm Yemeni-Hadhrami but was born in Ethiopia to an Ethiopian mother."

With an ear-to-ear smile he looked at me and said, "My son is Ghanaian." Then he qualified his statement, "I was married to Ghanaian woman and adopted her son."

He had married his wife in Ghana, and then the three of them moved to the US. The wife and son were living in the US, but Mark had come to North Yemen in the early 1980s to teach English. It was my understanding that Mark was still married to her but that she had requested an open marriage, so they were living separate lives at that time on different continents.

We quickly bonded and started to meet on weekends. During our visits, he began to share with me about his background in the US, including his involvement in the Communist Party USA. He had studied Russian literature in his undergraduate degree and had his master's degree in

English. When he spoke, he always held a glass of wine and a cigarette in the same hand. That was most amazing to me, and I used to worry he would burn himself or spill the wine when he got into intense conversation.

From the moment he became aware of my plans to go to the US until the day I departed North Yemen for the US about eighteen months later, he educated me about American history. The topics he focused on were the civil war, the Fourteenth Amendment, civil rights movements, the Jim Crow laws, and other internal conflicts including political and civil right leaders such as Abraham Lincoln, John F. Kennedy (JFK), Frederick Douglass, Martin Luther King Jr. (MLK), Malcom X, and Angela Davis.

He encouraged and supported my notion of heading to the US, but he also warned me that the reality in America was quite different from what I was imagining. "Adel," he said one day, "I'm afraid I'm going to burst your bubble. In America, if I have 0.1 percent Black blood in me, I'm Black and I have no rights."

He believed that since I belonged to a stronger tribe, perhaps I was better off staying in Yemen than heading to the US. "Always remember where you came from, my friend. Your family has deep roots here. Perhaps you would make a stronger impact here, carrying on their legacy."

Through his Ghanaian wife, he appeared to know about West African history. He knew little about Arabian or East African history, but he made sure I understood *my* history. He knew I was determined to leave North Yemen but constantly warned me to know my family legacy and background. According to him, that was the only way I could hold my head up in the US. In his view, I would always be inferior to the white race if I didn't know my heritage. "If you won't be deterred from going, then go. But carry with you a strong sense of self. Know your family history. Know what you stand for, and stand strong in your beliefs and your sense of identity. Go forth as a confident young man. And always beware of those who seek to hamstring you simply because of your race or religion or the part of the world you came from."

Mark was an avid reader. He introduced to me biography books about Malcom X and MLK. He didn't think highly of MLK, but he favored Malcom X. He compared MLK to the king of soccer from Brazil named Pelé, and Malcom X to Mohammed Ali. In his view, all four individuals were wonderful athletes and good people, but while one pair was a bit submissive and was well-liked by white people, the other appeared to be punchy and sore or *salty*, as he called them.

"Malcolm X had it right. There's more to the civil rights movement than Blacks being allowed to sit on any seat on the bus or restaurant. Those are just token gestures—surface level actions which create a false sense of equality. What's more important are identity, integrity, and true freedom. Complete independence from white oppression."

"That's what's dangerous about deeds such as removing 'whites only' signs from public property. Society then thinks that's where it ends—that by allowing equal access to the water fountain or seats on the bus, 'We've arrived. With the snap of a finger, Blacks are now equal.'"

And with that he snapped his fingers—fortunately on the hand that wasn't holding the cigarette and wine glass!

"That's a false sense of progress. True progress will only come when the hidden discrimination has been wiped out."

Mark called JFK "the good-looking rich boy," and I told him that JFK was my hero, citing the civil rights speech he gave on June 11, 1963.[1]

I was trying to draw a parallel between the relationship between F. Douglass and A. Lincoln with MLK and JFK. Mark politely but firmly crushed my idealistic and naïve views.

He told me, "Adel, dig deep and look at the big picture. Lincoln didn't free Blacks because he cared about Blacks. Rather, it was for economic reasons. He needed soldiers to fight the South." He went on, saying, "JFK was too busy dealing with Cuba and the [former] USSR about nuclear arms, and he paid zero attention to Blacks. If anything, LBJ made some dents in the progress for Blacks, but not JFK."

He also told me, "The issue between unionists and federalists is all about the boys from South getting angry at the boys in the North and vice versa. The same goes for the two political parties—Democrats and Republicans. Don't fool yourself."

He was well-versed in the discrimination that was taking place against African Americans in the US. Often, I wondered if it was worth going to the US.

In the years I spent in North Yemen working for an American organization and socializing with Americans, I had never met an American who had such a low opinion of his own country. He was the only American I encountered who embraced communist views! In his youth, Mark was one of the men who marched against the Vietnam War and protested for women's rights, Black rights, etc. He was a totally radical person. Ironically, while I abandoned the Marxist-Leninist views and countries like South Yemen and Ethiopia, he was hoping to be living under that ideology.

As much as I gravitated toward Mark for his intellectual predispositions, part of me also didn't want to be around him, as he was delivering the ugly side of the US blow by blow. It was hard to digest, and it was difficult to see my dreams and hopes being tainted by his views. Once, I asked him why he always had such negative views of his country and some of the leaders. His response was, "I speak the truth."

Despite his negative comments about the US, I was determined to move there and continued to pursue that goal.

*

At some point during the three years that I took lessons from and was friends and colleagues with him, Mark fell in love with a Yemeni-Ethiopian girl—one of his other students. He broke the news to me and told me he wanted to marry her. I told him that was nearly impossible given the cultural and language differences, as well as many other factors such as religious differences, the age difference, and the fact that he was so radical in his political views. She barely spoke any English. He was fifty-three, and she was in her early twenties. Initially, I thought he was just infatuated by this girl or lonely in North Yemen, but he insisted he was determined to marry her and he asked me for advice on how to go about doing so.

He pressed me to speak to her and her family, so I finally relented and visited the girl's parents, breaking his intentions to her family. I also asked the girl if she had any feelings for him and intended to marry him. She didn't answer me directly, but she wanted me to ask her father and see what his demands were and if he would agree to the marriage, which indicated she was willing to enter the marriage. I agreed to speak to her father.

When I spoke to the father, he said he didn't oppose the marriage provided Mark became a Muslim. I thought that was his way of putting up a barrier or a hurdle to the proposal. I knew Mark enjoyed his drinks and would never be a Muslim given his ideological and religious views. When I mentioned the father's request to Mark, to my surprise Mark agreed! At the time, I only had a week before leaving for the US, so I quickly arranged with a local mosque and sheikh to have Mark obtain an Islamic certificate. To make it possible for him to obtain the document, I asked the officials to write *Mubarak Hussein* in place of Mark Hansen on his Islamic certificate.

I then left Yemen, and later I found out the deal didn't go through; Mark didn't marry the girl. I never heard what had happened to change his mind.

*

As one of my biggest supporters, and despite his disdain for his own country, Mark wrote the following letter to help me pursue my dream of going to university in the US:

June 30, 1984

TO WHOM IT MAY CONCERN

I have known Mr. Adel Ben-Harhara for approximately three years as a colleague and student, and feel I am thoroughly familiar with his abilities and potential for academic study.

Mr. Ben-Harhara is currently Procurement Assistant at USAID, and had he not decided to further his education in the United States, he was scheduled for a promotion to the position of Assistant Systems Manager, an area of particular interest to him as he has both a deep interest and unusual ability with regard to computer systems, including programming, etc. His command of the English language, while not at a native English speaker level, is fully proficient enough to handle any university level classes in the US, and this, combined with extremely high motivation, a commitment to study and learning, and a passion to succeed in his chosen area of interest, should ensure that he will not only do well in university studies in the US, but exceptionally well.

Since Mr. Ben-Harhara (who is a Yemeni citizen, though he grew up in Ethiopia) was only able to complete a little more than ten years of formal schooling in Ethiopia as a result of political conditions, he took the General Education Diploma (GED) test in Sana'a in order to acquire high school equivalency. His scores were exceptionally high in all five categories, surpassing, in fact, most American students who take the test. All of his percentile ranks were in the 90s. Mr. Ben-Harhara did not achieve these successes without a great deal of hard work on his own time. He eliminated almost all of his social life and spent his afternoons and evenings studying, reading, and learning.

Adel is one of the brightest and most highly motivated young men I have ever come into contact with during my entire teaching career. He has sacrificed a lot to achieve what he has already achieved and expects to sacrifice even more. He will, I hope, continue past the BSc and eventually go into an MSc and a PhD program, and I expect he will bring honor to any educational institution in the US he chooses to attend.

Sincerely,
Mark Hansen, Coordinator, English Language Training Program

When I was digging up old records and found this letter, I discovered that Mark had a PhD in mind for me. Even though I put in my proposal in 2009 to do my PhD in cyber security law, due to divorce, financial strains, and single parenting, the mission to get a doctorate degree was thwarted. Perhaps if I ever do my PhD, I will dedicate it to him ….

XXI

Western Education

If Russia is to be a great power, it will be, not because of its nuclear potential, faith in God or the president, or Western investment, but thanks to the labor of the nation, faith in knowledge and science, and the maintenance and development of scientific potential and education.

— Zhores Alferov

Ever since I started receiving life-related advice from Bansser, the notion of heading to the UK or the US was tattooed onto my psyche. The first sixteen years of my life in Ethiopia and the following six years I spent in Yemen didn't seem to change my mind or provide me the fulfillment I was looking for in my life. In addition, the living situation for someone like me whose heritage was from communist South Yemen was more dire than for someone who was born in North Yemen to two Arab parents.

For those of us born outside of Yemen, getting an academic scholarship to study abroad was nearly impossible. Going to Russia or China was somewhat easier, but going to the US or Canada was only for the elite. But the living conditions in North Yemen including discrimination, mistreatment, and the lack of opportunities for those who were born outside Yemen were the main contributing factors for my needing to migrate again.

North Yemen wasn't a communist country, but the people and the government never sympathized with the Americans, largely due to the huge influence of the Egyptian president, Jamal Abdul Nasser. Even though it was the early 1980s, the notion of Arab independence from colonial power was so fresh in the minds of most adults at the time. Most adults in North and South Yemen recalled the Americans supporting the oppressive Royalist king of North Yemen during the revolution alongside the Saudis, and they also viewed the American government as being pro-Israel.

On the other hand, I had read several books about the treatment of Black Americans in the US. Malcolm X's speeches and biographies, for example, had been translated and widely distributed in bookstores. In North Yemen, no one dared speak about the mistreatment of Yemenis born abroad or the dark-skinned Yemenis living in coastal cities like Hodeidah, Tehama, Mocha, etc. However, anything to do with injustice toward Black Americans by white Americans and/or the Palestinian's predicaments under the Zionist Israeli government were widely discussed.

I was better versed about the story of Malcolm X than the teachings of MLK. In fact, other than what Mark had told me and the books he had recommended to me, I never heard of MLK up until I enrolled in university in the US. The other interesting aspect of this time period—the early 1980s—was that we had great respect and admiration for the Kennedys. I suspect it had to do with JFK's stance on the question of Algerian independence from France and his younger brother's position on the issue of Black Americans. Most of us were quoting Kennedy's speeches during conversations at this time. In addition, after reading some articles on South Yemen's struggle to earn independence from imperial Britain, I completely wrote off the notion of going to the UK to further my education. By then, I was brainwashed to believe that the British Empire was the worst enemy of Arabs if not of all humankind. The more I read about the British Empire, the more I questioned why my father was so loyal—why he had thought that they were better than the Arabs or even better than anyone. I set my sights on the US.

The dedication, aptitude, and initiative I exhibited in setting up and maintaining the Wang computer system at USAID, as well as the recommendation and encouragement I received from the Berkeley University professor James Zeigler, improved my confidence level. James was a computer science professor who was in North Yemen for a short-term work assignment, and he recognized my knack for working with computers and doing computer programming. He was the reason I chose to study computer science. Several staff references also prompted the USAID mission director to nominate me for the USAID scholarship to travel to the US.

Even though I had completed a UK-based standard high school exam, I needed to take the GED in case my high school studies would not be recognized by universities in the US. I started taking advanced English language courses. I scored 640 on the TOEFL[1] exam and obtained an average of 96 percent on the GED, which put me in a much superior position than any of the native Yemen-born candidates who put forward their applications for the scholarship.

Up until that time, I was holding a South Yemen passport. However, the US Embassy didn't issue entry visas to those carrying passports from communist countries. Therefore, I had to pay a hefty bribe to obtain a North Yemen passport. In the process, I had to drop my last name as it would identify my origins as Hadhrami from South Yemen. On the North Yemeni passport, my name read *Adel M. Ahmed* instead of *Adel M. Ahmed Ben-Harhara*. I was under the impression that this particular step would eliminate any chance of North Yemen's Ministry of Education identifying me as originally from South Yemen.

However, officials at the Ministry of Education wrote to the USAID mission director stating that I wasn't a North Yemen national and I hadn't been born in Yemen; they knew my mother was Ethiopian and my father was from the communist South Yemen. Therefore, my name was removed from the list of potential candidates to be sent to the US.

I wasn't sure how the Ministry found out that I was from South Yemen. It was crushing news for me and disappointing for the mission director at USAID. Even though the rationale was lame and outright prejudiced and inequitable, we had no choice but to accept the verdict. I was unable to sleep or eat for a couple of days after hearing the news that my application had been rejected.

The American expats who had knowledge of my situation encouraged me not to give up on my dreams. Some of them suggested that I start applying for admission at various US universities and pay for my own education myself—at least for the first couple of years—and find a way to become a US resident once I was on American soil.

I felt like paying my way for education and covering associated living expenses was going to be harder than flying to the moon. However, I and those around me were not deterred. The mission director and my manager, Richard Maddy, carved out a plan. The first step was to promote me from bookkeeper to a resident computer specialist and to increase my wage two-fold. I was unable to cash the increase in wages, though; Richard structured the situation so that I couldn't use the money. He was afraid I would spend it rather than save it for my education, so rather than receiving the money directly, I paid the costs of utilities and other expenses on behalf of the American expats in local currency. In return, the Americans wrote me personal checks in US dollars using the equivalent official exchange rate.

Richard had a daughter living in Connecticut who assisted me in opening a bank account in the US. Bi-weekly, I commenced sending her those individual checks via the US Embassy pouch. Every month, I received bank statements showing the amount of money that was deposited into my account.

While all of this was happening, I made a habit of making trips to Aden and Al-Shihr in South Yemen to spend time with my family. I was twenty-one years old, was growing facial hair, and had hormones kicking in. I was engaged to a beautiful girl my family had selected for me, and we were set to have a wedding the following year. I started to fall for this girl; not only was she beautiful, but also her behavior and intellect captivated me. She was levelheaded and grounded. She often spoke to me about building a life together—how we would raise our children and what our family dynamics would look like. She stressed the importance of education and had a mature outlook on all of these topics.

Upon returning to Sana'a from one of my trips to South Yemen in 1993, I received a couple of acceptance letters from

US universities: Oregon State University, The University of Arizona in Tucson, and Boise State University in Idaho.

It had been about a year since I had started applying. By that time, I had no less than US$25,000 in the US bank account, which would cover tuition fees and living expenses for two years. (International students pay three-fold of any US resident.) It wasn't nearly enough to get me through the full four years of the university program. To cover the full program cost, I had to remain two more years in North Yemen working and saving more money.

Richard was aware of my university acceptance letters and my engagement to the South Yemen girl. He called me to his office to meet with him. I wasn't sure what was on his mind; he seemed serious and concerned. He began the conversation by asking how much money I had in the bank and how serious I was about marrying the girl. I told him that I was dead serious about marrying the girl as I loved her, and I was also eager to pursue my education in the US. Perhaps I could do both and take her with me.

He leaned back in his reclining chair, and he said, "You probably need at least US$10,000 for a dowry payment for this girl. Am I right?"

I said yes.

"You probably need an additional US$10,000 to buy her gold and clothing and to pay for the wedding ceremony and reception. Am I correct?"

I said, "Yes, but I have already purchased the gold and clothing."

He stood up and walked around his desk to sit in the chair in front of me.

"The money you saved for your education will be wiped out, and you will be spending another four years here saving money. That is with the assumption you won't end up having babies right away. Moreover, what are you going to do with your wife when you're heading to the US? If you take her, your expenses will be higher. Have you thought of that?"

Finally, standing over my shoulder, he said, "Son, you're the same age as my children. My advice is to remove the notion of marriage from your mind. Go to the US and finish your schooling first. Once that is done, if it is meant to be and if she is still single, you can always marry the same girl."

He asked me, "What is her name, anyway?"

"Entisar."

He added, "Once you have a university degree, you can have not only one Entisar but four Entisars. I hear in your country you can have four wives. The opportunity for you to go to the US comes once in a lifetime, and I suggest you take advantage of it. You're a bright young man and you shouldn't be spending another single night in this country. Those are my suggestions, and you can take them, or you can leave them. We all want to see you succeed. It's unfortunate the Ministry didn't approve the USAID scholarship."

I told him he made a good point. "I will think about it."

I also mentioned to him that the money I had saved up wouldn't last for the four years of the university program.

He said to me, "Buy your flight ticket tomorrow, get your visa from our embassy, and leave. You may find a fine young girl in the US to marry you. If that is the case, you will pay less for university, and you'll be able to work part time and support yourself. With your work ethic, discipline, and determination, I have no doubt you will make it."

I left his office pondering my options.

*

I lost touch with Richard Maddy through the years. When I was researching for this book, the only information I could find about him was a notice about a memorial service for him that was held in Raleigh, North Carolina, in November 2006. He is yet another significant person from my past who I would love to thank in person for his impact on my life.

*

Even now, people ask me, "How is it that Muslims are allowed multiple wives? And why four?" From my experience, a lot of non-Muslims think that Islam increased the number of wives a man can have from one to four. However, prior to the spread of Islam in Arabia, there was no limit to the number of wives and mistresses a man could have, and it was prestigious to have hundreds of wives and thousands of children. Of several men in the Old Testament who had multiple wives, King Solomon is one of the most well-known: "And he had seven hundred wives, princesses, and three hundred concubines."[2]

Centuries ago, taking multiple wives served a practical purpose. Because of constant wars and conflicts, the number of women in the general population far exceeded the number of men. It was seen as honorable to take on multiple wives so as to support widows and orphaned children. Islam did not introduce polygamy; "rather, polygamy was the widespread customary practice in pre-Islamic Arabia, which continued in the later ages by distorting the actual revelation of the Qur'an."[3] In truth, Islam capped the number of wives a man can have at four.

However, the Prophet Muhammed (pbuh) didn't say that a man should have four wives. "Islam does allow polygamy … but it does not encourage it."[4] The Prophet Muhammed (pbuh) stated that if a man loves more than one woman—if a man absolutely needs to marry more than one woman—he may marry up to four women. Certain conditions may exist that may make it logical or even necessary for a man to have more than one wife:

> A man has been given permission to marry again if his wife is chronically ill and cannot fulfill the obligations of marriage; or if she is unable to have children; or under certain conditions of wartime, when marrying widows to look after orphans may be necessary to protect the morals of society.[5]

Conversely, if a man cannot give equal and sufficient attention (financial, emotional, etc.) to more than one wife, he is to have only one wife:

> If you fear that you will not deal fairly with orphan girls, you may marry whichever [other] women seem good to you, two, three, or four. If you fear that you cannot be equitable [to them], then marry only one."[6]

And why four wives? Four is not a random number.

> Four was a sacred and complete number with the Hebrews, as well as with several other peoples. It occurs very frequently in the Old Testament and the New Testament. It indicates completeness. Number four is the number of stability, order, and completion of justice. ... Allah, in His wisdom, has determined four to be an adequate number to provide proof beyond doubt (four witnesses) or to provide adequate time. It represents comprehensiveness, wholeness, and fullness or completion.[7]

There are four directional points (north, south, east, and west), four seasons, and four phases of the moon. The number four connects us in harmony to nature.[8]

The other caveat to a man having more than one wife is that the woman has to agree to the marriage. This is, however, not limited to polygamy. In Islam, a wife's consent to the marriage is required even if she is the only wife.

*

I was able to secure my visa for the US within a day because of my work with USAID and because I carried a North Yemen passport without my last name. After getting my visa, I purchased a one-way ticket to the US via Rome.

My sister Muna drove me to the Sana'a airport thinking she was seeing me off to Ethiopia for a visit. She was okay with that notion the entire time but broke crying the moment I told her my final destination was the US. She cried as if I had killed her child. Her wailing caught the attention of airport officials, and I was pulled over for questioning. I told them she was missing her mother and was upset due to her inability to fly with me to Ethiopia, and they let me go.

I left North Yemen in July 1984 without notifying any of my friends or family except for Muna. The only people who knew I was departing for the US to seek my education were the Americans I worked with. At that time, because of the political turmoil, there were conditions on some people for travel, and in particular, anyone under twenty-five shouldn't have been traveling. I didn't trust anyone and thought it was best to leave quietly lest someone or something thwart my plans.

While I was flying, I started to imagine the American dream. I saw myself being a good student, living in a free society. I envisioned the girlfriends I would have, the chance to speak like an American and be like an American .... I was so worked up.

The desire to further my education in the US had trumped my plans to get married. I canceled the wedding plans over the phone once I arrived in the US.

The Shame

Boise, Idaho.

I was dreading this phone call; I knew I had shamed my family, but my lifelong desire to obtain a Western education was finally coming to fruition.

I picked up the phone to call Hind.

The phone rang three times, and my aunt picked up.

"Hello," I began. "It's me. May I please speak to Hind?"

"Where are you?" Hind demanded as she took the receiver. "I heard you are going to the US. Is it true? You will be leaving?"

"I am already in the US," I gulped. "I'm calling to let you know that the plan for the wedding should be canceled because I'm not planning to return to Yemen."

There was a pause, and I heard her hang up the phone.

I called back. The phone rang and rang, but no one picked up.

I called again. Nothing.

The third time I called back, she picked up.

"You are a disgrace!" she scolded me.

Then she hung up again.

Once again, I called and she answered. I tried to convince her of the importance of my getting an education in the US. That wasn't what she had a problem with.

"If you had this plan all along, why did we go through this process of printing the invitations, purchasing the items for the girl, planning the wedding?"

"Until I arrived in the US, I wasn't sure my plans would work out. Now that I'm here, it is actually becoming a reality. I just want to make sure the girl's family knows that I'm now in the US."

She hung up again.

Yet again, I called.

She answered and said, "Don't ever call me again."

*

In the end, I don't know how she communicated to Entisar and her family that I had left.

When I returned to Yemen years later, I had to kill a goat and kiss my sister's knee, seeking forgiveness. I visited Entisar in 1993 to apologize. At that time, she was married and had three children.

My actions were unprecedented; it was and continues to be a big story. To this day, I'm known in the area as "the man who signed a marriage contract and disappeared."

Part Two

XXII

Starting Over

So here you are, too foreign for home, too foreign for here, never enough for both.

— Ijeoma Umebinyuo

In 1978, I had migrated to North Yemen, the land of my father and his ancestors, full of hope. After living there for six years, the discrimination, primitive ways of life in North Yemen, and the need to improve my life forced me to leave. Now, in 1992,[1] after attending and graduating from university and working in the US for eight years, a miscalculation and poor judgement on my part as well as the mishandling of my immigration and residency status by an incompetent lawyer put me in a legal quagmire with the US legal system. After an eight-year absence, I was left with no choice but to return to Yemen. By the time I returned, North and South Yemen had united.[2]

When Banajah (the family I connected with when I first moved to Sana'a in 1981) picked me up at the Sana'a airport upon my return, I was so exhausted I was barely able to walk.

I went to stay with them and slept for three straight days before I started talking. The family gave me the space and comfort required to recover from my ordeal. The mother constantly encouraged me to stay positive and regain my confidence.

Several weeks after I returned, she also wanted to make for me a special meal and asked me what kind of Yemeni food I had been missing and wanted to eat. I requested fish. When my sister Hind heard about this, she was disgusted with me because fish is a common, lower-class food in Yemen; she felt it would have been more appropriate to welcome me with a lamb or a goat. As usual, I didn't care as much about protocol as my sister did. Idaho isn't a source of great, fresh seafood, other than the fish caught in the rivers, and I missed eating good fresh fish while I was living there! Banajah granted my wish as an attempt to make me feel better about having been forced to return to Yemen.

(Upon my return from the US, Hind also asked me about my life there, including "Did you try alcohol?" As I was aware of her insistence to project a good image, I lied to her and said, "No!" Her response was not what I expected. I thought she would be pleased to hear that, but instead she retorted, "What a fool!" Apparently, although she sent me off to the US with a copy of the Qur'an, she thought I missed my chance to try things that were prohibited by Islam!)

Readjusting to life in Yemen was an immense struggle.

*

Sharese was a girl I met when I was doing my university studies in the US. She was a few years younger than me, but once we met, I was interested in getting to know her. Her focus seemed to be on her coursework rather than socializing, though. She was in a two-year diploma program and was about to finish her schooling and join the work force when we met. Before I got the chance to really establish a line of communication of some sort, she graduated and no longer showed up at the university campus.

Luckily, she was playing soccer in local city leagues, and I was able to track her down. Soon we started to play on a coed team and were able to develop a friendship. She didn't know at that time that I had strong feelings for her. Our relationship was strictly friendship, but she tagged along with me to many of the soccer games I played with a team made up of international students. Once she started to get to know me and my teammates (I captained the team), she was captivated by the sheer number of international students' accents, cultures, and different ways of conducting ourselves.

From the day I returned to Yemen, she kept in touch with me and encouraged me to stay positive. In her letters to me, she kept me apprised of what was transpiring in the city of Boise. During those exchanges, she wanted to know more about Yemeni culture and the status of women in Yemen. She became a main source of much-needed moral support for me as I struggled through trying to reintegrate into Yemeni society and at times felt depressed and isolated. She gave me hope and optimism. And she encouraged me to continue to pursue my goal of living and working in Canada or the US.

November 1992

Dear Sharese,

Thank you very much for taking the time to write me. I am so fortunate to have a friend like you. I am free of the INS[3] officers in the US interrogating and hassling me about my visa status, but it seems that I have moved into a society not better than an open prison.

On October 16, I left the US from Seattle. My passport had been in the possession of US immigration since 1987. I asked the INS officials if I could collect my passport and send it to the Yemen consulate for renewal. However, they didn't return it to me and as a result, I wasn't able to get an entry visa to France when I left the US. (I had to fly through France since there was no direct flight from Seattle to Yemen.)

At the Paris airport, the United Airlines flight attendant handed me over to the French immigration services with my expired passport. Since the officials had no clue that my passport had been in the possession of INS all these years while trying to sort out my status in the US, they conducted their interrogation and search by breaking my luggage. They also held one of my suitcases in France for several weeks before sending it to Yemen. I think they suspected I was a terrorist, because they were comparing my passport picture with several wanted pictures.

I was detained at the Paris airport for several hours and finally sent on to Yemen. The worst part of this process is that they didn't speak English, or at least they didn't want to. Nor was I able to say a single word in French. I don't know if it was because of the influx of illegal immigrants from North Africa to France or pure bad luck that I was faced with confused or ill-mannered French officers that evening. Perhaps I just looked suspicious. It may have been a combination of factors, but the process didn't go as smoothly as I was hoping for. I had sensed that the Americans had some respect for me, but the French didn't seem to consider me as being a human. One of them didn't even look directly at me; instead, he looked at my shoulder. The lack of acknowledgment of me was perfectly clear and evident!

After six hours of confusion and misunderstandings, the authorities put me on the flight and handed my passport to the Air France flight crew, instructing them to only return my passport to the Yemeni authorities upon my arrival in Sana'a. I landed at the Sana'a airport a little past 10 p.m. I hadn't slept in almost forty-eight hours.

As I disembarked the plane, one of the French flight attendants asked me to walk with her to the immigration booth.

When we got to Immigration, she turned to the senior officer.

"I've been told to hand this man's passport to the authorities because his passport is expired," she said to him.

She asked him to handle the matter, as a huge line of passengers was queuing behind me.

The man in the booth didn't understand a word she said and looked at me for help. I repeated for him, in Arabic, exactly what she had said. At that, the French flight attendant walked way. I stood by the booth and waited for the official to hand me my passport so that I could proceed.

"Why is your passport expired?" he began his questioning, "and why did the Paris officials insist that the passport be handed to us?"

I launched into an explanation of the entire situation: that my passport was expired because it hadn't been in my possession in the US for the past several years and hadn't had time to renew it because I had to leave the country on short notice. I told him that the process that had started in Seattle, with flight crews from all legs of my journey holding on to my passport and passing me through to immigration officials at each port of entry as I made my way on multiple flights, ultimately landing in Sana'a, at their booth.

The explanation I was trying to give didn't make sense to him.

I was detained and sent to a room where no fewer than five men took turns interrogating me because I also wasn't carrying my Yemen ID card with me. (The immigration officials in Seattle held on to my ID card.) And to make matters worse, there were two deportation orders: one issued by the French and the other issued by the US government.

I had no food or sleep for two days—since October 15. The officials at the Sana'a airport were asking me where I used to live and work in Yemen years ago before I left for the US, who my supervisor was, how I left Yemen, why I left the US, what I was doing in France, why I didn't renew my passport, why I was now wearing glasses, and many other questions I cannot remember. I was barely able to stay awake or carry on a meaningful conversation.

After fifteen hours of interrogation, I was sent to a holding cell for further investigation. When I asked them why they were detaining me, they said, "We have to detain you here until we find out why you left the US."

I was praying to God that the US immigration services hadn't disclosed my application for political asylum because that would have led to my immediate persecution in Yemen. Now, my passport is with the Yemen government. However, if the Yemen government finds out about my application for political asylum, that would jeopardize my life and personal safety.

The Yemenis wanted to know if I had committed a crime. These days, a lot of Yemeni men coming from Chicago and New York are involved in drugs. They suspected I was caught up in the drug business and kept asking me, "Have you committed any crimes?" "Are you involved in the drug trade?"

They found nothing suspicious or inconsistent with my story, travel documents, or my demeanor. However, a couple of officers became more interested in finding out if I had brought a load of cash, as most Yemeni do when return from abroad. Their suspicion had moved from thinking

I was a drug dealer to suspecting I was money laundering. My carry-on bag and the two suitcases I had with me were searched multiple times (my third suitcase was still in Paris). From the interrogation, they knew I worked as a computer programmer, how much money I earned in a year, and the amount of time I had spent in the US. They kept asking me what had happened to all of my money. I told them I had worked for almost seven years to pay my legal bills and probably still owed more money to the American lawyers. They intended to break me and extract money from me. They were just unable to accept that I had no cash in my pockets.

The following day, to my surprise, one of my relatives came and spoke to some officials. Ferdows, my cousin in the US, knew my flight details and had told other family members in Yemen when I was set to arrive. After waiting for me at the airport, they knew something was wrong because I never appeared. Bazara had asked some airport officials where I was, and they probably told him I was being detailed due to my expired passport and lack of a Yemeni ID card.

He produced a copy of my Yemen ID card, and I was finally released. Perhaps he even bribed a few of them with some cash to agree to let me go free and enter the country. I have no idea what my situation would have been if this copy of my ID hadn't surfaced and rescued me. I also didn't have the foggiest idea why my nephew maintained a copy of my ID for all of these years. When I left Yemen, he was only nine years old! When I asked him about this, he said, "I knew someday you would return. Besides, I didn't have a picture of you other than this. So I kept it for sentimental value."

Well, I will close here for now. Thank you again for your letter. Please write again soon!

Adel

XXIII

Struggle

Sometimes the people around you won't understand your journey. They don't need to—it's not for them.

— Joubert Botha

I felt more foreign in North Yemen when I returned in 1992 than I had the first time I moved there in 1978. Prior to departing Sana'a for the US, the city had been cleaner and less crowded. Now, after an extended hiatus, I was surprised to see the number of women wearing head-to-toe coverings. I saw more people wearing Saudi clothing than the typical Yemeni outfits I was used to seeing. And many men were carrying guns. The differences were beyond my imagination; it didn't feel like the same country I had left less than a decade earlier.

When I asked friends and family about the changes the country had experienced in the previous eight years, they told me how and why life changed after the Gulf War. The invasion of Kuwait by Saddam Hussein and the Yemen leadership's public support for Saddam and criticism of Saudi Arabia for inviting American-led forces into the Kingdom provoked the Saudis' swift and punitive deportation of millions of Yemeni workers.

Nearly two million Yemeni immigrant workers were forced out of Saudi Arabia and other Gulf states, and many of them returned to Yemen. The returning workers brought with them the *Wahhabi* version of Islam to Yemen. Wahhabism is the strict orthodox version of Islam practiced mainly in Saudi Arabia and Qatar. It originated from within Sunni Islam and promotes a stricter, more "pure" form of Islam than what most Muslims had been practicing in that region. The Saudi Royal Family has exerted its power for the past four hundred years to maintain adherence to the Wahhabi sect.[1] The two million Yemeni who spent a good portion of their lives working in Saudi Arabia brought their beliefs with them when they were kicked out of Saudi.

The people I knew prior to going to the US had completely changed. Nearly all of the Muwalladin had changed their Yemeni ID cards to indicate that they were born in Yemen even though they hadn't been. They didn't want to speak Amharic as they didn't want people to know they had any connection to Ethiopia. A good portion of the youth that I knew had returned to Yemen after serving in the Afghanistan war against the former Soviet Union. They had been recruited, gone to Afghanistan to fight, and returned changed. Most of them wore beards. We had been friends as children, but now we were almost enemies. We no longer had anything in common, so conversations were limited. As an Americanized man wearing jeans, I was an infidel in their eyes, and when I saw their clothing, their beards, and their attitudes, I saw the Taliban.

All conversations were around religion. Everyone talked about this extreme version of Islam—Wahhabism. As a young child, I had been taught Islam, and I'd had a great deal of exposure to it when I migrated to North Yemen in the late 1970s, but the tone now was totally different. Everyone was focused on killing the Jews and every American. To them, "American" included the entire Western population, all of whom were seen to be supporting Israel.

When I was a child and a young adult, we had all thought that when someone kills an innocent life, it is as if he has killed all of humanity. However, what I found upon my return to North Yemen was totally contrary to the Islamic teachings I had received. Every person who had returned from the Afghanistan war was capable of killing, without any reason, any ordinary American or Jewish civilian he could find. The religion had turned into an ideology. Why?

As per my earlier teachings of Islam, I understood that the religion does not condone, and it in fact condemns, practices such as "honor killings," racism or tribalism, oppression of women, banning women from obtaining an education, and many other un-Islamic practices that make their way into the sensationalized news.

Of course, having lived in the US for the previous eight years, I had a completely different image of the US and Westerners than people in Yemen possessed, but I was unable to reason with anyone. They kept dismissing me as having been brainwashed by the US or simply being ill-prepared with zero or a low level of Islamic knowledge.

In the 1970s, every family and almost all shops and restaurants in Yemen had a picture of Jamal Abdul Nasser, the Egyptian leader, on the wall. Those pictures were gone;

now most houses, shops, and restaurants had either verses of the Qur'an or a picture of Saddam Hussein on the walls. I was told girls should not be sent to purchase cucumbers, eggplants, or carrots, and they weren't allowed to milk cows. The response I got to my inquiries was that these vegetables and the cows' udders would remind girls of male genitalia or bring sexual desires. This concept was never thought of when I was a child.

I also observed that the way the Somalian and Ethiopian refugees were treated in Yemen was beyond any acceptable pattern to humanity; they happened to be dark-skinned humans from the continent of Africa, yet they were treated as sub-human. Most Ethiopian and Somali females who were hired to work as domestic servants were often underpaid and overworked. I came to know that several of these employers never fully paid the women their deserved wages. I also learned that most of these women were subject to sexual assaults and other types of abuse.

All forms of media including books, newspapers, magazines, films, and television were censored. In the late 1970s and early 1980s, when I was a teenager in Yemen, I was able to hear and enjoy songs from Egypt, Lebanon, and Syria at groceries stores, shops, and cafeterias. In the 1990s, though, I didn't hear any music played in malls, department stores, or grocery stores. Also, music classes were no longer allowed in public schools because music was forbidden since school curricula had to follow the rules of this new form of Islam.

As a teenager, I had been able to attend movie theaters in Sana'a, Ta'izz, or Hodeidah. Upon my return, I noticed that movie theaters were nearly nonexistent in Yemen; people only watched movies in private, residential houses. Movie theaters were a no-no for those devoted to Islam, as they enabled the unsupervised mingling of men and women, which Muslims believe may lead to immoral actions outside of marriage.

Even more disappointing for me was to see the state of South Yemen after the unification of North and South Yemen. Apparently, it is much easier to dilute clean water with dirty water than the other way around. Back in the early 1980s, when I used to travel to Aden, women had almost an equal footing or status in society, as they were working as judges, police officers, etc. Nearly all of them dressed without covering their faces. The situation was totally different in 1994, and I found it hard to believe how easy it was to relegate half of the members of society into suppression.

I was disheartened to find that Yemen seemed to have gone backward a thousand years in less than a decade. I was confused as to whether my observations were the result of my exposure to a different lifestyle in the US, so I had a different outlook, or whether the country had turned the clock backward in only eight years due to the increasing Saudi Arabian influence on Yemen. It was likely both.

I was sophisticated, and I began to wish I hadn't gone to the West to learn how to live life differently. I didn't chew qat, and I wasn't invited to any social gatherings. I become lonely and depressed. I continued writing to my friends in the US as an outlet to express my frustrations.

November 1992

Dear Sharese,

You've asked about my family. Let me tell you how I'm getting along with them.

I used to tell my relatives how free I was in the US, and I was boasting about all of the opportunities I had in the US. Of course, they don't see anything other than me returning to Yemen like an undesirable dog because my return was not my choice.

My sisters have already started to speak to me about marriage. In the US, I was always able to avoid this issue using school as an excuse. When I tell them I have plans to return to the US, they almost go crazy. I will find a way to delay the issue until I leave Yemen again.

I've already stopped sharing my problems and intentions with my sisters because they don't understand my perspectives. In one way, they are happy that I have returned to Yemen, but they also know how much I hated Yemen and loved the US, and they also knew I had no intentions to return to Yemen.

I am having communication problems with friends and relatives because we don't seem to have common ground for anything. The years I spent in the US have completely molded my values, attitudes, presentation, and in many ways, I'm facing difficulties in adjusting. I feel I am a total stranger in my own native country.

The country is experimenting with democracy for the first time in its history by bringing together the two states that differ greatly in terms of their official attitudes toward women, law, religion, and human rights.

The difference between the two states is causing all the laws passed by parliament to either have been contained or frozen. There is a large gap in their respective visions. They have different points of view about the implementation of the laws, the role of the presidential council, the judiciary, and the parliament. The ruling government interferes in judicial independence despite constitutional guarantees.

There are major problems facing Yemen at present. The country and its people inherited a very troubling attitude of lowliness. The basic problem today is that certain elements in this society are either ignorant of the laws or unwilling to abide by them. The worst part of it is that some of those law makers are often the first ones to break them. As a result, the whole system suffers from a state of helplessness. In fact, social habits enjoy more respect and adherence in Yemen than the laws.

The question of the democratization of Yemen is a critical and vital part of its political evolution. The two Yemen countries were subjected to one of the most ruthless dictatorships in the world. Marxist communism in the former South Yemen and feudal-military rule in North Yemen.

Since unification, despite Yemen's stated support for human rights, there have been lapses. The government continues to selectively monitor citizens, search homes, open mail, and listen in on telephone conversations.

Women in the former South Yemen, where my origins are, had enjoyed extensive legal rights based on a progressive family code and greater access to work and education. Although women in North Yemen held full electoral rights, they had fewer educational and vocational chances. A basic tension thus exists between the legacies of the two states, as progressive and Islamic groups differ in philosophy regarding the role of women in such matters as divorce, child custody, and polygamy.

Well, that gets you up to speed on some of the difficulties I am seeing and experiencing.

Until next time,
Adel

*

November 1992

Dear Norma and Rich,[2]

How are you, my friends and families? I received your fax yesterday. I was happy to know that I can still communicate with you.

Struggle

I am staying with relatives. The language, culture, food, and just about everything else is new to me. I cannot remember being here in this country before.

My relatives are doing everything to make me feel better. They make sure I eat and get rest. They provide everything, and I have no idea how I can return the favor. They do understand my emotional distraction and disappointments. As a matter of fact, they are amazed that I am still together. It's a large family that I'm staying with. There is a grandmother and grandchildren, as well as other adults. All of the attention and love is able to take me away from my immediate problems. But between you and me, I feel as though I am a foreigner in my own homeland.

I have no reading materials. There is nothing here in English. I have no decent clothing. I have already lost one bag and arrived here with only underwear and socks. I forgot everything and I have to be escorted everywhere I go. I am very disoriented. I hope you have contacted the US immigration officer to find out the whereabouts of my ID card, and military exception papers. I need these documents. Because I am here with no ID card, or any other kind of identification, I am worried about my status here, more than ever before. The Yemen government is conducting massive arrests of whom they think to be Somalis. Millions of Somalis have fled to Yemen, and none of them are in the refugee detention center. The UN is requiring the refugees to be at the detention center in order to provide them supplies to meet their needs. Since I am dark-skinned, I am often mistaken for being Somali and am in danger of arrest. Not only that, with no ID, I cannot obtain a job, travel, or do anything.

Please say hello to all of my coworkers and friends!!

Sincerely,
Adel

XXIV

Coping

Much of the stress that people feel doesn't come from having too much to do. It comes from not finishing what they've started.

— David Allen

The first six months of my life back in Yemen, from October 1992 to April 1993, were excruciating. I was on the verge of mental breakdown. I was both depressed and stressed. The notes I was sending to my friends were frenzied and frantic; they clearly indicated a confused mental state. Without the letters I was receiving from friends and former coworkers in the US, I am not sure how I would have recovered from a long depression. There were times when I walked to the post office twice a day to see if there was a letter for me.

One day, my friend Bahamam was with me when I collected a couple of letters from the post office and together, we were walking in downtown Sana'a through Tahrir Square. I really wanted to read the letters, so I didn't wait to get to my car before opening them. The first letter was a couple of pages long. As I was reading it, I felt someone breathing around my neck. When I turned around, I found another man peering over my shoulder trying to read the letters with me.

I was both surprised and annoyed. He didn't say anything.

I looked at him and said, "You probably know only how to read twenty-five words in the Arabic dictionary. What makes you think you can read English letters?"

*

The following are only a few of the multitude of letters of support and encouragement I received from friends and former colleagues in the US.

Adel,

You keep your spirits up no matter what happens!!! Losing faith and being depressed will only make matters worse, and your health will suffer, too. Please keep in touch with us so that in case we lose track of exactly where you are or aren't able to get a mailing address, we won't lose touch completely—even if it is a two-word postcard so that I know you are still alive and on the same planet. I know the mail system can be sort of strange after a letter leaves the country, and since I have never been out of the country, I have no idea how other people do things.

I worry about you a lot,
Michele [a friend from Idaho]

*

Adel,

I understand why your situation is so depressing. I have no idea what it would feel like to be so caught in these types of circumstances and unfortunate decisions. I wish there was something I could do; it is such a helpless feeling to sit by and watch and listen but do nothing to fix it. The best I can say is that we, your friends in Boise, remember you and love you. I continue to pray for you.

I appreciate your letters. I am glad you feel you can be relaxed when you write to me. After I have read your letters, I always feel as though I have just had a one-sided conversation with you, and I enjoy that even when the conversation is sad.

Take care and know what we all care about you.
Jane [a former coworker from Idaho]

*

Dear friend Adel,

I hope this letter finds you healthy and surrounded by your friends and family. I hope that you are doing fine, and take good care of yourself. Don't get involved with people who like to do wrong, because I really like you, Adel, just as if you were one of my brothers.

I thank God for the sincere friendship we find in each other. You are a special friend to me, and God is gonna bless you whatever you do.

As far as how I am, I would like to tell you that I wrote a letter to my family and I told them that I had a Black brother, and that your name is Adel. And I also told them that if someday you get there, where my parents live, they'll receive you and treat you as if you were me.

See you soon, brother,
Ismael [another international student/friend in Idaho]

Coping

*

Greetings, my brother,

Thank you for taking the time to write me a letter. I wonder often how you are doing, both physically and emotionally, and wish there was a magic word I could utter to make it OK for you and get you back in this country, and in Boise.

I miss you, my good friend!

And some of the words you put together to express your feelings since returning to Yemen make me sad. They are great words, great thoughts. But sad. Two thoughts in particular I recall. One where you said, "I am dying softly for lack of freedom." The other in the letter you wrote to me: "My stomach is full, but my heart is empty." I know that your words will one day wind up in some poetry of mine because they carry such depth of feeling.

Stay well, my brother. Please extend my best wishes and hopes for happiness to your family.

May our paths cross again! If there is anything I can do for you, all you have to do is ask.

Bill [a former coworker from Idaho]

*

Adel,

It's nice to know that you're receiving my letters. I can't tell you how much I appreciate finding a letter from you in my P.O. Box. Recently, I have been checking my mail box two-to-three times daily in anticipation of news from you.

I want you to know that I don't usually write on cards and with stationery. However, I thought that in your drab surroundings, you might appreciate a glimpse of the US, so I'm sending a postcard. And not only that, I was hoping that they would be reminders of what you're fighting for—to come back, not only to the country but to the people, too! You have made so many friends—people who really do care for and respect you. And none of us want you to give up hope or lose that ambitious spirit in you!!

Please tell me more about the culture in Yemen.

Sharese

*

Dear Sharese,

After returning from the US, it was quite difficult for me to find an apartment to rent. It has nothing to do with my skin color or place of birth. Rather, my marital status is the hurdle. After two months of searching and having elderly folks vouch for me, I was able to secure a two-bedroom apartment. It's common here for most landlords to live in the same building as their tenants, so my landlord lives on the top floor of my building. Landlords check who is coming and going, and they keep a spare key to the unit so they are able to enter without notifying the tenant.

This particular landlord was aware that I had been living in the US for almost a decade, and at every opportunity when we crossed paths on the stairs or in the hallway, he always asked me about the US. Often, his inquiries focused on my lifestyle abroad and how easy it was to access alcohol, women, and pornographic materials. I kept telling him access to alcohol, women, and pornography isn't an issue, as they are easy to get, but whether a man engages with such activity is a matter of self-respect and the choices we make in life, as there are severe consequences of each decision we make and how we lead our lives. I shared with him my personal experience with alcohol and female companions. Yes, I tasted alcohol, but I was never drunk. Nor I have developed any interest in drinking. I had a couple of girlfriends, but those relationships were based on a mutual love interest by both parties; nothing was forced or paid for. Moreover, my head space was never focused on those topics, as I was focusing on my schoolwork, my employment, and sports along with my social life. He wanted to know if I had any materials in relationship to pornography. I said no and asked him, "Why should I?"

He was also aware that I am working for an oil and gas company which has operations in Yemen exploring natural gas on Socotra Island. Therefore, he continued to inquire about the possibility of me asking my British or American colleagues to procure alcohol for him. Alcohol is a banned substance in Yemen, and in most Islamic countries, in fact. The punishments for possession and consumption are harsh.

Drinking was common in Arabia before the adoption of Islam. However, according to Islam, drinking alcohol is haram, or forbidden. Specifically, the Qur'an forbids praying while intoxicated: "You who believe, do not come anywhere near the prayer if you are intoxicated, not until you know what you are saying ...."[1] A later verse of the Qur'an holds that "intoxicants and gambling, [and] idolatrous practices ... are repugnant acts—Satan's doing—shun them that you may prosper."[2] Even though alcohol has some medicinal benefits, the negative effects of it outweigh the good[3] and it is therefore to be avoided entirely.

Khamr, an Arabic word for wine, refers to forbidden substances including wine and other types of alcohol and drugs. "The Prophet Muhammed (pbuh) said, 'Intoxicants are from these two trees,' while pointing to grapevines and date-palms. Alcohol derived from dates or raisins is also prohibited, regardless of the amount consumed."[4] Saudi Arabian scholar Muhammad Saalih al-Munajjid claims that most classical Islamic scholars agree that consuming alcohol is punishable by flogging.[5]

Despite the awareness and acknowledgment of those restrictions, my landlord was persistent in his request for me to bring him some alcohol. Often, he knocked on my door to ask for updates on my bootlegging.

I kept saying, "No, I'm not asking anyone to provide you any alcohol."

Then, after a while I noticed items had been moved around my apartment from time to time. I asked the landlord if he had been in my unit. He kept denying he had been. I kept marks in the unit to see if someone had been in my private space. I was sure the landlord was searching my place in hopes that he would find pornographic material or alcohol.

I was frustrated and felt violated to learn that the landlord continually conducted himself in such a manner. I approached my American colleague, Oscar Bernard, and asked if he would give me an empty bottle of alcohol, which he did. I urinated in the bottle and left the bottle under my bed. Lo and behold, the landlord went into my unit and found the alcohol bottle. I would suspect perhaps he started his indulgence with excitement only to be met with a very disappointing outcome. I was kicked out of the apartment building.

With the help of friends and relatives, I found another apartment to move into. Unlike North America, in Yemen, apartments do not come equipped with appliances like a fridge and stove. In most cases, a landlord demands a yearly rental to be paid in advance. For someone like me, who returned to Yemen with eighty-three dollars in his pocket, it is nearly impossible to come up with the funds to cover a yearly rental and purchase furniture as well as appliances. To make matters more difficult, while in the process of moving to the new apartment, it was discovered my fridge was about three inches wider than the main door. The movers suggested that taking the two-inch wooden door frames off from each side of the door would make the move easier.

I contacted the landlord to inform him about the issue and the alternative plan we had come up with. Moreover, I wanted to be up-front and make him aware that we would be removing the frames temporarily and putting them back after the move was done. The landlord forbade us to even temporarily remove the wooden frames, and he suggested that perhaps we should cut the fridge instead.

The movers laughed at me for consulting with the landlord. It was a waste of time, and they chided me, "What else do you expect from a primitive person like him?" Yes, I had forgotten that most Yemenis are like that and to expect the unexpected.

So long for now,
Adel

XXV

Bookstore

What I say is, a town isn't a town without a bookstore. It may call itself a town, but unless it's got a bookstore, it knows it's not fooling a soul.

— Neil Gaiman, *American Gods*

*I*n addition to letters from the US, I also found comfort in writing in my journals and, of course, reading.

One Friday afternoon, as I was walking along Ring Road near my house, a bookstore across the street caught my attention because of its name: ADEL'S BOOKSTORE. Below that sign was another that read, "Readers don't steal and thieves don't read." It was an English translation of an Arabic saying based on the fact that most Iraqi bookstores don't lock their doors. Most Iraqi bookstores have that sign on their doorsteps.

I crossed the road without getting killed by crazy Yemeni drivers and entered the store. The bookstore contained many Arabic magazines and newspapers. A good portion of the books were in Arabic, but there were some in English, too.

As I glanced at printed materials, the owner asked if I needed help.

I replied, "No thanks," and kept reading and browsing.

In the corner of my eye, on the top left section of the tiny, dusty, smelly bookstore, I saw a few books lined up: *The Myth of Sisyphus*, *The Fall*, *The Rebel*, *The Stranger*, and *The Plague*, all by Albert Camus. They looked familiar. I recalled having those titles purchased for me by my American friends during the early 1980s. Even the way they were shelved reminded me of how I had placed them in my bedroom, as I had them in almost the exact same order.

Since the books were in the far, high, and unreachable shelf for me, I asked the owner if he would assist me. He looked at the books and me twice.

He said, "Those books haven't been looked at for years."

I told him, "That wasn't my question."

He looked at me and said, "I don't have a stepladder to get those books now."

I told him he could step on top of the table in the middle to reach them if he could not find his ladder.

He looked at me again and he said, "Those are written in English."

I said, "I know, and that is the very reason I asked to see them."

He got frustrated and asked me, "Do you even read English?"

His question made me think that I may have given him the impression that I was just wasting his time.

I paused for a moment and told him, "Those are very interesting books and I'm curious as to why they ended up on your shelves."

"What do you mean?" he asked.

"Have you read them?"

He said, "No. I don't read English. Plus, I don't know how to get rid of those English books as they have been collecting dust, and no one has been interested in purchasing them from me."

Instead of answering his question about my ability to read English, I said to him, "I used to own similar books."

"You used to?"

"Yes, before leaving for the US almost ten years ago. When I left for the US, I sold my books for twenty-five cents each to a guy as I was unable to take them with me."

His approach and treatment toward immediately changed. He then asked me if I knew the previous owner of the bookstore.

I said, "No, I do not."

"I bought this bookstore in 1990," he told me. "The previous owner named it ADEL'S BOOKSTORE, and I kept the name as is. When I asked the previous owner about the English books and the store name, he told me that he had purchased the books from a young man named Adel and gave the store the same name, as his business started with that young man's books. Apparently, that young man went to study in the US. There were about 1,500 English books to begin with, but most have sold. I have about seventy-five left."

I told him, "I thought perhaps you had named the shop after your son, as most men in Yemen are named either Ali or Mohamed."

We both laughed.

"My name is also Adel," I told him. "Do you think those books might be mine?"

He said, "Let's find out," and jumped on top of the table to pick a couple of them off the shelf.

Yes, my signature was in them.

We both were amazed at such a coincidence. When I offered him money to re-purchase my old books, he refused to take any. We made arrangements that I would pick up my own books, read them, and return them to him, as I had no interest in hoarding books I had previously owned.

We ended up becoming good friends.

In 1996, just before I departed for Canada, I went to his bookstore to say goodbye to him. In a typical Yemeni humorous way, he said, "If you ever decide to return to Yemen, I cannot guarantee you that either the books or I will be here waiting for you!"

Reflecting on the war that started in 2014 claiming over 100,000 thousand lives, I wonder if he and my books survived the war, the famine, or flood in his country.

XXVI

Socotra

I explored Socotra Island — a place unlike anywhere else.

— Jurassic Park

Shortly after my return to Yemen, I received my Yemen ID card back from friends in the US, and I started working for a major oil and gas company in Sana'a. (Without an ID card, it was impossible to work, and it also wasn't possible to get a new ID card without showing the old one, so I was desperate to get it back!) I was hired as the head of the IT and finance departments. My role was to look after the local computer networks and travel to remote drilling sites to install radio communication devices. Part of my job entailed working as a telecom engineer, where I set up satellite stations to send drilling and geological data back to headquarters via high radio frequencies. In addition, I oversaw the financial systems and reported on all aspects of my company's oil and gas operations in Yemen.

Only foreign companies such as mine could hire indiscriminately. Government agencies and nearly all local companies only hired those who were of full Yemeni origin and were residents; they did not hire foreign-born Yemenis. In my case, I was the most attractive staff member because these foreign firms were able to spend a fraction on my wages in comparison to bringing in someone from Europe or North America to perform the same work. I had earned my university education in the Western world, and on top of that, I had over five years' work experience in the US. Had I held a Canadian or US passport, I would have earned US$11,000 per month plus accommodation and transportation allowances. Interestingly, I now earned much less money than I had before departing for the US. Back in 1984, I was earning an equivalent of US$3,500 and in 1993, my salary was not quite US$2,000. As the currency devalued, which it did quickly, I was earning as little as US$1,000 a month without any benefits. Moreover, I was told I could only earn my wage in the local currency, not in US dollars. Only expats got paid in foreign currency. *Why am I being devalued for being a Yemeni*, I asked myself?

Still, my wage was considered high by Yemeni standards. But some of the expats who worked there only had a diploma and were earning ten to fifteen times more. I know because I was the head of the finance department and all transactions passed through me (including the bribes the foreign firm paid to the corrupt Yemeni officials).

Overall, I didn't mind the salary as having work of some sort was much better than being unemployed, which many people were. As an added bonus, with this work, I was able to travel on business trips to remote sites of Yemen including the island of Socotra.

Socotra, 380 kilometers (240 miles) south of the Arabian Peninsula, is located between the Guardafui Channel and the

Arabian Sea, and it is the largest of the four islands in the Socotra archipelago. It is 132 kilometers (82 miles) long and forty-eight kilometers (thirty-one miles) wide.[1] The territory is near major shipping routes and, being attached to the Hadhramaut Governorate, is officially part of Yemen even though it is geographically closer to Africa.

Aside from the time I spent with my immediate family, my most beautiful memory of Yemen is of Socotra, with the Mocha port coming in a close second. While I worked for them, the oil and gas company was doing gas exploration on Socotra. During the trips I made to the island, although we spent most of our time at drilling sites and only stopped in the city to refuel and eat, I quickly came to love and appreciate its unique beauty. I especially enjoyed the views of the ocean, but Socotra has a unique landscape as well:

> In the 1990s, a team of United Nations biologists conducted a survey of the archipelago's flora and fauna. They counted nearly 700 endemic species found nowhere else on Earth; only New Zealand, Hawaii, New Caledonia, and the Galápagos Islands have more impressive numbers.[2]

Socotra was designated as a UNESCO World Heritage Site in 2008 due to its unique plant life, including the dragon's blood trees, cucumber trees, desert rose trees (also called bottle trees), and Boswellian trees, from which frankincense oil is extracted. "It has been described as 'the most alien-looking place on Earth.'"[3]

> In 2001, a group of Belgian speleologists[4] of the Socotra Karst Project investigated a cave on the island. There they came across many inscriptions, drawings, and archaeological objects. Further investigation showed that these had been left by sailors who visited the island between the first century BC and the sixth century AD. Most of the texts are written in the Indian Brahmi script; there are also inscriptions in South Arabian, Ethiopic, Greek, Palmyrene, and Bactrian scripts and languages. This corpus of nearly 250 texts and drawings constitutes one of the main sources for the investigation of Indian Ocean trade networks in that period.[5]

Most inhabitants of Socotra live on the main island. As of the 2004 census, the population was around 50,000, roughly 20 percent of whom live in Hadibu, the main city.[6]

> The islanders followed Indigenous religions until AD 52, when, according to local beliefs, Thomas the Apostle was shipwrecked there on his way to evangelize India. He then supposedly constructed a church out of his ship's wreckage and baptized many Socotrans. After this, Christianity became the main religion of the island. They followed Nestorius, the Archbishop of Constantinople, who was later excommunicated for heresies. The Socotrans remained loyal to his teachings and joined the Assyrian church. During the

tenth century, Arab geographer Abu Muhammad Al-Hasan Al-Hamdani recorded during his visits that most of the islanders were Christian.[7]

In the sixteenth century, the Mahra Sultanate established power in the area, and subsequently Islam largely replaced Christianity. "In 1800, the fanatical and puritanical south Arabian tribe, the Wahhabis, attacked Socotra, destroying tombs, churches, and graveyards on the coast around Hadibo."[8] As a result, the only evidence of Christianity that still exists are some cross engravings from the first century AD, a few Christian tombs, and some church ruins.[9]

During our business trips to Socotra, we flew with a small airplane and a military helicopter. We had to go to drilling sites where no people set foot other than those who were working there. The views from the plane and helicopter were breathtaking. The water and the beaches reminded me of the days in my youth at the Red Sea, when I was living in Ta'izz, Hodeidah, and in particular, Mocha. However, in comparison, the water in Socotra was totally clear and the sand was white.

Each time we landed by the Indian Ocean, I spent hours walking on the beach, collecting many seashells, which I still have today. Although Socotra is a small island, I wasn't able to explore it as much as I would have liked to because our time was largely devoted to work. And some of the archaeology on the island has been discovered since I lived in Yemen. I'm hoping to visit Socotra again to do more exploring and enjoy the beauty of this island.

XXVII

Civil War

A wall is a hell of a lot better than a war.

— John F. Kennedy, August 1961

During the latter part of 1988, while I was living in the US, the Soviet empire was dissolving, and the USSR was unable to support countries of marginal interest. As a result, South Yemen went virtually bankrupt. In November 1989, the leaders from South and North Yemen met and agreed to merge. On May 22, 1990, they announced their plans to the international community.

Yemen suffered a huge financial blow with the return of Yemeni workers from Saudi Arabia and other Gulf countries and the loss of income from migrants sending money back to Yemen from the other, wealthier Gulf countries.

In addition to slashed international development assistance, the return of the millions of Yemeni workers put a huge strain on local infrastructure as they returned looking for jobs and needing housing. Ideological tensions were compounded by a new wave of land disputes, triggered by the homecoming of traditional tribal leaders who returned from exile and, to reassert their influence, began to reclaim land that had been confiscated by the communist regime. In addition, the Yemeni *mujahideen* (Islamic guerillas engaged in *jihad*[1]) were also returning home from Afghanistan. When the South Yemen leadership fell prey to an assassination campaign in the early 1990s, Northern politicians blamed Southern vendettas, but the socialists accused the Islamists and, increasingly, the president's security service.

When I read the news of the unification while I was in the US, I was perplexed about how two countries that had followed distinctly different trajectories for much of the twentieth century would—or even if they could—work together. The North was a conservative tribal society, while the South had endured colonialism and Marxism. At the time of the unification, Northerners outnumbered Southerners by roughly four to one. Before then, the economies of both Yemens were dependent on foreign aid and loans and remittances from migrant workers in Gulf states.

When North and South Yemen united, the country adopted a new flag—the current flag of Yemen, which consists of three horizontal stripes: red, white, and black. The black stripe symbolizes the dark days of the past, the white symbolizes hope for the future, and the red stripe symbolizes the blood shed by martyrs. Despite the 1990 unification and adoption of this flag and the hope that came with it, however, that turning point was not the end of civil unrest in Yemen.

In such an atmosphere of intense distrust, parliamentary elections marked the end of the two-year transition period. It was the period after the elections during which I returned to Yemen. After the 1993 election, the Northerners, combined with the Islamists, took the majority of the seats, leaving the socialists with one seat on the five-member presidential council. Angry and humiliated, the leader of South Yemen withdrew himself to Aden, complaining the North didn't respect or honor the terms of the unity agreement. With that, the preferred federal model vanished.

A full-scale military offensive started two months later, and the Northern troops swiftly proved they had the advantage. In May, the Southern leadership proclaimed the creation of a new entity as an independent state with its capital at Aden. Northerners dismissed the Southern allies from the cabinet and tightened their military stronghold on Aden, which fell to Northern forces in July 1994.

The two-month civil war in 1994 destroyed much of the optimism surrounding the idea of unity and, by extension, democratization. The irony of unification lay in the fact that both the Northern and Southern political elites seemed to believe that unification would solidify their respective authority. However, with four years of unification, the remnants of the socialist regime were destroyed and many of the socialist leaders were forced into exile, while the Northern military's victory allowed them to declare peace as the victors.

How did the civil war impact people's daily lives? People like me were stuck in the middle. Being from South Yemen, I was loyal to the South's cause and needs. I wanted them to break away from the North, the country I always had issues with at many levels. At the same time, I was residing in North Yemen and my work in Yemen was based in the North. I was caught between my loyalty to my ancestral land (South) and my employment and need to survive.

I wasn't alone; many Southerners were living in the North. We could not loudly support the South due to fear of execution, but we were unable to stomach what was being done to Southerners, namely our relatives.

There was no electricity or water. Those with money ran generators to listen to radios or watch TV with a new satellite dish. During the day, we walked around the city to see the damage on property and humans. We often clustered around family members and exchanged war news with people who were connected to authorities and military officials.

After the war, there were endless cases of those with good connections seizing property in the South, and the effect was felt by Southerners as a Northern invasion. During that time, the unemployment rate stood at 35 percent. More than a third of the population was living in poverty, and half the population was illiterate. Yemen was second only to Sudan among Arab countries in the scale of its hunger count. Yemen had one of the lowest rates of water availability in the world, and Yemeni women consistently came last in the World Economic Forum's Global Gender Gap Index.[2] Southerners were not alone in waiting for Yemen's as-yet unfulfilled promise of democracy and prosperity to come to fruition.

XXVIII

Newspaper Columnist

By giving us the opinions of the uneducated, journalism keeps us in touch with the ignorance of the community.

— Oscar Wilde

In 1993, I started to contribute to the *Yemen Times*,[1] a weekly newspaper printed in English. The editor-in-chief, Abdulaziz Al-Saqqaf,[2] who passed away a couple years after I left Yemen the second time, convinced me to write a weekly column. I told him, "I'm not a writer, and I have very little to share."

He argued, "Adel, you're a computer science and engineering graduate, you have a number of years' work experience in the US, and you have the skills and knowledge to teach the Yemeni people. The entire nation, if you will!" He also knew that I was passionate about political and social issues.

I wasn't convinced, but I agreed to assist him, as he was a dynamic person. Moreover, although it wasn't public knowledge and no one would say so aloud, he too was born in Ethiopia, but as part of a survival mechanism he had to change his birthplace to Yemen. We both knew this fact, and I wanted to help him by bringing an added dimension to his paper, which was dominated by political and social affairs.

*

Abdulaziz Al-Saqqaf had initially asked me to regularly contribute to the Science & Technology column. Interestingly, I was a new graduate of a computer engineering degree in the early 1990s, the exact time that people worldwide were jumping on the computer craze. More and more people were purchasing personal computers for home use, and that period of time also saw the introduction of the Internet to everyday life.

One of the articles I wrote for the *Yemen Times* is about the history of the personal computer.[3]

Even though I vowed not to engage in political or social issues, I ended up writing a handful of articles unrelated to science or technology. The first was about qat. The second was about women and the wearing of veils. The third was about a woman who was found with a man and jailed for violation of religion and cultural values.

The fourth article was a translation of an Arabic article written about me by my friend Gamil Al-Razahi. I was worried, though, as the content was a hot topic—it highlighted racism and presented an implied attack on Southerners. Moreover, the article was published only a few weeks before the 1994 civil war between North and South Yemen when tensions were building.

In the end, we didn't translate the entire article—only a condensed version.

*

When I returned to Yemen from the US, one of the major differences I saw in my life was my interaction with native-born Yemenis. Between 1978 and 1984, I rarely bonded or connected with locals. My circle of friends was limited to Yemeni who had lived overseas and/or who were born outside Yemen.

In the early 1990s, with the return of many Yemenis from Gulf states and many Yemenis who went abroad to study and returned home after completing their education, combined with the unification of the two Yemen countries, the pool of people I could interact with widened. Although I initially felt disconnected from everyone around me upon my return, over time, I was able to meet and connect with many more people than I had in my previous stint living in Yemen. Probably 80 percent of the people I encountered were following the Wahhabi form of Islam, but there were more educated Yemenis with more international experience than previously; I eventually was able to connect with people I had more in common with. As I interacted with more and more of these people, I was able to freely mingle without cultural end educational elements restricting me. There were many individuals who I befriended, but Gamil Al-Razahi stood out.

I always got along with those with whom I had common ground, particularly other Muwalladin. I never thought I would be befriending let alone bonding with a person who wasn't a Hadhrami and/or who wasn't born outside Yemen. Perhaps I was prejudiced, or perhaps I was unable to distinguish between the system in Yemen and the Yemeni people. Gamil Al-Razahi completely erased the ill feelings I had in me about Yemeni society, perhaps because he was fairly educated and spent considerable time overseas, or maybe because I, too, spent time in the US. Perhaps more schooling matured me. Our friendship grew quickly, and it was profound. Over the course of a few years, we spent countless hours discussing Yemeni political and social matters. Together, we translated into English and summarized articles from various Arabic newspapers of current affairs of the country for our oil and gas executives. When I was writing articles in the Science & Technology column for *Yemen Times*, he persuaded me to also write about social issues, so I did.

Al-Razahi went on writing articles on my behalf about challenges I was facing with discrimination. Most of my political opinions about Yemen were based on the discussions and readings I shared with him. He didn't see me as less of a person due to my color or birthplace. He treated me as an equal human being and respected me. Most Yemeni I encountered were definitely racist with unpleasant discriminatory attributes, but some were not. Al-Razahi in particular didn't share any of those qualities, and I'm sure there were plenty like him I didn't encounter. I thank him for changing my attitude toward Yemenis, whom I had considered primitive, narrow-minded, and racist.

XXIX

Oscar

They came to work with red and bulging eyes, and they were tired and unable to give their full attention to their work.

— Unknown oil and gas company executive

Oscar Bernard was an American drilling manager whom I met in 1992 and worked with for a couple of years. He was the colleague/friend who gave me the alcohol bottle so that I could leave a tasty "treat" for my nosy landlord. He was also the man I frequently traveled with on helicopter flights to Socotra and other drilling sites. Every time we met, we tended to ponder and discuss topics about the US, Yemen, and Canada. He was an Acadian who traced his ancestors back to Canada. Oscar departed Yemen quickly because of the conflict there, and when he did, he left his apartment key with me. The apartment was full of enough food to feed a family for six months.

During the civil war, while he was stationed in Reading, UK, he made every effort to stay in contact and ensure my team was safe/alive. In his letters, he continually encouraged me to look for opportunities to move to Canada or back to the US. He even begged me to consume the food he left behind and to take his belongings (including the Rolex watch!). Despite the harsh circumstances we were under, I didn't lift a thing from his place because I thought I would be betraying our friendship.

Oscar didn't return to Yemen after the war, but he stayed in touch with me. Shortly after I landed in Calgary in May 1996, he sent me $1,500 to purchase a car and some items for the new baby my wife and I were expecting. He had written many recommendation letters to the Canadian consulate supporting my application to migrate to Canada, and he then wrote countless more to prospective employers while I was hunting for employment in Canada!

While in Yemen, when I was pushed around by Yemeni authorities, he encouraged me to stay strong. He even assisted me in editing the articles I was contributing to the *Yemen Times*.

We spent many weekends and evenings together at his apartment talking about his sons, ex-wife, and music/band playing experience. I always felt as though he thought of me as a younger brother.

Oscar always wondered about qat in particular and kept asking me about it. He thought that other than food, substances we put into our bodies that make us do or feel differently cause us to behave as if our bodies are captivated by drugs. To him, a drug could range from painkillers, alcohol, or heroine, all of which eventually ruin our body and spirit.

I agreed with him, and I told him, "Qat is a drug, too. This opinion is just mine though, as it is not supported by scientific evidence. That is just an opinion, but it's based on common sense to point out that 99 percent of our society is suffering from a vicious drug called qat and its consequences."

He asked me to elaborate on what qat was. "Qat is a drug with its own power! It's powerful enough to force millions of people in Yemen to allocate the best and largest room in every home for qat-worshipping purposes. Most homes in our country do not even have enough spaces for cooking, sleeping, or other uses. But qat has imposed its place."

"How important is qat for Yemeni people?" he asked.

"It is powerful enough to make adults—both men and women—fill up their mouths with leaves that have visible and strong negative effects on their health. They look stupid and ugly with their cheeks puffed out, and every now and then, the green saliva leaks out." I asked him, "Have you tried to speak to a person with his mouth full of qat?"

"No."

"If you come too close, you risk being covered with a lot of stuff that flies out of their mouth as they stutter. But if you keep your distance, you don't hear or understand what they are saying."

"It seems like it's such a big part of society. What is the impact on society?" he continued with his questions.

"Qat is destroying the country's economy. Its prevalence is a waste of human resources. It damages work and workplace ethics, and forces the misallocation of scarce agricultural land, which is used to grow this drug instead of useful crops."

He asked, "Are there any substitutes to occupy your people rather than qat?"

"Not really. Alcohol is forbidden, but it's acceptable for men to smoke cigarettes. And qat is not only allowed; its use is rampant. Because of the effects of qat, people forget social activities, family ties, and responsibilities. If you inquire at a police station about feuds and quarrels, you will find most of the confusion and misunderstandings arise either immediately before or after the qat chewing. A large group of our society spends several hours every day doing nothing except chewing. Chewing is, for many people, a chronic drug addiction."

"Do you grow it here, or is it an imported material?"

"It comes from a shrub that is grown on the mountains of Yemen, as well as in various parts of the Horn of Africa and East Africa. Possibly as far south as Mozambique."

"What kind of people in your society chew qat?"

"There is no need to carry out a thorough study to realize that 80 percent of our adult population chews qat. While the public and health officials are oblivious to the issue, qat is increasingly becoming a weapon in the destruction of the minds and bodies of our people. In fact, you will even find medical doctors treating their patients in afternoon clinics with their mouths full of qat. It looks both ugly and unprofessional."

"Holy cow! That is fucked up!" he exclaimed. "If I may ask, what do you do for social activities?"

I said, "Not much! Social activities not involving qat are about to disappear, if they even ever existed. All social events now revolve around a qat-chewing gathering. Weddings, birth celebrations, death rituals, holidays gatherings, weekends, etc., all have qat chews as their core event. The most typical question friends ask each other in Yemen today is, 'Where will you chew today?' As a result, community activities are reduced to a minimum. Society does not feel pressed to create parks, zoos, clubs, recreation facilities, playgrounds, etc. The population doesn't care about those types of facilities because they are indoors chewing. I don't chew it, so I spend my time reading and teaching English to my friends' children. That's the extent of my free time activities!"

"How about on the home front? How does it impact family lifestyle?"

"Well," I said, "Parents and children spend few hours together because adults are busy in their daily qat-chewing sessions. Most worrying is that families are spending more on qat than on food."

"How much money is qat claiming from the family income?" he asked.

"According to some estimates of the household budget, on average qat claims from 25 to 40 percent of the total family income. This habit comes at the expense of other badly needed purchases, especially food. Children don't get a sufficient food intake. They don't have proper clothing to wear or toys to play with. Most parents, especially the father, spend too much of the family income on qat."

"You said qat grows in Yemen. What is the economic impact as a whole?"

"Economic development is the lifeline of Yemeni society, yet, qat is one of the major factors which slows down our growth rate. Qat takes up the best part of our resources, such as humans and land. The famous Arabic coffee is from

Yemen, so coffee exports could greatly benefit workers and the country's economy, but farmers choose to plant qat trees instead of growing coffee. Since qat is not an edible agricultural product, it doesn't help us minimize the demand for imported food. Today, some 1.5 million hectares of good agricultural land are used to grow qat. Moreover, qat is neither an important source of revenue for the government, nor it is an exportable product."

"Holy shit! Your country soon will become a shithole!" he added with a frightened expression on his face.

I continued, "Human effort is frozen for half of the day, every day, while people chew qat. To aggravate the situation further, a good part of the other half of the day is also used to prepare for the qat chew. Not only that, but qat addicts cannot sleep well, and therefore, they are not ready for work the next morning."

He said, "You seem to know a lot about this topic. Have you tried to communicate with influential people and make moves to change this ugly pattern for the better?"

"Ha!" I told him, "I'm too busy surviving and trying to leave this country. I don't have time for this. And in my mind, my effort would be like trying to burn the ocean. I love Yemen, but not the way people conduct themselves these days."

"I see. You seem very passionate and angry about the whole issue," he said.

I told him, "I'm not necessarily angry only about qat alone. It just triggers me on all the other disappointments I have about this country."

He told me, "I remember an oil executive we used to work with complaining about Yemeni employees. He always said they came to work with red and bulging eyes, and they were tired and unable to give their full attention to their work."

"Exactly!" I said. "It is all part of the qat syndrome!"

This conversation with Oscar prompted me to write another article for the Yemen Times. He was always encouraging me to write for the newspaper because he felt I should educate others. He often told me, "You have the knowledge to teach the entire nation. You never know if future generations will read your articles."

Qat is a Drug and Most Yemenis are Addicted to It![1]

No one can deny that Yemen is one of the poorest countries of the world. It has survived the last thirty years on donations and foreign aid. I had hoped that this generation would pick up the pieces and start rebuilding the nation, but alas, qat is in the way.

Thousands of people are treated from poisoning every year because often expired or unhealthy pesticides are used on qat farms. Others suffer from gastrointestinal complications directly related to qat chewing. And still more suffer from dental problems. Many doctors have expressed their astonishment at the number of Yemeni patients with backbone problems. Many Yemenis' spines are not vertical. There are signs they grow sideways. Of course, many Yemenis spend half of their lives in qat sessions, during which people force their bodies to recline sideways by putting their elbow on the *matka* (pillows, thirty centimeters or twelve inches high), and then supporting their weight on that elbow.

Physical and emotional disturbances in Yemen are plenty, and many of them are associated with qat. If a Yemeni person says qat has no effect on our behavior, I will call them a liar. Simply observe the activity of an average person before and after qat hours, i.e., the way they talk and conduct themselves. One of the best examples is to look at people's attitude while they are driving to qat markets. They speed; they don't pay attention to pedestrians or other traffic. They are fixated on their destination and driving in a panicky state.

Another aspect is wife- and child-beating, which has become an acceptable phenomenon in Yemeni homes. These beatings happen mainly during the evening because the father, following the qat chew, wants to be left alone. The slightest noise or disruption irritates him. Imagine that kind of person in a house full of kids. If you add the demands of the family, particularly if the income level is low, the cause of the conflict is evident. Because of the money that people spend on qat, kids are deprived of their meals and families go without other household necessities. The lack of money for basic needs creates domestic disputes and adds to the stress and demands of running a household. Women don't have a voice, and so qat and the money spent on it create huge dissention within households.

Crime is the result of deviant behavior. In developed countries, several drug- and alcohol-related crimes are committed on the streets. Yes, we have fewer crimes committed on the streets of Yemeni cities related to qat in comparison to countries like the US. However, our "drug addicts" are committing crimes at home and in government offices.

Government workers take advantage of their position to collect bribes and personal benefits. Bribery has become such a prevalent disease that most companies—both local and foreign—have "fixers." If you look at their accounts, they always have entries such as gratuities which are invisible on the expenditure side. If you have paperwork to process in any government office, get prepared to part with some money. It is called *Haq alqat* meaning *for qat*. If you don't hand over the money or agree to hand it over later, there will be deliberate delays in completing your formalities, or the whole bundle of paperwork may even vanish.

Qat is doing damage everywhere. Make a quick trip to our government offices, and you will see employees preoccupied with the chewing. In fire departments, police stations, and even in hospitals, you will see senior officials, military and security officers, and medical doctors all chewing. Next time you drive, watch the traffic policeman; he is probably chewing while guiding traffic. Qat chewing while on the job has become acceptable. Walk into any shop and you will find the shopkeeper too lazy to move his butt while sitting on the mattress and chewing.

The rulers of Yemen meet at qat sessions to decide on how to manage the affairs of the nation. No wonder everything is in such shambles. In Yemen, qat has become an essential aspect of life. Some say that to conclude any business in Yemen you must chew. Yemenis even boastfully present the qat to visiting dignitaries. What a joke!

I think we should handle qat as the weighty problem that it is. Government officials should take the issue seriously and implement steps to limit its use. Of course, nothing can be done by force, but the public should be taught the damage done by qat to our society. Every moment is the right time to address this problem before it becomes a plague.

*

My article didn't change Yemen's approach to qat. I didn't change the world with *any* of my articles. But the *Yemen Times* was a great outlet for me during a difficult period. It presented me the opportunity to express my views on social and political issues and share my knowledge of computers with a society that I felt needed to become more modernized and outward thinking.

A few years after I moved to Canada, I learned that Abdulaziz Al-Saqqaf was killed when he was hit by a car in 1999.

> Despite appeals by Dr. Saqqaf's heirs to re-open an investigation into the accident due to indicators that it may have been a carefully coordinated assassination, the authorities in 1999 refused to do so, resulting in a withdrawal of trial proceedings against the car driver. Saqqaf's elder son Walid and younger daughter Nadia, who [ran] the *Yemen Times* [from 2005 until 2014], have mentioned on more than one occasion that they believe the accident was orchestrated due to their father's frequent critical writings against the former president of Yemen Ali Abdullah Saleh.[2]

I have always believed their suspicions were correct.

XXX

Capitalism

It's easier to imagine the end of the world than the end of capitalism.

— Marc Fisher

Over the decades, I've worked for oil and gas companies, and I've worked for NGOs. In my work with these organizations, I saw how international aid money is used in Yemen, how scholarships are awarded, and how employment is granted within those organizations. I also noticed the Western world only provides aid to developing countries if the interests of those Western countries is kept. Most of the time, when political views are misaligned, that foreign aid is cut.

I have very negative views of how detrimental internal aid programs are to developing countries. Based on what I have seen, the money is rarely distributed properly and most of the time, those developing countries remain further dependent on foreign handouts and unable to sustain themselves.

One major indication of the problem is the fact that, when Yemen produces over half a million barrels of oil a day, most Yemeni people do not have clean running water, hospitals, infrastructure, schools, or other basics of human needs. Millions of dollars are funneled to a few within the presidential circle (including family members). Those running the companies spend money on military equipment or put it into overseas investments.

The money that people in Western countries donate to social development does not necessarily make it to the intended recipients. I know my family suffers, so I send money directly to them. This is a sore point for me. The way aid organizations or oil and gas companies conduct themselves has nothing to do with developing society or giving back to anything. These groups are only about resources being extracted, and the country is being drained and left poor. It is a predatory capitalism. This type of capitalism—the way the Western world exploits the environment for minerals and oil—is like how you treat a disposable cup. You drink out of it and then you leave it somewhere; you don't remember where you left it, and you don't even claim it. The local people are kicked out of their land for nothing. They end up working as guards or other grunt workers for the oil companies, and those oil companies treat them as if they don't exist. Once the oil has been extracted, the job ends, and that family is left with nothing.

What is humanity when many of us, in developed countries, worry about putting garbage in the ocean, but we don't provide basic human necessities for one another?

It concerns me not only as Yemeni but as a human. I'm not anti-capitalist. I suspect capitalism generates more revenue and enhances life standards for many, but it has to be ethical.

The type of capitalism the world is currently practicing is sad and very scary to me. When you think of Karl Marx, Lenin, and so on, Lenin brought revolution. But the reason people in developing countries don't rise up these days to rebel against being taken advantage of and fight to have a better life is that they don't have the means to learn that the resources are being taken away from them. The suffering we see today is maybe 100-fold what it was at the turn of the century. I worry about what humans will do. It wouldn't be surprising for me to see another Nazi Germany-type situation in the world. Humans revolt and they destroy their institutions because of no respect for law and order. When they start seeing injustice, they revolt. We may not have Karl Marx's kind of thinking today, but the worst kind of communism might come because how society lives right now is beyond sustainable. The greed of capitalism we have now is very frightening compared to the greed and capitalist mentality Karl Marx and Friedrich Engels criticized 100 years ago.

The IMF,[1] European Union, or the US gives these poorer countries loans, and a few selected officials are stealing the money and putting it into Swiss banks. The interesting part is when a country is in bad shape and cannot pay, the richer countries say "That's fine. We can drill for oil." Then, when the wealthier country extracts the minerals and the local president resists, outside powers come in to exert control and, in some cases, a new government comes to power.

Ethiopia is one example; US$30 billion in financial aid given to Ethiopia by the US several years ago went straight into the pockets of Ethiopia's leaders—a handful of influential people working in government.[2] It is evident the money is needed for development within the country, but it was never used for those purposes.

So when we preach human rights and democracy, when we tell developing countries that their elections are wrong or corrupt, and we can't even give them back the money they are entitled to, they are screwed backward and forward.

While the majority of Yemenis don't have much to eat and suffer from all types of social and economic hardship, the county's president and his cronies are stashing oil money abroad. When those corrupt officials invest billions of dollars in offshore accounts, Yemen's children are dying of starvation and disease. The country is geographically far from North America or Europe; therefore the suffering is far from sight for most people in the West. The nation itself is a dysfunctional and failed state, if not a terrorist nation; therefore, the years of suffering don't get news coverage—a fraction of the amount of coverage the Ukraine was getting in early 2022. I don't mean to be critical or compare, but it's hard not to be as I just ponder this issue.

You can't tell me the world is in a better place these days than it has been previously. What I saw was the sickest part of capitalism played out in a developing country. I'm not professing I know the solution. I wouldn't entirely blame the system, which is capitalism, and I don't want to come across as communist. I just want to state plainly that the balance of the power and the balance of the planet are not sitting very well.

I remember I read somewhere that if everyone on the planet lived like North Americans or Europeans, we would need three planets like Earth. I look at how many different choices of toothpaste we have, how much food we waste in restaurants, etc., yet I go to Africa and I see people who don't have a single meal. If they do, it is a loaf of bread with water. So are we better off in Western societies? Why do we have to be so greedy? To have nothing doesn't mean you are deprived of happiness. Why do we need to deprive people of basic human necessities to be happier ourselves when we are destroying others in the process?

This is a pain I carry around when I go to Ethiopia; if I don't write about this, I won't feel fulfilled. I get emails and have phone conversations just about every other day with my family from Yemen and Ethiopia. When I ask them, "How is life?" in their responses, they say, "We are surviving," but the one big the thing they don't say speaks volumes; they never complain.

There is no food, and sometimes they borrow money against their own salaries. "There's no electricity," they admit to me. "If we have two hours electricity each day, we will be happy." Other than that, they are hesitant to say what isn't working; they don't talk about how high inflation is. Denial seems to be a way of coping with the pressure and rising costs.

XXXI

Arranged Marriage

I realized I would be forced to run away from home if someone tried to arrange a marriage for me. I didn't want to think about it.

— Elizabeth Wein

Almost immediately upon my return to Yemen from the US, I began to explore ways to leave Yemen again. At the same time, I was craving a social life as well as a partner in life. While I kept looking for opportunities to emigrate to Australia or Canada, or return to the US, I was also open to finding a suitable woman to marry. I was targeting a partner with a few main criteria: a woman of about thirty years of age, a college graduate, and possibly a Hadhrami lady.

Life in the US had changed my views about arranged marriages, so I no longer had an appetite for one, but my options in Yemen were limited. In light of the previous marital arrangement my oldest sister had made for me and how I had ended it, I didn't have the courage to ask my siblings to find me a mate a second time. I was embarrassed, as I had brought shame and disgrace to my family.

Hadhrami families stay in touch with each other and support one another as typical Jewish tribes do, so soon after returning to Yemen, I reconnected with the Basherahil family, the family my mother had worked for as a nanny. They had already moved back to Yemen and were living in the same city I was in. I managed to secure a job as a driver at my workplace for one of their sons. They therefore felt indebted to me and were looking for an opportunity to return the favor. Every now and then, they invited me for a homemade meal, and I spent several evenings at their house talking about life.

The mother was fond of my father; she never stopped talking about him. She seemed to know many intimate details about him too—as much as my stepmother did. She was aware that I knew little about my dad, so she was generous in feeding my craving for more information. During my visits to their residence, she kept asking me about my plans for marriage, as I was thirty-two years old by then, and it was the right time and age for me to marry.

One Monday, she called me at work and asked me to join the family for Friday lunch. (Friday is the equivalent of what Sunday is to the rest of the world, and Saturday is the first day of the work week.) I agreed. At the time, most Yemenis didn't have home phones, and cell phones were not even part of the vocabulary yet let alone in existence, but their family had a telephone. She phoned again on Thursday to remind me about Friday lunch. She suspected I may have forgotten and wanted to be sure I didn't miss it. During the call, she told me she would be making a typical Yemeni dish that I love (zurbian, or as Indians call it, biryani).

The next day, after the meal and tea had been served, she reached into her purse and pulled out a couple of pictures. "What do you think of this girl?" she queried as she pushed one of the pictures toward me.

I said, "She is pretty."

She gave me a big smile.

"What is going on?" I asked her.

She replied, "You wouldn't like her."

"Well, I didn't say I liked her. I only complimented her looks."

"I think you should marry her. I will ask the mom. This girl just finished high school with a 92 percent and is planning to attend medical school. She is pretty, young, and smart. What else can you ask for? Moreover, her mom was born in Ethiopia. She knows your other culture and respects you."

"Is she Hadhrami?" I asked.

She said no.

I asked if the girl's grandfather, who had migrated to Ethiopia, knew my father.

"No. Your dad was in a different class altogether, and her grandfather was a humble person. But he was a very good man. Would you like to speak to her mom? I have known the mom since she was a baby, but she was brought to Yemen at the age of twelve. The girl's grandmother was also my friend. I believe your biological mother knows the girl's grandmother."

Half-heartedly I relented, "Sure, talk to the mom," and we moved on to a different topic.

Only a week later, I received a call from the Basherahil family again.

"The family you were interested in agreed for you to travel to their city to visit them."

"That was quick!" I said. "That is fine."

The mother suggested, "How about you and my son drive to Aden to meet the family?"

"Why?" I asked. Living in the US for almost ten years had reprogrammed my brain. Plus, I was never up to speed on the protocols involved in engagements to begin with, so I didn't understand why I needed to begin the courtship by meeting the family.

"I spoke to the mother already about possible arrangements," she said. "They didn't want to say anything until you come to visit them and get to know you."

"That makes sense," I agreed, "but I am busy for a week or so closing yearly financial books."

We decided I would make my way to Aden with her son after my workload eased up.

*

Two weeks later, Basherahil (the son) and I drove to Aden to meet this family. I stayed with Fawzia. I didn't tell Fawzia or my stepmother, Maryam, the purpose of my trip, though.

The day after we arrived in Aden, I went to meet the family. The house was kind of a shack and was shabby. Doorbells are not common in Yemen, so when someone approaches a home, they holler to announce themselves so that the family members inside know that visitors have arrived.

After announcing our arrival, Basherahil and I were invited to enter the house and the living room. It was a two-room house with one bedroom and one living room. A veranda or patio of some sort seemed to have been converted into the living room, which had a TV set. It was November, when the average temperature in Aden is about 30 degrees Celsius (86 degrees Fahrenheit), and it was hot that day. I was happy to be seated in the living room, as it felt cooler.

Floor seating can be seen all over the Muslim world. In fact, it is a Muslim practice to sit, sleep, and even eat on the floor, because doing so is a *Sunna*, any practice that was exemplified by the Prophet Muhammed (pbuh). Since the Prophet Muhammed (pbuh) is a role model to all Muslims, they follow in his footsteps and mimic his practices. That does not mean that you will not find chairs in a Muslim home. It merely explains why some Muslims prefer to sit on the floor and why you might find pillows scattered on the floor in a Muslim home.

Also, compared to Ethiopia and the US, the seating area of an Arab home is different. Since I am partially Arab, those sorts of differences come naturally to me and have never bothered me. But I noticed in this house the pillows didn't have a color pattern.

It was around two p.m., and the father was setting himself up for a qat-chewing session with his cigarettes also ready. The two men sat side by side, leaving me in the corner of the room by myself. Cigarette smoke always irritates and triggers my sinuses, so I was more than happy that they were keeping their distance. We exchanged short conversations for about thirty minutes, breaking the ice, making small talk about the road trip we had just taken, and so on. After about half an hour, the man yelled to his wife, "*Ya mara!*" (Hey, woman!) I was taken aback by that as most Hadhrami men don't call their wives in such a harsh, direct manner.

A lady in her late thirties, dressed in a typical Aden or South Yemeni outfit with her hair partially covered, came to say hello. She greeted me and asked about the drive from Sana'a to Aden. She seated herself not too far from me, and she and I continued to exchange simple conversation. She was graceful and dignified, speaking calmly and with level-headedness.

For about an hour or so, she asked me about my schooling in the US, where I grew up in Ethiopia, and how long it had been since I left Ethiopia. I answered all her questions. Even though she had been born in Ethiopia like me, her Arabic didn't sound like those who were born in Ethiopia. She spoke clearly, and her comments and questions were elegantly put. I suspected that had to do with her leaving Ethiopia at the age of twelve and spending most of her life in South Yemen. We also exchanged a few words in Amharic, which her husband didn't know.

Her husband jumped into the conversation and asked me about the main purpose of my trip. "I hear you're interested in one of my daughters and are about to ask for her hand."

I replied, "Kind of. In fact, I came to meet the family so that we could both get a feel for each other before going too far with the other parts of the process."

He interrupted me and abruptly asked, "How much are you willing to pay?"

The room went quiet. I felt as though he had punched me in the stomach. I didn't know how to respond.

His wife quickly jumped in and said, "Are you crazy? He came to see us and get to know us. And we need to get to know him, too. What kind of manner is this? Stop it!" she shouted at him.

He responded with a soft voice, "Why don't we just focus on the matter of money and have a useful discussion?"

I looked him in the eye, and I said, "I didn't come here to purchase a woman. The purpose of my trip was to get to know each other and see how it goes."

The mother sensed that I was tense, and the conversation wasn't going well. She took control of the situation and started to talk about the place where she grew up and asked further questions about my work in Sana'a. Even though she knew and had heard enough about me, she went on asking more questions about my life in an attempt to ease the tension in the room.

At about 5 p.m., three hours after my arrival at their house, the father asked, "Are the girls presentable and able to come to say hello?" The wife said she would check. She left the room, returning in about ten minutes to sit in the same spot she had been all afternoon.

About three minutes later, six children came into the room one by one to greet me. Their ages ranged between six and twenty. There were three boys and three girls, and the two six-year-old boys were twins. I didn't know which one of the girls I would be married to. I had only seen her picture before coming to see the family. To make matters more complicated, the two oldest girls looked almost identical, and both were good-looking. I said hello, but they remained quiet. None of the children spoke, and five minutes later, they all left the room together. I kept asking myself where these children slept, knowing that in addition to the mother, father, and six children, two extended family members were also living in the same residence.

I was getting a headache from the cigarettes and the heat, so I asked if I could return to my sister's house. It was agreed, and the father escorted me and Basherahil to the main gate and into the street. As we left the main door, we ran into the father's younger brother. The father introduced me as the fiancée of his daughter, potentially proposing to marry his daughter. I greeted the brother with a brief smile, but the comment from my future father-in-law didn't sit well with me as I hadn't yet proposed or accepted any agreements. I left his home feeling as though he was treating the potential marriage as an exchange of commodities—buying and selling a woman rather than respectfully arranging for her marriage.

As we drove to my sister's house, I commented to Basherahil about the uneasy feelings I had about my future father-in-law. I repeated the man's comment about money and added, "I was sad that he asked me how much I'm willing to pay for his daughter." In fact, I was appalled to hear such a comment from him.

I kept repeating the issue until Basherahil said to me, "You're not marrying him. You're marrying his daughter. Look at her mother."

He added, "You know what is said about girls—get to know the mother first prior to proposing to the daughter."

I said, "I understand. The mother is a fine lady, but I cannot stand that man."

I told him I had been engaged to a Hadhrami girl in the past, and in that situation, money was never mentioned. In fact, her family was even embarrassed to hear what we had to offer. It was my sister who had set the mahir, and no one else ever discussed it.

"This is incredible," I said.

Basherahil is a man of a few words. He simply said, "We Hadhrami people are different. We have our own manners and protocols. Remember, this man could be a bit off balance, as most Yemeni don't engage in the topic in the manner that he did. Let's hope he misspoke and the whole thing was just a mishap."

I shared my encounter with my stepmother Maryam upon my return to her home.

She said to me, "Son, if you have a bad feeling, just halt the process here. I cannot tell you who you should marry or not, but trust your gut feelings."

Quickly, she wanted to know about the mother and the girl herself. Most importantly, she asked how I ended up in this family's circle. I told her the entire story. She made it clear what her preferences were regarding my future wife.

"I hope you take a Hadhrami girl. If you do, at least we can ask people about the family before tying the knots," she said.

I told her, "The girl is as beautiful are you are." She laughed.

*

Upon my return to Sana'a, the Basherahil family contacted me to let me know the family had agreed to marry their daughter to me. I went silent. My lack of enthusiasm worried me, but what concerned me more was the speed of the girl's family and their wanting to speak to me. When I told the Basherahil family about my apprehension, I was overwhelmed by the amount of clarification and justification they then provided. In fact, they labeled my future father-in-law as unstable and confused. They suggested that I not put too much stock into his words. I was informed the wedding would take place quickly, as delaying matters was never good.

I was dreading breaking the news to my sisters and the rest of the family, as they would be disappointed that I had made such an arrangement without their knowledge and involvement. I was also worried about the pushback and the concerns they may have about me taking a wife they knew nothing about. Marriage is a family affair and is not just for the husband and wife; it involves the union of two families.

All my sisters wished me the best of luck, but with enormous reservations. They didn't want to say anything about that situation, as they knew I was stubborn and wouldn't change my mind. But they were perplexed as to why I would go through the process of marrying this girl knowing that I was already preparing to leave Yemen for Australia, Canada, or the US. They also hadn't forgotten what took place some eleven years prior, when I disappeared after the wedding date was set and invitation cards were distributed. They were, however, happy that I would be marrying a Yemeni girl, and they hoped that marrying her meant that I may not leave the country again. They wished me luck time and time again, but none seemed overly excited.

XXXII

Weddings

Never marry at all, Dorian. Men marry because they are tired, women, because they are curious: both are disappointed.

— Oscar Wilde

On January 26, 1995, my father-in-law and I signed the marriage contract and began making arrangements to have two wedding receptions: one in Aden, where a large portion of my wife's family resided, and the second in Sana'a. Members of my family who were living in South Yemen could attend the first reception, as it would be too expensive for everyone to travel to the capital. Moreover, it was also an opportunity for my two sisters, who never talked to each other in the past, to attend each wedding separately.

As was the custom, during the initial ceremony, I joined hands with my bride's father. The officiant held our hands together, which were wrapped with a white cloth, and he blessed the wedding. My father-in-law and I then both signed the certificate. But before this took all place, the officiant, asked the bride in private if she was willing and able to enter the marriage.

At this point the bride has to say yes; the officiant won't consent to the marriage if the bride says no or if he senses she is being forced into the marriage. The bride's consent is a critical part of an Islamic marriage.

Over 300 ladies attended the first reception in Aden, and I was the only male allowed to enter the wedding hall. One of the ladies in attendance approached me and said to me, "You look better without glasses," and removed my glasses from my face. As a result, I couldn't see any of the ladies dancing! (So sneaky of her!)

I'm not sure if it was something I ate or if it was my nerves as I was mentally exhausted, but I was sick from the evening before and was wishing for the party to be over quickly. The entire celebration lasted five hours, and I was relieved when it ended. When we left for the hotel, the photographer following us and was continuing to shoot pictures; he didn't want to leave our hotel room. I vividly recall him making a comment to another cameraman, the person holding the flash, saying in English, "They didn't find a lighter-colored Yemeni man to marry this beautiful girl than this dark man?" He didn't know I spoke English. I pretended I didn't hear him. I had to politely ask him to leave, as I could barely stand.

The second wedding was at the Sheraton Hotel in Sana'a and was held according to Ethiopian tradition. The band and singers we hired consisted of a group of Ethiopian refugees who had abandoned an Ethiopian navy ship in the Red Sea and voyaged to Yemen. I thoroughly enjoyed dancing to Ethiopian songs. We also made it a mixed-gender wedding.

The evening was wonderful and included my coworkers from the UK, US, Canada, and other countries. Some brought their alcoholic drinks in a Coca-Cola bottle, as alcohol wasn't available. We danced all night. That celebration was the best part of my entire marriage.

*

Having two wedding ceremonies is common in Yemen; however, my two weddings were not representative of what usually takes place. My first wedding was typical of one of the marriage celebrations held in Yemen. Because men and women don't mix in social settings, it is common to have a wedding in the evening at a wedding hall with only women in attendance except for the groom. Dancing is a central part of this celebration.

In Yemeni tradition, another celebration for only men is usually held during the afternoon on the same day as the "ladies only" wedding. Men gather at noon to honor the groom. Three or four goats are killed and cooked, depending on how many people are attending, and the men sit and chew qat. Usually someone plays guitar, and the attendees sing, dance, and talk while chewing qat. However, I decided to forego the second Yemeni style wedding. Because qat was not (and is not) a part of my life, and because of my Ethiopian heritage, I chose to have an Ethiopian style celebration in Sana'a instead of this type of gathering.

*

By the time we went to Amman, Jordan, for our honeymoon, we had been married no more than two weeks.

Already, it was clear to me that this marriage wasn't going anywhere. I found my wife to be acting and behaving much younger than her actual age (nineteen). There was nothing to talk about; we had zero common ground. It was obvious she had been very sheltered and had no world knowledge or experience. I was aware that most women in Yemen didn't have many rights to learn and grow, but I found this situation was totally different. I was looking for a partner, but the feeling I had was the possibility of my having to raise a child rather than build a family with an equal partner.

We had also had our first major quarrel a week before our wedding took place. I had booked and paid for the wedding hall where the reception in Aden was to take place, but friends of my soon-to-be-wife told her about another venue that they thought would be better, so she pressured me to change the venue for our wedding. We argued about the change; the major problem was that the rental fee had already been paid and was not refundable. She didn't agree with me that it made no sense to forfeit the money and spend more on reserving a different venue when there was nothing wrong with the one we had booked; the only problem was that someone else had gotten it into her head that a different venue would be better.

My gut was telling me that I should not be entering into this marriage, but I ignored the warning signs. I was thirty-two years old, which was old in Yemen culture for a single man. Remembering how badly I had handled breaking my previous engagement to Entisar, I felt that to end this engagement as well would bring even more shame to my family. I felt I had to move forward with the wedding. Little did I know that this argument about the venue was the first of many similar disagreements my wife and I would have about money during our marriage.

As soon as I returned to Yemen from my honeymoon, I phoned Hind to tell her that I had made the biggest mistake of my life. She asked what that was. "I married the wrong woman," I admitted, and tried to explain my experience.

My sister was living in a different city, and she told me, "Give it time. She is nineteen, and you're more than thirty. There is a thirteen-year gap between the two of you. Remember, you were born outside Yemen and left the country to further your education and hold professional jobs both in Yemen and the US. She hasn't had any of those types of opportunities. You must be patient with her. She will come around."

Her last comment was, "She is soft and malleable at the moment. She can learn. It is your opportunity to permanently mold her personality toward your way. With the right temperament, you will eventually make her a lovely and practical wife."

I told her, "That is a tall responsibility. I need a readymade, compatible wife and partner to start a family and grow old together."

She ended the conversation by saying, "Damn those Americans! They washed your brain! You'd better sharpen your understanding of your own culture and routines! Leave your Western thinking where you found it. We are Arabs and Muslims. With that kind of useless thinking, nothing will work for both of you. Stop being rash and uninformed. Otherwise, you'll end up making your lives miserable."

XXXIII

Leaving

Leaving everything that makes them who and what they are, leaving because it is no longer possible to stay. They will never be the same again because you just cannot be the same once you leave behind who and what you are, you just cannot be the same.

— NoViolet Bulaway

The Yemen Civil War, the treatment of North Yemenis toward the South Yemeni, and the continued mistreatment of Muwalladin made it impossible for me to continue residing in Yemen. Yemen simply wasn't a place I wanted to raise a family and spend the rest of my life. I could not even protect myself let alone a family.

One day in August 1995, my wife and I were walking home from a friend's house. My car was in the shop, so we decided to walk, as we were not far from where we lived. A civil security officer jumped out of his SUV and started to follow my wife and me. I made sure my wife was protected from seeing him, and I kept her busy by talking to her so she wouldn't notice him. He kept flashing his gun at me as an attempt to intimidate me. We continued marching home so that we could avoid any altercations with him.

Upon arrival at our building, we were greeted by the guard, and we locked the gate behind us hoping that would be the end of the chasing. It wasn't. Since my wife and I were residing on the first floor, I couldn't help but hear the commotion from the living room window of our apartment. I peeped through the curtains to see what was going on.

The civil security officer was still at the gate challenging the guard. It was a heated exchange, and the officer was trying to force himself in. Suspecting it may have to do with me, I decided to go out to inquire as to what he was seeking.

I mentioned to the guard that I had noticed the officer following us, and I asked the officer if there was anything in particular he was looking for. He asked for my ID card, and I asked him why he needed to see it.

"I'm from the civil security department, and when I suspect something abnormal, it's our responsibility to check," he replied.

I asked what kind of violation he suspected me of. He didn't want to hear my questions; in fact, he was astonished that I was brave enough to ask him anything rather than just obey his request. The guard mentioned to me that the officer suspected me of being a Somali pimp and my wife to be a Jordanian hooker.

"What makes him think that way?" I asked

"He is trying to force a confrontation with you and possibly arrest you both. I told him that you're a respectful Hadhrami person and she is your wife from Aden. However, he didn't listen to me."

Leaving

I pulled out my Yemeni ID card and handed it to the officer. He asked for the original. (In Yemen, we always made a copy of our ID, laminated the copy, carried it with us, and kept the original at home.)

"That is a duplicate copy, and that is all you get."

He also asked for my marriage certificate. I pulled out a copy of my marriage certificate and handed it to him. After examining both documents, he returned them to me. In the midst of all this, the landlord came down to the ground floor and started to inquire about the situation. He got furious about the matter and ordered the officer to leave the vicinity.

If we hadn't made it to the house in time and gotten the support of the building guard and the landlord, what would the outcome have been? What if we had been on an isolated road?

This was just one incident. There were others, including the incident that Gamil Al-Razahi had written the article about:

In April 1994, I was driving to the airport to pick up my niece and her husband. They were arriving from Hadhramaut to spend their honeymoon in Sana'a. A man claiming to be a police officer pulled me over. There was no traffic violation on my part, but he needed some money. Often, in these situations, I would let the police officer into my car, drive him around the block, give him a couple hundred rials, and then kick him out of the car.

This time, for some reason, I decided not to give him any money. As he was hurling racial insults at me, I was tempted to take him on. I'm short by North American standards, but I can beat the shit out of any Yemeni man, as they all are my dimension if not smaller and weaker. I decided not to, as the punishment for attacking an armed officer with a uniform is severe. I remained resolute and calm.

Instead, I drove to the nearest police station to report him to his supervisors. After I explained the situation, the senior officer at the station, who was also as corrupt as the first one, decided to impound my car. Furthermore, he requested I pay qat money to both officers if I wanted my car to be released.

I was outraged. I wanted to reason with the senior officer that this wasn't an appropriate action I expected from authorities. When I said, "I pay taxes to fund your wages, and it is totally unacceptable for you to demand money randomly just because you can," the officer stood up from his chair and told me, "Don't make me arrest you and put you in custody!" I left the building without further risking myself.

I contacted Amin Bahamam, a friend and family member, and explained to him what had transpired. I asked him to give me a ride to the airport. He said, "Adel, your problem is that you're still operating as if you're living in the US. This is Yemen. We have no rules or justice system. We'll never have one. We will stay in the same place for the next 10,000 years."

He shared with me a joke to crack me up. "According to popular legend, Sana'a was founded at the base of the mountains of Jabal Nuqm by Shem, the son of Noah. Shem decided to return to Earth and visit to see how things had developed on this planet. As he was flown by various experts on the crew, he was so impressed by progress made in the US and Europe. As they were passing by the Middle East and heading to Asia, as the guide tried to direct Shem's attention to the city he founded. Shem quickly said, 'Never mind. You don't have to introduce me to Sana'a. I can tell the city and the people are the same as I left them.'"

I told Bahamam, "We need to make a dent in this type of rotten system." I said, "I will write a major paper and publish the story to raise awareness. Yemen must improve."

He concluded his comments by saying, "This is a lost cause. You're wasting your time."

I had to pay more bribes to get my car released and needed to enlist the help of influential officers.

*

I was aware of many humiliating and harassing occurrences in North Yemen against Somalis, Yemenis born in Africa, or Ethiopian refugees living in the country. One had to always be alert and, if possible, lay low.

And I had had enough of being on the receiving end of this treatment.

*

By 1995, I had narrowed my selection of the countries I had in mind to migrate to. The US, Canada, and Australia were my top three choices. John Rees, one of the geologists and a coworker of mine at the oil company was from Calgary, Canada. We spent lots of time chatting, and I ended up sharing my plans with him.

The primary concern was looking for employment opportunities. I decided that wherever the next employment opportunity came from would be my new home. The

Australian government sent me an acceptance letter, and I had a visa for the US pending, but John told me to hold off and explore options in Canada before committing to one of the other countries. He convinced me to drop Australia and weigh my options for either the US or Canada, as I was familiar with the region and systems. When I had been living in the US, I had a positive experience in Vancouver when my soccer team traveled there for competition. Also, two of the most influential people during my time in the US had favorable opinions of Canada. I had criminal clearance from the FBI and returning to the US was a real possibility, but John told me I had better opportunities in Canada.

"Go. Establish yourself. Get your citizenship. If you don't like it, you can always go south to the US."

After considering all factors, I took John's advice and applied for Canada, as well.

The Canadian embassy in Saudi Arabia screened all applications and selected for interviews candidates who had the potential to be successful in Canadian society. I was selected and subsequently interviewed by the Canadian authorities. During the interview, the official examined all materials. He then provided results of the interview, including his recommendation, to officials at the embassy, who decided who could enter Canada. There was a point system in place evaluating education, age, work experience, French and English language skills, etc. After the Canadian embassy officials determined I was a suitable candidate for immigration to Canada, I decided to make the move based on my education and the demand for my skill set in Canada. Immediately, Canadian Immigration Services asked me to complete and pass all medical requirements. I did, and all was clear. I was set to go.

Leaving

*

Since moving to Canada, I've learned there are a lot of misunderstandings about the Canadian immigration process. Many Canadians I've met assume it is like getting a movie ticket and flying to Canada—that the country is open to people coming from all walks of life. It is not.

I was not a refugee, investor, or caregiver. Nor did I have family in Canada to sponsor me. People in all of these situations undergo different processes and have to meet different requirements. I came as an independent professional under Express Entry, which is for skilled workers.

There are five steps one needs to complete before applying for Express Entry:

1. *Find out if you're eligible.* This step requires interested parties to answer a series of questions and acts as a screening tool to see if the potential applicant meets the minimum requirements.

2. *Check your score.* Applicants can determine if they are eligible for Express Entry based on their score on the questions in the previous step. Candidates who achieve the minimum score will be invited to apply.

3. *Get your documents ready.* Applicants need to submit numerous documents such as proof of language proficiency, a passport, medical exam, proof of funds, and more.

4. *Fill out your profile.* Applicants must create and submit a profile through the Government of Canada website.

5. *Get an invitation and apply.* The Government of Canada sends invitations to eligible candidates based on the candidates' score and other criteria. Once the invitation has been extended, applicants have sixty days to apply for Express Entry.[1]

*

There was one problem. What was I going to do with my marriage?

Hind came from Hadhramaut to visit us. I told her that I had found employment and secured a visa to migrate to Canada. She asked how far Canada was from the US.

"They are neighboring countries in the same way that Yemen and Saudi Arabia are," I told her.

"No wonder you wanted to go that way. You have always been fond of Americans," she commented. "What will you be doing about your marriage?"

I told her, "I'm going to end it here before I leave."

"Have you spoken to your wife about any of this?"

"No," I admitted.

"You'd better speak to her," she said she walked away.

The following day, I mentioned to my wife that I will be migrating to Canada. She didn't know where Canada was, and she asked when I would be returning. I told her I was most likely not coming back. She didn't comprehend what I was saying. I repeated the message again.

Then she said, "How will you be seeing your child? I think I'm pregnant."

I went silent for a moment and told her to take care of it. She didn't understand what I had asked of her so she said, "Will I raise the child by myself?"

"Abortion," I said.

She left the room.

As I was getting ready to sleep that night, Hind stormed into the bedroom and wanted to talk.

"I just spoke with your wife," she started in on me. "You requested the child she is carrying be aborted. Mr. Educated Man, the one who always considered himself to be a better person than his father, guess what? Perhaps you're worse than him. When your mother got pregnant as a fifteen-year-old, he initially requested the fetus be aborted. Then he wanted to know if you were a boy or not before admitting that he was the father. We can say that he was a man of the previous generation. He was a married man when you were conceived and was shameful about his actions, and he wanted to cover it up. What is your excuse? If your mom had gone through with the abortion back then, you wouldn't be here. Perhaps it would have been better if she did that!"

And she stormed back out of the bedroom before I could say anything.

I didn't have a response to what my sister had just expressed. I couldn't justify or rationalize what I had said to my wife; my sister was right. I was placed between a moral dilemma and my plans to leave the country. After all, I didn't respect my wife, let alone love her, but my sister's words hit her target. I had spent the last twenty-five years seeking my identity, learning about my father, and wanting to emulate him—the good side of him. And I wanted to conduct myself as a man he would be proud of if he were still alive. I started to re-evaluate my existence and my previous encounters with marriage. I felt as though I had failed in all aspects of my life.

I kept asking myself what I was going to do with my wife in Canada. She spoke no English, Canada was a cold country, and I wasn't sure if she was the kind of partner I was looking to keep. My wife was a beautiful woman. But she was innocent and gullible. Due to her upbringing within her immediate family circle and primitive society, she was very sheltered and naïve. She would have been the perfect wife for any Yemeni man who wanted to live in Yemen and carry on with life following Yemeni traditions. She and I were just a mismatch at all levels.

Still, my sister's words kept playing in my head and left me with no possibility to escape from her message. I was wounded by her words; she wasn't wrong, but her scolding was hard for me to accept. I didn't sleep all night.

I delayed my trip to Canada and started the paperwork to plan for my wife to travel with me. I was hoping she or her family would oppose the notion of her moving as far as Canada and perhaps that would be the end of it. But they presented no opposition, so on May 1, 1996, we set out to migrate to Canada as a family: me, my wife, and my unborn child.

Preview of Volume One

Release date: May 2022

When life is defined and debated through sound bites and social media, who would want to hear a story about a boy who traversed multiple cultures, languages, religions, and geographical areas?

To Have Nothing, the first volume of Adel Ben-Harhara's three-volume memoir, delves into the voyage of a boy who was separated from his mother as a toddler and was essentially orphaned at the age of five when his father died. With his mother's inability to provide support, the boy was homeless, often left on the streets between the ages of eight and eleven. How did he survive?

The boy was born in Addis Ababa to a poverty-stricken, fifteen-year-old Ethiopian mother and a wealthy fifty-year-old businessman who was a retired British soldier from the Middle East.

As a child, the boy received extensive religious teachings in Judaism, Islam, and Christianity. As an adolescent Marxist in Ethiopia, he was imprisoned for taking part in a Communist party youth movement and barely avoided the death squad's bullets before moving to his ancestors' land: Yemen.

This is the story of that boy, an inspiring tale of perseverance and survival.

Preview of Volume Three

Release date: 2023

The contrast between how the West views newcomers versus how immigrants picture themselves is stark. New residents in Canada and the US are often misunderstood, disrespected, or poorly labeled due to inaccurate assumptions and stereotypes held by all parties.

What does it take to attend university in a second or third language? What are the common denominators amongst people arriving in the West wanting to pursue "the American dream"? What are the impacts of cultural and social adjustments, academic and professional advancement? How do new Canadians and Americans maneuver through prejudices and discrimination coming from not only those born on Western soil but also from other immigrants?

My Silver Lining, the final volume of Adel Ben-Harhara's three-volume memoir, is a window into the hurdles that settlers face and the support they get from those who welcome immigrants to their new chosen homelands. Peer through this window by reading the story of a young man who navigated from Ethiopia and North Yemen to the US and Canada to establish his identity and purpose.

The story shows how Adel Ben-Harhara succeeded after leaving behind everything he knew and attempted to embrace an unknown way of life on a new continent.

Acknowledgments

Bawazier was the Yemeni version of Bansser, my father figure and role model when I was living in Addis Ababa, on a smaller scale. Bawazier was a friend of my father who did what he could to assist me with completing my high school. He put forward a sizable amount of money for me to attend a private English school. I also thank him for making the cultural adjustment easier for me in Yemen.

Equally, the ***Al-Mekaleh*** family were important to my life in Yemen. I didn't know them prior to arriving in Yemen, nor they were Hadhramis, and they didn't know my father. They just happened to be decent people with generous and kind hearts.

The ***Basherahil*** family was the contributing factor for the union of my father and mother as my mother worked for them as a nanny before I was born. I was able to connect with them in Yemen in 1981, and we carried on the friendship that was born in Ethiopia. Just like Bawazier and Bansser, Basherahil told me stories about my father. Moreover, as I was heading to South Yemen to meet my sisters, he wrote a letter to friends and family to ensure I was safe and able to connect with my family. Basherahil was the person who introduced me to the Ben-Shahna family, who helped me find my sister Fawzia on my first trip to Aden.

Abdallah Al-Arasi was responsible for my outlook on literature. Even though I didn't know or like the literary world, I grew to appreciate it because of him. He expanded my horizons. He was a man of many talents and possessed a great depth of understanding of the Arab and Ethiopian cultures. I respected and upheld his principles.

Gamil Al-Razahi was a man who assisted me in reassimilating and aligning to my homeland upon my return to Yemen from the US.

Richard Maddy was my manager at my first formal job in Yemen working for USAID. He was also the first white man I worked for, which exposed me to a new culture and working style. As a teen, I was soaking up everything I heard. I respected authority and what was written in newspapers. I was in the stage of innocence.

The last time I reported to him was forty years ago. Yes, my memory is flaky and fickle, but some of the things I learned from him lasted a lot longer than any knowledge I acquired from textbooks I have read. He set the bar as to how a manager/leader should conduct himself. Today, I play the role of manager and take a leadership role; every time I'm dealing with staffing issues, I ask myself how Richard Maddy would handle them.

I was disappointed when I was denied the scholarship to study in the US, but Richard was saddened with the outcome as if I were his son, and he helped me overcome that obstacle.

Mark Hansen was more than just an ESL instructor. He significantly raised my awareness of life in America and how to navigate through challenges in Yemen and abroad. Although I didn't grasp the magnitude of his wisdom and direction when he was part of my life, I have grown to appreciate his intellect and support more now than ever.

Acknowledgments

Dr. Abdulaziz Al-Saqqaf was a human rights activist, economist, and journalist who established the *Yemen Times* as a weekly newspaper in 1991. Not only it was Yemen's first of its kind, but it was also the most widely-read independent English newspaper in Yemen. When he approached me to contribute to the Science & Technology column of his paper, I didn't grasp the vision he had for his country! His calls for meaningful change to the economic and social spectrum within Yemen, his honest opinions, and his determination quite possibly resulted in his life being cut short at the age of forty-eight. He was ahead of his time and was an agitator to the corrupt leadership. I suspect that his numerous critical writings against the former president of Yemen, Ali Abdullah Saleh, and others within his circles, led to his assassination.

Although I gravitate toward radical minds, my association with him began to frighten me. I was afraid I would be guilty by association and began to fear for my safety as well. Yet he inspired and challenged me to express my honest opinions and perspectives.

There is one thing I always remember ***Oscar Bernard*** told me: "You have the education and the experience in computer science and telecommunication engineering to teach all of Yemen." I'm sure Oscar has no idea what those words did for my self-esteem while living in Yemen.

I started Volume One with a lengthy gratitude to introduce and recognize my team: ***Lorna Stuber***, ***Tracey L. Anderson***, ***Nesma Abdalaziz***, ***Solomon Kedamawi***, and ***Haifa Al-Maashi***. After several months' work, thousands of words across multiple manuscripts, and endless exchanges of emails and other types of communication amongst myself and my team members, I want to renew my gratitude, as well as express my appreciation!

The words THANK YOU are often misused or relegated to minor deeds; with me, those words mean a lot. Needless to say, the products (*To Have Nothing*, *Hope in the Sky*, and *My Silver Lining*) should stand tall and speak loudly about my team's dedication and commitment. Furthermore, I'm not an easy person to deal with as I tend to have a set vision in mind with specific taste and preferences for the final outcome. My communication etiquette can be blunt and forward, often absentminded and somewhat blurred, but my team helped me achieve my objectives without altering my voice.

Of course, to capture the dedication Lorna applied to this project requires a book of its own; that information is now parked for a short, light-hearted book called *Behind the Scenes*.

Stay tuned!

From Lorna (Co-Author)

I do so much better at "Jeopardy" these days when watching it every evening. Now that I've worked through *To Have Nothing* (Volume One) and *Hope in the Sky* with Adel, most times when there is a question on the show about Ethiopia or Yemen specifically or the history or culture of that general area of the world, I shout at the TV screen with great satisfaction, *"I know this one!"* I feel so much more enlightened as a result of working on Adel's books. Believe me, there have been hundreds of hours of conversation between me and Adel on his home countries' histories, cultures, and politics that have not made it onto the pages of these books.

Like Oscar, who wrote the foreword for *Hope in the Sky*, I knew almost nothing about Yemen when I started on this volume of Adel's trilogy, as I call it. From what I have learned, I know that it is a country I would love to visit one day. I've seen the pictures Adel has shared in the photo gallery on his website (adelbenharhara.com). I've viewed other pictures and websites and read multiple articles and other books. I find myself yearning to travel to Yemen to see the architecture, try the food, interact with the people, and visit the places that Adel fondly remembers, such as Mocha and Socotra. And wouldn't it be wonderful if I could meet some of his family members, as well? I feel as though I already know some of them to a certain extent after hearing, reading, and writing about them for close to a year now. I sense I would get along well with these warm, kind people.

Having never traveled to Arabia, I admit my knowledge of that part of the world has largely been formed by what I see in the media. I've also been impacted, though, by students of mine from Afghanistan, Iraq, Iran, Syria, Lebanon etc., when I was still teaching English to new Canadians several years ago. What we see in the media is only a fraction of reality, though, and a biased glimpse at that. I've appreciated and taken advantage of opportunities to question Adel about topics I was hesitant to ask my students as I know he will not be offended by my ignorance about Islam; roles, rights, and opportunities for women in the Middle East; and other political and social issues. I have been given a huge gift: the opportunity to earn the equivalent of several university credits in anthropology (one of my favorite subject areas) through private study with someone who is knowledgeable, multi-faceted, and highly amusing. And wouldn't we all be so lucky to work every day for months with someone who consistently makes us laugh until our stomach hurts?

One of the greatest lessons I've learned throughout my time spent traveling and living abroad as well as teaching and working with people from all over the world has been the fact that we need to look at people as individuals rather than basing our views on stereotypes and assumptions.

The Iraqi ambassador is a terrific example of this. What prompted him to visit Adel, the young man who had been jailed for rear-ending him? The ambassador was likely a compassionate man, having recognized that the conditions where Adel was jailed were not fit for humans to live in. He also certainly saw what others, including Mark Hansen, James Ziegler, Richard Maddy, John Rees, and Oscar Bernard recognized: Adel was (and is) a man of great integrity, respect, and intelligence. The Canadians and Americans in particular who worked with Adel in Yemen identified someone who would benefit from greater opportunities. And they knew Adel was also a man who had a lot to offer to Canada or the US, so they helped him move toward reaching his potential and achieving his goals.

In my experience, there are the proverbial "good and bad people" in any culture. Corruption, discrimination, and oppression are certainly more rampant in some places than others. It's hard—seemingly impossible—for one person to combat those ills, but as we know from the cliché, one drop of water added to another and another eventually fills the bucket. Adel's droplets when he was writing for the *Yemen Times* and now, with these books, will surely create a ripple effect, one that will be felt across multiple borders.

Nine months into our working relationship, I'm still as excited about this project and as humbled as I was when Adel initially chose me to be his sidekick. The more I learn about him, the more I respect this fascinating man and admire the positivity he consistently exudes. It's with great anticipation that I look ahead to how the latter part of Volume Three will unfold as he brings us all into his current life.

Website: lornastuber.com
Facebook: facebook.com/lornastubereditor

Glossary

Except as noted, the terms in this glossary are nouns. Those that refer to a specific person or place are capitalized. Those that refer to a generic item are not capitalized. Any terms that are not nouns are noted with information in brackets after the term. Where applicable, the language of origin of the term is included before the definition. Additional spellings are included with a /.

Abdallah Al-Arasi - عبدالله العراسي
(Arabic) a writer and literary critic whom Adel roomed with for four years in Sana'a. Al-Arasi passed away in June 2016 and was buried in Ethiopia.

Abdulaziz Al-Saqqaf - عبدالعزيز السقاف
(Arabic) the founder and editor of *Yemen Times*. He was born in Ethiopia but he chose not to admit that and always pretended that he was born in Yemen to avoid negative stigma and stereotypes the Muwalladin were facing in North Yemen.

Abera Lemma - አበራ ለማ
(Amharic) Abera Lemma is one of the best-known Ethiopian authors and poets. He was a friend of Al-Arasi's and is based in Norway.

Abubaker Bagarsh - ابوبكر باجريش
(Arabic) the son of Salem Bagarsh and classmate of Adel's brother, Hussein.

Glossary

Ād/Ādd/Āde - عاد
(Arabic) one of the ancient Arab tribes (the "lost Arabs") located in southern Arabia (tribe members were called the Ādites). The people of this tribe were regarded as one of the original groups of Arabs who rejected the teachings of a monotheistic prophet named Hud. They formed a prosperous nation until they were destroyed in a violent storm; the storm is mentioned several times in the Qur'an in verses 41:16, 46:24, 51:41, 54:19, and 69:6.[1]

Addis Ababa - አዲስ አበባ
(Amharic) the capital and largest city of Ethiopia; means "new flower"; known in Oromo as Finfinne, "natural spring."

Ahmed Bansser/Bansser - أحمد بانصير
(Arabic) Adel's father's close friend and countryman from Hadhramaut; a father figure who played a significant role in Adel's young life and was instrumental in connecting Adel with his relatives in South Yemen.

Aksum/Kingdom of Aksum
The ancient Kingdom of Aksum was in power from the second to the tenth centuries and covered what is now northern Ethiopia as well as modern-day Eritrea, eastern Sudan, and Yemen. Its capital was the city of Aksum (Axum).

Al-Mukalla - المكلا
(Arabic) one of the major sea ports in South Yemen. Once, it was the capital of Hadhramaut. The Harhara (Yafa) family ruled the area and built a palace for sultans and sheikhs.

Al-Mukha/Mocha - ميناء المخا
(Arabic) an ancient port in North Yemen, responsible for introducing Arabica coffee to the Europeans.

Al-Razahi - الرازحي
(Arabic) one of Adel's friends in Yemen who encouraged Adel to write for the *Yemen Times*.

Al-Shenawi - الشناوي
(Arabic) Adel's Egyptian coworker and mentor in the first job Adel had working for Bawazier.

Al-Shihr - الشحر
(Arabic) the birthplace of Adel's father in Hadhramaut. Al-Shihr is a strategic port city, and Adel's ancestors inhabited this city for several centuries.

Amara/Amhara - አማራ
(Amharic) Adel's mother's tribe in Ethiopia.

Asr - صلاة العصر
(Arabic) afternoon prayer. Asr is one of the five mandatory Islamic prayers. Because an Islamic day starts at sunset, the Asr prayer is the fifth prayer of the day. It is the third prayer of the day when counting from midnight.

bab - باب
(Arabic) a city gate.

Bab Al-Yemen - باب اليمن
(Arabic) the Gate of Yemen, also called Yemen Gate, located on the southern end of the wall of Sana'a. It was designed by Shem, the son of Noah. Travelers going south from Sana'a need to leave through this gate.

Glossary

Bab Makkah/Bab Mecca - باب مكة
(Arabic) the Gate of Mecca, through which Muslims pass to enter Mecca. Non-Muslims are not permitted to pass through the gate.

Baharon - باهارون
(Arabic) Haron Baharon was Adel's childhood friend in North Yemen. Salem Baharon, Haron's uncle, was a good friend of Adel's father and lost his life during a cosmetic surgery.

Banajah - باناجاه
(Arabic) family friends of Adel's. The Banajah family were part owners of the Ethiopian restaurant where Adel met Al-Arasi.

Baobaid - باعبيد
(Arabic) a good friend and classmate of Adel's older brother, Hussein; instrumental in getting Adel a South Yemen passport and sending him to North Yemen. He also flew to North Yemen to ensure Adel was okay.

Basherahil - با شراحيل
(Arabic) Abduallah Basherahil was a friend of Adel's father. Adel's mother worked for the Basherahil family as a nanny prior to giving birth to Adel. Anwar Basherahil is the son who accompanied Adel to Aden when meeting Adel's future wife's family to arrange the marriage.

Bawazier - باوزير
(Arabic) family friend who helped Adel get settled in North Yemen when he arrived in 1978.

Bekele Mola - በቀለ ሞላ
(Amharic) Bekele Mola was the man who borrowed money from Adel's father and then offered to pay back only a fraction of the

loan after Majid died. He was the first Ethiopian to construct hotels and motels in towns and tourist centers throughout the country. At least thirteen hotel establishments in the Ethiopian Rift Valley region carry his name.

Ben/Bin - بن /Ibn - ابن /Al - ال
(Arabic) prefixes attached to a surname to mean "the son of" (e.g.) Ben-Harhara means "the son of Harhara."

Ben-Braik - بن بريك
(Arabic) one of Adel's nephews.

Ben-Shahna - بن شاهنا
(Arabic) the family who helped Adel find his sister Fawzia on his first trip to Aden, South Yemen.

Dhuhr/Zuhr - صَلَاة اَلظُّهْر
(Arabic) noon prayer; one of the five mandatory Islamic prayers. Because an Islamic day starts at sunset, Dhuhr is the fourth prayer of the day. It is the second prayer of the day when counting from midnight.

Eid - العيد
(Arabic) Eid marks the end of Ramadan and is celebrated by decorating and gathering for feasting. Special food and drink is prepared.

Emperor Haile Selassie/Emperor Haile Selassie I - ቀዳማዊ ኃይለ ሥላሴ
(Amharic) the Ethiopian king/emperor from 1930 to 1974.

Fajr - صلاة الفجر
(Arabic) dawn prayer; one of the five mandatory Islamic prayers. An Islamic day starts at sunset, and the Fajr prayer is the third

prayer of the day. If counted from midnight, it is the first prayer of the day.

Fatuma M. Ali (Banajah) - فطومة باناجه / ፋጡማ ባናጃሁ
(Arabic) an Ethiopia lady who lived in North Yemen and assisted Adel with basic needs while he was living there. Even though Fatuma assisted Adel starting in the 1980s, she played a significant role in Adel's life upon his return from the US in 1993, when he had no home and no food.

Fawzia - فوزية / ፋውዚያ
(Arabic) one of Adel's half sisters. Bansser's daughter has the same name.

Fourteenth Amendment to the United States Constitution
Ratified in 1868, the Fourteenth Amendment was passed on July 9, 1968, to abolish slavery. It granted citizenship to all those who were born or naturalized in the United States, including former enslaved people. The Fourteenth Amendment guaranteed all citizens equal protection under the law.

Great Mosque of Mecca/Mecca/Makkah - الحرم المكي
(Arabic) the holiest city in Islam. Mecca is revered as the birthplace of the Prophet Muhammed (pbuh). Muslims from all over the world visit Mecca for the Hajj and Umrah pilgrimages.

Ghusl/Gusl - الغسل
(Arabic) "full ablution"; involves the mandatory full-body purification before performing various rituals and prayers. Ghusl is required for full purification in any of the following cases: after sexual intercourse or ejaculation; after menstruation has finished; if one has touched a dead body; after irregular bleeding in women; after vaginal discharge following childbirth. It is also performed on the body of a dead Muslim.[2]

habeshi
(Arabic) a racial insult used in Yemen to refer to Ethiopians and Eritreans. The nuance is "you are dirty; you are a criminal."

Hadhramaut Governorate - محافظة حضرموت
(Arabic) the province in South Yemen where Adel's ancestors hail from. Adel's family ruled Hadhramaut for roughly 400 years; many still live there. Hadhrami - حضرمي
(Arabic) a person whose origins trace back to the area of Hadhramaut in South Yemen.

Hajj/Hadj/Hadji/Haj - الحاج
(Arabic) the annual pilgrimage to Mecca, Saudi Arabia, which is the holiest city for Muslims. Muslims must participate in Hajj at least once in their lifetime unless they are physically or financially unable to make the journey.

Hadith حديث
(Arabic) a record of the words, actions, and practices of the Prophet Muhammed (pbuh).

haram - حرام
(Arabic) forbidden or unlawful. Muslims are prohibited from being involved in activities such as drinking alcohol, gambling, viewing. pornography, and eating pork. The opposite of haram is *halal*.

Himyarite/Himyar
The Himyarite Kingdom was the government in the southern highlands of Yemen from 115 BC to AD 570 and was at its height in AD 525 before being overthrown by Christians from Ethiopia.

Glossary

Hind - الهند / Mujudah - مجودة
(Arabic) Hind, also known as Mujudah, was Adel's oldest half sister. In the local culture, if the oldest child is a girl, a slight change is made to her father's name and his altered name is given to her. In Hind's case, her (and Adel's) father's name was Majid, so she was called Mujudah.

Hodeidah - حمير
(Arabic) a historic port city in North Yemen where Adel spent almost a year working for Bawazier.

Hussein - حسين
(Arabic) Adel's older half brother.

Ibb - مدينة إب
(Arabic) one of North Yemen's ancient cities; a place where Adel went for vacations when he was a high school student and young adult living in North Yemen.

Ingy
an Indian office clerk working for Bawazier. His full name was Inderjit; Ingy was his nickname. Adel learned the workings of financial management from Ingy while working for Bawazier.

Isha - صلاة العشاء
(Arabic) one of the five mandatory Islamic prayers. Isha is the second prayer of the day—the night prayer—as the Islamic day starts at sunset. If counted from midnight, it is the fifth prayer of the day.

Jamal (Gamal) Abdul Nasser - الرئيس جمال عبد الناصر
(Arabic) a late Egyptian president and arguably considered by modern generations as a great leader.

jambiya - الجنبية
(Arabic) a decorative dagger typically worn by Yemeni men from the North. The jambiya is secured in the man's belt and worn at the front of a man's waist.

James Ziegler
Adel's computer programming teacher in North Yemen in the 1980s.

Jamil - جميل
(Arabic) Adel's high school friend. Jamil was a Yemeni-Vietnamese boy who had moved to Yemen with his family to escape the conflict in Vietnam.

Jamila - جميلة
(Arabic) younger sister of Adel's Yemeni-Vietnamese friend, Jamil.

John Rees
a Canadian geologist from Calgary, whom Adel worked with in Sana'a.

Kaaba - ألكَعْبَة
(Arabic) the building at the center of Mecca; the most important mosque and most sacred site in Islam.

Maghrib/Maghreb - صلاة المغرب
(Arabic) sunset prayer; one of the five mandatory Islamic prayers. Because an Islamic day starts at sunset, the Maghrib prayer is the first prayer of the day. If counted from midnight, it is the fourth prayer of the day.

Glossary

mahr - مهر
(Arabic) a payment made by the groom and/or his family to the bride and/or her family when a couple marries in Yemen.

Mahra/Mahra Sultanate - سلطنة المهرة
(Arabic) a region in eastern Yemen; one of the provinces in South Yemen.

Majid Ahmed Hussein Ben-Harhara – ماجد احمد بن هريرة حسين
(Arabic) Adel's father.

Marib - مأرب
(Arabic) a region in the center of Yemen. For Arabs, particularly Yemenis, it is the home of the Queen of Sheba.

Mark Hansen
Adel's American ESL instructor in North Yemen in the 1980s.

Marwa and Safa - مروة والصفا
(Arabic) two small hills in Mecca, adjacent to the Kaaba. Muslims travel seven times between the two hills during the pilgrimages of Hajj and Umrah.

Maryam Afif - مريم عفيف
(Arabic) one of Adel's Yemeni stepmothers.

Mekaleh - عائلة المقالح
(Arabic) The Mekaleh family was closely tied to Bawazier and to Adel during Adel's first two years in Yemen. The father was a subcontractor who worked for Bawazier. Adel lived with Bawazier's twin brothers while he finished high school in North Yemen.

Mohammed Ali Othman School (MAO)
the private school Adel attended in Ta'izz, North Yemen, to finish high school.

mu'akhaar - مؤخر
(Arabic) an agreed-upon portion of the mahr that the groom's family pays to the bride's family and is paid after a couple has gotten married.

mujahideen - المجاهدون
(Arabic) Muslims who fight/go to battle in the name of Islam or the Muslim community.

Muna - منى-/ሙና
(Arabic) one of Adel's half sisters.

mu'qadam - مقدم
(Arabic) an agree-upon portion of the mahr that the groom's family pays to the bride's family in advance of the wedding.

Muwalladin - مولدين
(Arabic) a person of mixed race, specifically one who has one parent of Arab descent and one non-Arab parent.

Oscar Bernard
an American drilling engineer with whom Adel worked in Yemen in the 1990s.

Prophet Muhammed (peace be upon him/pbuh) - النبي محمد صلى الله عليه وسلم
(Arabic) the Arab social, political, and religious leader who founded Islam.

qat - القات
(Arabic) leaves that Yemenis chew in the afternoons and during ceremonies. Qat is like chewing tobacco and dulls the senses.

Qur'an - القرآن
(Arabic/English) the main religious text of Islam, believed by Muslims to be a revelation from God (Allah). It is widely regarded as the finest work in classical Arabic literature.

Ramadan - رمضان
a period of one month of fasting, prayer, reflection, and community. During this month, Muslims are prohibited from eating, drinking, smoking, or engaging in sexual activity from dawn to dusk. It takes place during the ninth month of the Hijri calendar and is observed by Muslims worldwide. The end of Ramadan is marked by Eid, a celebration involving feasts. The Gregorian calendar is eleven days longer than the Hijri calendar, which is based on the motion of the moon. The Hijri calendar is composed of twelve months of 29.5 days, which is why Ramadan is on different dates on the Gregorian calendar each year.

Richard Maddy
Richard, an American, was Adel's first manager at Adel's first job in Yemen. The two of them worked together for roughly four years. Richard was supportive in helping Adel set up an American bank account so that Adel could save his money for his studies in the US.

Saba' - سبأ
(Arabic) the Arabic name of the Queen of Sheba.

Salem Bagarsh - سليم باجريش
(Arabic) Adel's father's friend. Along with Bansser and Baobaid, Bagarsh played a major role supporting Adel during his first

sixteen years in Ethiopia. He was instrumental in getting Adel a South Yemeni passport and sending him to North Yemen.

Sana'a - صنعاء
(Arabic) the capital city of the former North Yemen. It is the largest city in North Yemen, one of the highest elevation capitals in the world, and the oldest city in the Arabian Peninsula. The Old City of Sana'a is a UNESCO World Heritage Site; it is home to distinctive architecture: multi-storey buildings with decorations in geometric patterns.

Seiyun - سيئون
(Arabic) an ancient and the largest city in the Hadhramaut Valley, known as a resting spot for travelers.

shari'a - الشريعة
(Arabic) Islamic law, guiding the rules of human behavior, based on the Qur'an and Hadith.

Sheikh Al-Hara - شيخ الحارة
(Arabic) a community leader.

Sheikha - شيخة
(Arabic) one of Adel's half sisters.

Shemalin - شيمالين
(Arabic) a local reference to North Yemeni; the Northerners.

Shia/Zaydi - الشيعة / الزيديون
(Arabic) Zaydism is one of the Shia sects of Islam which emerged in the eighth century. Those who follow Zaydi Islam are called Zaydi Shia.

Glossary

Socotra - سُقُطْرَىٰ
(Arabic) an island in the Socotra archipelago in the Indian Ocean off the south coast of Yemen. Socotra is known for its unique flora and fauna and beautiful beaches.

Sunna - السنة
(Arabic) the day-to-day activities or practices of the Prophet Muhammed (pbuh).

Sunni - سني
(Arabic) Around 85 to 90 percent of Muslims follow the Sunni branch of Islam. According to Sunni beliefs, the Prophet Muhammed (pbuh) did not leave a successor, and Abu Bakr was appointed as his next-in-line.

Ta'izz - مدينة تعز
(Arabic) Considered the cultural capital of Yemen, Ta'izz is one of its oldest cities. It is in the former North Yemen, where Adel completed high school.

Taliban - طالبان
a militant, fundamentalist Islamic political movement in Afghanistan.

Tarim - تريم
(Arabic) an ancient city known as the theological, juridical, and academic center of the Hadhramaut Valley.

Tawaf - طواف في مكة المكرمة
(Arabic) refers to encircling the Holy Kabba seven times in a counter clockwise direction as part of Umrah or Hajj.

Umrah - العمرة
(Arabic) Umrah is one of the pilgrimages to Mecca and can be done at any time of year, unlike Hajj, which must be done on specific dates according to the Islamic calendar.

wadi - وادي
(Arabic) a valley, usually a river valley.

Wahhabi/Wahhabism - الوهابية / الوهابية
(Arabic) an extreme form of Islam based in Saudi Arabia, still spreading in Yemen and other Middle Eastern and African countries.

Wollo - ወሎ
(Amharic) one of the provinces in northern Ethiopia. Wollo is believed to be linked to King Solomon's dynasty. The mother of one of the owners of the Ethiopian restaurant in Sana'a, where Adel met Al-Arasi, was from Wollo.

Yafa/Upper Yafa/Lower Yafa - يافا / يافا العليا / يافا السفلى
Yafa is both a tribe name and a geographical area. Over the centuries, the Yafa region went through multiple changes due to a continued tribal conflict over power. Recent records indicate the land split into two powerful tribes: Upper and Lower Yafa.

Zeinab Afif - زينب عفيف
(Arabic) one of Adel's stepmothers. Cousin to Maryam, another of Adel's stepmothers, Zeinab was married to Adel's father (Majid) when Majid had an affair with Maryam.

zurbian - زربيان
(Arabic) a Yemeni dish similar to biryani in Indian cuisine. Adel's favorite Yemeni meal.

Appendices

The following appendices have been included to provide additional historical, cultural, and religious information about Yemen and my ancestry.

Appendix One "The Legacy of Computers": My main contribution to the *Yemen Times* was the weekly Science & Technology column. This article shows my knowledge of and passion for computers back in the 1980s, when personal computers were making their way into people's everyday lives.

Appendix Two The Himyarite Kingdom: I've briefly explained the development of religion and the importance of trade in the Himyarite Kingdom as both have been the constant cause of conflict and transformation of the area, even up to today.

Appendix Three Hadhramaut: I've included this information to show how tribalism still exists and permeates everyday life in Yemen.

Appendix Four My Ancestors in Upper Yafa: I'm including this information to point to the prominence the Harhara family had in South Yemen, ruling the Yafa area for more than two hundred years.

Appendix Five Saba': The Land of Sheba: The Queen of Sheba is referenced in both the Bible and the Qur'an; her story is one of the best-known examples of how the wealth in the area led to the dominance and then downfall of Yemen throughout the larger region.

Appendix One

"The Legacy of Computers"

Yemen Times March 20, 1994, Adel Ben-Harhara

A computer is no different from a calculator, typewriter, file cabinet, or a fax machine, which we use on a daily basis. However, for many reasons, people are afraid of computers as if they were loaded guns.

No other machine in history has so rapidly or thoroughly changed the world. Computers have made possible such epic achievements as lunar landings and planetary probes, and they account for a myriad of everyday conveniences and benefits. They monitor anesthesia in hospitals, help children learn to read, and create special effects for movies. They have replaced or supplemented the typewriter in newsrooms and adding machines in banks. They enhance television reception control and record the price of groceries at the supermarket checkout counter. In short, they are woven into the very fabric of modern life making computer avoidance if not computer ignorance practically impossible.

Recent gains in computer power and versatility have come at a dizzying rate. Spurred by the appearance in the early 1970s by a tiny technological miracle called the microprocessor, this chip of silicone, which is smaller even than a baby's fingernail, resides in hundreds of thousands of electronic components capable of outperforming the room-sized dinosaurs that had dominated the computer world only a few years before. Despite the head-spinning pace of modern advances, the foundations of the computer revolution were built in a slow and fitful fashion. A starting point was the development more than 1,500 years ago and probably in the Mediterranean world of the abacus. The abacus was so efficient that it soon spread far and wide, and in some lands, it is still in use.

Not until the seventeenth century, a time of great intellectual firmament, did it meet significant competition as a computation tool. European thinkers of the era were fascinated by the challenge of devising aides for calculation. Among the most resourceful was John Napier of Scotland, a theologian, mathematician, and would-be-designer of military weapons. Of lasting impact was the publication in 1614 of his discovery of logarithms.

Although Napier's theory of logarithms would have enduring application, the foundations of his idea were soon eclipsed by the slide rule and other types of calculators, most notably a mechanical type pioneered by a brilliant Frenchman named Blaise Pascal.[1] One of today's computer programming languages is named in his honor. Though widely praised, Pascal's first calculator did not make him rich. Nevertheless, his principal of interlocking wheels remained central to the operation of most adding machines for the next 300 years.

Throughout the eighteenth century, French silk weavers had experimented with schemes for guiding their looms using perforated tape, punch cards, or wooden drums. In all three systems, the presence or absence of holes created the patterns in the fabric by controlling the way the yarns were raised or lowered. In 1804, Joseph Jacquard built a fully-automated loom that could handle enormously complicated design. The loom was programmed by a mountain of punch cards, each card controlling a single throw of the shuttle to produce a new pattern. The operator simply replaced one set of cards with another.

But punch cards were destined to have their greatest impact in the programming of computers. Of all the pre-twentieth-century thinkers and tinkerers who added something to the development of computing, the one who came closest to actually inventing a computer in the modern sense was an Englishman named Charles Babbage. It was Babbage's great glory and lifelong frustration to have conceived the fundamental principles of the modern computer a century before the technology existed to build one. He spent many decades, much government money, and a good deal of his private fortune in the attempt.

Just nineteen years after Babbage's death, one aspect of the analytical engine punch cards appeared in a functional machine. The machine was a statistical tabulator built by the American Herman Hollerith to speed up the processing of returns for the 1890 US census.

John Billings, a high-ranking census official and Hollerith's future father-in-law, suggested that the tabulation might be done with punch cards, and Hollerith spent the 1800s working to develop such a system. It is not known where Billings himself got the idea—from Jacquard's loom or perhaps from watching railroad conductors punch tickets—but he was content to let Hollerith pursue it.

By 1890, Hollerith's tabulator had bested several rivals to win the 1890 census contract and forge a new link in the chain of computer history. The cards in Hollerith's tabulator were the size of dollar bills. Each card had twelve rows of twenty holes to be punched for the data on age, sex, country of birth, number of children, occupation, marital status, and everything else the census wanted to know about the US population. So swift was Hollerith's machine that a simple count was ready in six weeks and a full statistical analysis in two-and-a-half years. He formed the tabulating machine company to introduce his invention to railroads, government offices, and even tsarist Russia, which had decided that it too wanted a modern census.

The company was immediately successful. Over the years, it passed through a number of mergers and name changes. The last came in 1924, five years before Hollerith died, and created International Business Machines (IBM). Now, a century and a half after Babbage's epic struggle with the analytical engine, IBM is a world leader in an industry that has brought to life his vision of machines of the most general nature.

Through the twentieth-century magic of miniaturization, increasingly everyday objects and tools possess a kind of resident genie—a phenomenally small computer device called a microprocessor. A microprocessor is a far cry from the clumsy electronic powerhouse composed of hundreds of thousands of microscopic electrical circuits etched on a tiny sliver of silicon.

Semiconductor companies sometimes spend millions of dollars developing a microprocessor design but mass production may allow the chip to be sold for a few dollars.

A microprocessor works by responding to electrical impulses that open and close its circuits thousands or millions of times per second. Each opening or closing represents a single unit of information encoded in the digits zero or one of the binary system. The chip is thus a digital device only interpreting information that is presented as individual bits or binary digits rather than perceiving it as a smooth or analog continuum.

Like the dots and dashes of Morse code, the opened and closed circuits of a microprocessor can combine to spell out instructions for machines as diverse as automatic coffee makers and personal computers. So ubiquitous has the tiny digital genie become that millions of times a day, people take part in the computer revolution performing acts as mundane as making a telephone call, starting a car, passing through a supermarket checkout counter, or merely checking the time on a wristwatch.

Traditional watches used balance wheels, springs, and gears to keep time. Electronic watches have replaced those innards with a microchip, a quartz crystal, and a battery. Thanks to these new parts, computerized watches never have to be wound and they should be accurate within three minutes a year. A traditional watch may lose three minutes a week.

The central processing unit, as it is called, enables the computer to switch easily from plain and existing video games to rearranging the paragraphs in a business report. Each role is defined and controlled by a set of electronically-coded instructions called programs or software. Some computer users enjoy the challenge of writing their own programs, but most are content to choose from thousands of software packages available on the market.

With the help of different programs, personal computer users can track the performance of investment portfolios, organize tax records, store address lists, or drill themselves in

French verbs. They can bank, shop, or run a business from home. They can learn skills ranging from chess or bridge strategy to touch-typing. By placing telephone calls to a database maintained by other computers, personal computer users can do various kinds of research, rifling through distant electronic index files without the user leaving home or the office.

The personal computer, in short, is a servant of innumerable talents not the least of that being that it is simple enough to be used by a six-year-old.

Appendix Two

The Himyarite Kingdom

The Himyarite Kingdom, also known as the Sabaean Kingdom, was a political state in the southern highlands of Yemen that existed between 110 BC and AD 520. Three thousand years ago, South Arabia was comprised of several states. Two of the most significant were Hadhramaut and Saba'.

> In these ancient times South Arabia claimed several notable features: the famous dam at Marib, the cosmopolitan incense trade, and the legendary Queen of Sheba. Then about two thousand years ago the Himyarites became the masters of South Arabia, dominating the region for several centuries.[1]

The period around AD 380, several decades after residents of the Kingdom of Aksum in Ethiopia converted to Christianity, marks the end of evidence of the Himyarites worshipping local gods. The inscribing of names and deeds of kings on local buildings ceased at this time. The Himyarite kings appear to have abandoned polytheism and converted to Judaism. Temples were abandoned, and references to the previous gods were replaced by inscriptions in the Sabean language, and sometimes Hebrew, referring to Rahmanan, "the Lord of Heaven" or "Lord of Heaven and Earth." However, unlike what had occurred in Aksum, the people's script, calendar, and language did not change.[2]

The conversion may have been politically motivated and was perhaps a result of Arabia's desire to remain neutral and maintain good trading relations with Byzantium, "which first adopted Christianity under Theodosius the Great, and the Sasanian Empire, which alternated between Zurvanism and Manichaeism."[3] It is believed that one of the first Jewish kings to have converted did so after a military expedition into northern Arabia and as a ploy to eliminate Byzantine influence.[4]

The Arabian Peninsula was appealing to the Byzantine emperors, who were eager to control the lucrative spice trade and trade route to India. They "hoped to establish a protectorate by converting the inhabitants to Christianity. Some progress had been made in northern Arabia, but they had little success in Himyar."[5] Some historians believe that politics were not a motivating factor for the Himyarites. Rather, "Judaism, by its philosophical, simplistic, and austere nature, was attractive to the nature of the Semitic people."[6]

Later, the first Aksumite invasion took place sometime in the fifth century and was triggered by the persecution of Christians; in the countries controlled by the Romans, the Christians wickedly harassed and persecuted the local Jews, killing many of them.

The end of the Jewish monarchy in Himyar came during the reign of Dhu Nuwas, "who, in 523, persecuted the Himyarite Christian population of Najrān."[7] It was during his reign that the Himyarite Kingdom began to become a tributary state of Aksum. The process concluded with the commencement of the reign of a Christian appointed by the Aksumites.

The area was able to initially attain its wealth because of its location on the trade route on the shores of the Red Sea. Trade brought with it constant dynamic new development during the millennium before the Christian era. However, the decline in demand for frankincense ultimately brought about the gradual decline of the South Arabian civilization.

> Greeks and Romans used frankincense to cover the odor of burning flesh at cremations. Since Christians buried their dead, instead of burning or embalming them, the demand for frankincense and myrrh dropped dramatically as Christianity spread.[8]

Hundreds of years later, coffee became the source of wealth. These days, the popular beverage, mocha, bears the name of Mocha, the port city in Yemen.

Appendix Three

Hadhramaut

Hadhramaut, a province or region in South Arabia, is part of present-day eastern Yemen. The earliest reference to Hadhramaut is Sabean inscriptions, which suggest that it was an independent kingdom and acquired tremendous economic significance because its possession of frankincense grew. Greek historians were aware of Hadhramaut as early as the fourth century BC. Theophrastus of Eresos, a disciple of Aristotle and his successor as the head of the Peripatetic School, mentions Hadhramaut in his main botanical work as one of the regions where incense, myrrh, and cinnamon came from.[1]

Since the late fourth or early third century BC, the region was comprised of nomadic kingdoms as well as followers of Judaism, Christianity, and now Islam.

Today's Hadhramis live in dense towns established near traditional watering stations along *wadis* or riverbeds/streams. Agriculture, one of their mainstays, includes harvesting crops of wheat and millet; tending to date, palm, and coconut groves; and growing coffee. On the plateau, Bedouins tend sheep and goats. The society is still highly tribal. Hadhramis are still traditionally educated and are strict in their Islamic observances.

Appendix Four

My Ancestors in Upper Yafa

Yafa is both a tribe name and a geographical area. According to Arab genealogist Al-Hamadani (AD 893 to AD 945), the tribe is one of the biggest that descended from the ancient Himyarite.[1] Some historians reference the people to have been the descendants of Axumite who settled in the Yafa area. Over the centuries, the Yafa region went through multiple changes due to a continued tribal conflict over power. Recent records indicate the land split into two powerful tribes: Upper and Lower Yafa. "The Upper Yafa had a separate treaty with the Protectorate of South Arabia, and *it was ruled by the Harhara sultan (Empire between 1730 and 1967)* [emphasis added], and its capital was called Mahjaba."[2]

> The Qu'aiti Sultanate of Al-Shihr and Mukalla was a sultanate in the Hadhramaut region of the southern Arabian Peninsula, in what is now Yemen. Its capital was Mukalla, and it was divided into six provinces including Al-Mukalla, Al-Shihr, Shibam, Du'an, the western province, and Hajr. Apart from Al-Mukalla, Al-Shihr and Shibam were the Sultanate's major cities. The Sultanate spanned the Indian Ocean coast up to the border of Mahra, encompassed Shabwa, the central valleys

and oasis settlements of Hadhramaut, and controlled the southern Empty Quarter.[3]

The people of Upper Yafa are known for their religious scholarly knowledge, bravery, and military capabilities, and a few Yafa sultans went on to rule Hadhramaut (e.g., Qahtan, Al-Mehdhar, Harhara, etc.), around Mukalla and Al-Shihr. "The Yafai's were a confederation of hardy, warlike tribes who, although weakened by internal dissention, tended to close ranks in guarding their independence against any threat of foreign invasion."[4]

The following is a translation[5] of a report of the march of Omar Ben-Saleh Harhara, one of my ancestors, culminating in a battle with and defeat of a rival tribe in Yafa in the early 1700s. I'm including it to show only one example of the long history of conflict between the Shia and Sunni, and how my ancestors battled to gain and maintain power in Yemen. My lineage is full of chiefs and commanders.

*

Al-Sultan Omar Ben-Jaafar, a Zaydi sultan from Yafa, had seized and occupied all of Hadhramaut and kicked out Eissa Ben-Badr and whoever was with him, aggressively and oppressively sending them to the imam. The local notables, sheikhs, and gentlemen were so upset.

There wasn't any option for the beloved Al-Sheikh Ali Ben-Hamed [a Sunni sheikh] except to escape to an area near Hood.[6] He wrote to Omar Ben-Saleh Harhara a special book about Al-Sultan Omar Ben-Jaafar. Upon the receipt of his book, we [those of us accompanying Sultan Omar Ben-Saleh Ahmed Harhara] arose, we decided, and we trusted Allah. In the name of Allah the merciful, we left Al-Muhajiba[7] on the first day of Dhul-Q'adah[8] 1113 Hijri.[9] Gathered for us in Upper Yafa were around 500 people. Then we moved ahead to Al-Bayda.[10] We arrived on 15 Dhul-Q'adah, and from there we continued. The land we crossed from Mora to Hadhramaut hadn't any water or trees, but God saved us with rains before and behind us.

We arrived with 500 camels to Al-Awlaq[11] and we met the Sultan Ben-Monsser Al-Awlaki.

We woke up the next day, which was pilgrimage day—the big day of Hajj.

We got the news that the Sultan Omar Ben-Jaafar made his way to Bahran village.[12] He was gathering Al-Zaydi soldiers.

They continued gathering horses, men, and money from the imam, and they increased in number in Bahran village to over 4,000. They had around 150 horses.

We moved from Al-Akaba to Mehzaa Al-Hijriin, where there were 100 soldiers belonging to the imam. We were confronted with a huge number of horses and around fifty knights. We stopped them with guns by the end of the day.

When we planned to leave, we wrote to Sultan Ben-Jaafar nice words saying, "We arrived from Yafa and wanted to leave Al-Zaidiah and remove their doctrine willingly and forcibly. You're the sultan, and so the decision is yours. If you give us an answer, we will swear upon ourselves that you are the beloved Ben-Ahmed."

He refused and told us in his response, "These are my countries, my father's, and my grandfather's, and there is no way you are setting a foot on it. I arose to you from the bottom of Bahran, and I have all the men—all of them from Dhofar[13] to Al-Shihr and Qibla[14]—and their swift horses. I'm watching their back and will meet you by dawn."

Then the prince Ben-Moqbel and the honorables wrote to us something really ugly saying, "We stood on your book for the Sultan Ben-Jaafar. If it is you, Omar Ben-Saleh Ahmed Harhara, who is riding the white horse and raising the umbrella in front of Yafa's women, show yourself to us."

We answered saying, "Yes. We are heading to you tomorrow, Thursday morning. When the sun is setting and I, Omar Ben-Saleh Ahmed Harhara, will arrive, you will see the umbrella over my head in the bottom of Bahran."

After giving a speech to the people and encouraging them, we split into three positions:

1. My brother Abou Bakr Ben-Harhara, and with him Al-Musta and Labous.

2. My boys Saleh, Hussein, and Yahya Ben-Harhara; Al-Nakhby; and Al-Zaidi.

3. The boys and I: Kassem Harhara, Omar and Saleh Ben-Harhara, Al-Zaby (friend), Hadhrami people of Bahr, Al-Had, and Al-Enaq.

The enemies were around a mile away from our position and numbered around 1,200 persons. We were around 600. We confronted them in the early morning, the first of Muharram[15], 1114 Hijri. When both groups met, the conflict got intense. There was no talking, only fighting. The land was shaking, and they attacked us with their horses, but we caused their fall with our guns. Then we moved as one, continuing to attack them. They started escaping. You could see them running as if they were roots of palm trees torn up from the ground. We continued our assault, stabbing them with swords from morning till evening. We took over their station in Hodeidah. We also took over their tents and all they had: guns, swords, shields, and other valuable stuff. We spent this night in Hodeida.

We kept our rival, Abou Bakr, and everyone with him in Yafa in Hadhramaut and moved to Al-Shihr, where we stayed for three months. Al-Shihr is a great city. It has a lot of stores and markets etc.

We split ownership of the lands into two. A portion of people went to Hadhramaut. I and those who were with me went to Yafa.

That was the march of the brave sultan Omar Ben-Saleh Ben-Ahmed Harhara and those who were with him, heroes and brave ones from Yafa to the inside lands of Hadhrami.

Appendix Five

Saba': The Land of Sheba

In early centuries, the civilization called Saba' in Arabic (Sheba in the West) was exceptionally wealthy. According to the Qur'an, Saba's queen, known in the West as the Queen of Sheba, was "a woman ruling over the people, who has been given a share of everything—she has a magnificent throne".[1] Her kingdom prospered throughout what is now Ethiopia, Somalia, and Yemen.

According to the Bible, the Queen of Sheba visited King Solomon in Jerusalem about 900 BC, bringing with her an abundance of gifts: "Then she gave the king 120 talents of gold, and a very great quantity of spices and precious stones. Never again came such an abundance of spices as these that the Queen of Sheba gave to King Solomon."[2]. Her choice of gift-giving versus military confrontation with Solomon was viewed as "feminine politics," but "the Qur'an however, clearly prefers the Queen's peaceful tactics and generosity"[3] over aggressive confrontation.

> Saba' was known for dealing in the lucrative frankincense and myrrh trades. The Sabaeans were a seafaring people and were known to have influence and a population in the Northeast African kingdom of D'mt, across the Red Sea in Eritrea and Abyssinia, the only other source of both frankincense and myrrh.[4]

The Queen of Sheba's kingdom flourished for centuries and ultimately collapsed only when "social injustices reemerged and became so oppressive there were only two remaining classes: the very rich and the very poor."[5]

Marib, the former capital of Saba', is in modern-day Yemen. "The city flourished as a center of trade on the caravan routes, that linked the Mediterranean with the Arabian Peninsula and held a trade monopoly on the movement of frankincense and myrrh in the region."[6] The caravan trade played an integral role in the development of South Arabian culture. Of greatest importance were the riches that were traded and wealth that was spread, but of equal importance were the connections made as a result of the trade between the south of the peninsula and Egypt, Mesopotamia, and Persia. Saba' gained its wealth by trading the much sought-after frankincense and myrrh to Egyptians, who used it for embalming, and the Chinese, who used it for medicine. Both commodities were also burned for their aroma in temples and imperial courts around the world. By the fourth century AD, however, Marib lost its economic power as the market for frankincense and myrrh plummeted due to the rise of Christianity, which forbade the use of frankincense because of its association with pagan worship.[7]

The Sabaean kings who established Marib as their capital city built the Marib Dam, which was in operation for more than a thousand years. They also established other irrigation projects and build various castles and temples.[8]

When Marib and Saba' in general began to suffer economic decline, the Marib Dam in Yemen fell into disrepair and ultimately collapsed. Its collapse is considered to be the end of major civilization in the region. Why it crumbled has been debated by scholars for years. Some claim it was due to erosion caused by heavy rains; others believe an earthquake shook the dam apart. Legend states that rats gnawed and clawed through the stonework, ultimately wearing it away. According to the Qur'an, the collapse was a punishment inflicted on the Sabeans by God because of their ungratefulness.[9] Whatever the cause, the demise of the dam marked the end of a prosperous ancient civilization in South Arabia.

Bibliography

"About the IMF." International Monetary Fund. 2022. imf.org/en/About.

"AskIslampedia: Dhul-Quadah." Accessed June 30, 2022.
askislampedia.com/en/wiki/-/wiki/English_wiki/Dhul+Qadah.

Ben-Harhara, Adel. "Qat is a Drug and Most Yemenis are Addicted to It!" *Yemen Times.* January 30, 1994.

Ben-Harhara, Adel. "The Legacy of Computers." *Yemen Times.* March 20, 1994.

Countries and Their Cultures. "Yemen." 2022. everyculture.com/To-Z/Yemen.html.

ExecutedToday.com. *1978: Salim Rubai Ali, President of South Yemen.* June 26, 2019. executedtoday.com/2019/06/26/1978-salim-rubai-ali-president-of-south-yemen/.

FTD Facts. "10 Surprising Facts About Yemen." November 1, 2020. YouTube Video. youtube.com/watch?v=tylvRmNDeIk.

"How Express Entry Works." Government of Canada. Last modified February 7, 2022. canada.ca/en/immigration-refugees-citizenship/services/immigrate-canada/express-entry/works.html.

"Is Polygamy Allowed in Islam?" *Al Islam.* The Official Website of the Ahmadiyya Muslim Community. 2022. alislam.org/question/polygamy-in-islam/.

Jeffs, Jeremy and Gregory Doran, dirs. *In Search of Myths & Heroes.* "Season 1 Episode 1. The Queen of Sheba." Aired 2005 on PBS. pbs.org/mythsandheroes/myths_four_sheba.html.

John F. Kennedy Presidential Library and Museum. *Historic Speeches.* "Televised Address to the Nation on Civil Rights." June 11, 1963. jfklibrary.org/learn/about-jfk/historic-speeches/televised-address-to-the-nation-on-civil-rights.

"Ma'rib—Capital of the Kingdom of Saba." *Heritage Daily*, 2021. heritagedaily.com/2020/06/marib-capital-of-the-kingdom-of-saba/133781 - :~:text=Ma'rib%20is%20an%20archaeological,edge%20of%20the%20Sayhad%20desert.

Malek-Ahmadi, Pegah. "The Himyarites." January 5, 2020. rebuildthemiddleeast.com/history-of-the-middleeast/2020/1/5/the-himyarites-1.

Bibliography

Natan, Yoel. *Moon-o-theism: Religion of a War and Moon God Prophet, Volume I of II*. July 29, 2006. page 345. books.google.ca/books?id=GB_R90_DlGEC&pg=PA345&lpg=PA345&dq=Theophrastus+of+Eresos+on+Hadhramout&source=bl&ots=NU-2Z46mga&sig=ACfU3U0HAnJKmM6ffUZThf9jkvIWSlK4pQ&hl=en&sa=X&ved=2ahUKEwi2sLvIjab3AhXXCTQIHUrNDzgQ6AF6BAgoEAM#v=onepage&q=Theophrastus%20of%20Eresos%20on%20Hadhramout&f=false.

Our Yemen Campaign and New Hadith Collection. "The Story Behind #IamYemeni." June 26, 2020. muslimhands.ca/latest/2020/06/the-story-behind-iamyemeni.

Pandya, Sophia. "Yemenis and Muwalladīn in Addis Ababa: Blood Purity and the Opportunities of Hybridity." *Journal of Arabian Studies*. (2014) 4. 96-114. 10.1080/21534764.2014.918337.

"Passage to Yafa' (1891-1967)." Vol 15, 2007. *The British-Yemeni Society*. al-bab.com/albab-orig/albab/bys/articles/editor07.htm.

Patowary, Kaushik. "The Collapse of the Marib Dam and the Fall of an Empire." *Amusing Planet*. November 26, 2018. amusingplanet.com/2018/11/the-collapse-of-marib-dam-and-fall-of.html.

Rehmatullah, Dr. Nasim. "Significance of Number Four." *Al Islam*. The Official Website of the Ahmadiyya Muslim Community 2022. alislam.org/articles/significance-of-number-four/.

Sanford International School. "The History of Sanford International School." 2022. sandfordschool.org/the-history-of-sandford-international-school/.

Sarwar, Mohammad Golam. "What Does the Quran Say Regarding Polygamy?" *The Daily Star*, April 13, 2021. thedailystar.net/law-our-rights/news/what-does-the-quran-say-regarding-polygamy-2076941.

"Southern Arabia," Nabataea.net. 2020. nabatea.net/explore/travel_and_trade/southern-arabia.

Steinman, David. "Ethiopia's Cruel Con Game." Forbes. March 3, 2017. forbes.com/sites/realspin/2017/03/03/ethiopias-cruel-con-game/?sh=621fb7df29d0.

Summerland Hotel. "Socotra History (Socotra Island)." 2014. summerlandsocotra.com/SocotraHistory.html.

TFF. "In Islam and the Qur'an: The Queen of Sheba." *The Fatal Feminist*. August 2, 2011. thefatalfeminist.com/2011/08/02/in-islam-and-the-quran-the-queen-of-sheba/.

"Wikipedia: Abdulaziz Al-Saqqaf." Wikimedia Foundation. Last edited September 17, 2021, 06:39. en.wikipedia.org/wiki/Abdulaziz_Al-Saqqaf.

"Wikipedia: Abraha." Wikimedia Foundation. Last edited May 15, 2022, 19:53. en.wikipedia.org/wiki/Abraha.

"Wikipedia: Ād." Wikimedia Foundation. Last edited November 18, 2021, 17:28. en.wikipedia.org/wiki/%CA%BF%C4%80d - Legend.

"Wikipedia: Al Hudayah." Wikimedia Foundation. Last edited May 10, 2022, 02:16. en.wikipedia.org/wiki/Al_Hudaydah.

"Wikipedia: Al-Qalis Church, Sanaa." Wikimedia Foundation. Last edited December 7, 2021, 15:07. en.wikipedia.org/wiki/Al-Qalis_Church,_Sanaa.

"Wikipedia: Amhara people." Wikimedia Foundation. Last edited July 1, 2022, 10:20. en.wikipedia.org/wiki/Amhara_people.

"Wikipedia: General Certificate of Education." Wikimedia Foundation. Last edited April 28, 2022, 00:15. en.wikipedia.org/wiki/General_Certificate_of_Education.

"Wikipedia: Governorates of Yemen." Wikimedia Foundation. Last edited February 28, 2022, 15:33. en.wikipedia.org/wiki/Governorates_of_Yemen.

"Wikipedia: Gushl." Wikimedia Foundation. Last edited November 28, 2021, 15:26. en.wikipedia.org/wiki/Ghusl.

"Wikipedia: Hadhramaut." Wikimedia Foundation. Last edited June 3, 2022, 15:02. en.wikipedia.org/wiki/Hadhramaut.

"Wikipedia: Haile Selassie." Wikimedia Foundation. Last edited June 26, 2022, 11:59. en.wikipedia.org/wiki/Haile_Selassie.

"Wikipedia: Himyarite Kingdom." Wikimedia Foundation. Last edited June 21, 2022, 19:24. en.wikipedia.org/wiki/Himyarite_Kingdom.

"Wikipedia: Ibb." Wikimedia Foundation. Last edited April 10, 2022, 12:15. en.wikipedia.org/wiki/Ibb.

"Wikipedia: Immigration and Naturalization Service." Wikimedia Foundation. Last edited June 17, 2022, 15:53. en.wikipedia.org/wiki/Immigration_and_Naturalization_Service.

"Wikipedia: Khalifa." Wikimedia Foundation. Last edited May 16, 2022, 16:29. en.wikipedia.org/wiki/Khalifa.

"Wikipedia: Khamr." Wikimedia Foundation. Last edited May 26, 2022, 02:46. en.wikipedia.org/wiki/Khamr.

"Wikipedia: Law enforcement in Yemen." Wikimedia Foundation. Last edited March 22, 2022, 09:52. en.wikipedia.org/wiki/Law_enforcement_in_Yemen.

"Wikipedia: Lower Yafa." Wikimedia Foundation. Last edited June 16, 2022, 10:01. en.wikipedia.org/wiki/Lower_Yafa.

Bibliography

"Wikipedia: Marib." Wikimedia Foundation. Last edited June 27, 2022, 13:03. en.wikipedia.org/wiki/Marib.
"Wikipedia: Marriage in Islam." Wikimedia Foundation. Last edited June 29, 2022, 14:44. en.wikipedia.org/wiki/Marriage_in_Islam.
"Wikipedia: Mocha, Yemen." Wikimedia Foundation. Last edited July 1, 2022, 13:12. en.wikipedia.org/wiki/Mocha,_Yemen.
"Wikipedia: Moment magnitude scale." Wikimedia Foundation. Last edited June 24, 2022, 14:30. en.wikipedia.org/wiki/Moment_magnitude_scale.
"Wikipedia: Muladi." Wikimedia Foundation. Last edited March 30, 2022, 23:02. en.wikipedia.org/wiki/Mulad%C3%AD.
"Wikipedia: *One Thousannd and One Nights*." Wikimedia Foundation. Last edited July 2, 2022, 19:49. en.wikipedia.org/wiki/One_Thousand_and_One_Nights.
"Wikipedia: Qu'aiti." Wikimedia Foundation. Last edited June 16, 2022, 06:36. en.wikipedia.org/wiki/Qu%27aiti#:~:text=Qu%27aiti%20%5Bnb%201%5D%20or%20the%20Qu%27aiti%20Sultanate%20of,Ash-Shihr%2C%20Shibam%2C%20Du%27an%2C%20the%20Western%20Province%20and%20Hajr.
"Wikipedia: Seiyun." Wikimedia Foundation. Last edited February 12, 2022, 02:00. en.wikipedia.org/wiki/Seiyun.
"Wikipedia: Sheik." Wikimedia Foundation. Last edited March 18, 2022, 12:40. en.wikipedia.org/wiki/Sheik.
"Wikipedia: Sheikdom." Wikimedia Foundation. Last edited May 31, 2022, 20:50. en.wikipedia.org/wiki/Sheikhdom.
"Wikipedia: Shia-Sunni relations." Wikimedia Foundation. Last edited June 16, 2022, 04:58. en.wikipedia.org/wiki/Shia%E2%80%93Sunni_relations.
"Wikipedia: Socotra." Wikimedia Foundation. Last edited July 1, 2022, 23:41. en.wikipedia.org/wiki/Socotra.
"Wikipedia: South Arabia." Wikimedia Foundation. Last edited May 7, 2022, 22:45. en.wikipedia.org/wiki/South_Arabia.
"Wikipedia: Sultan." Wikimedia Foundation. Last edited June 22, 2022, 15:18. en.wikipedia.org/wiki/Sultan.
"Wikipedia: Taiz." Wikimedia Foundation. Last edited February 19, 2022, 07:50. en.wikipedia.org/wiki/Taiz.
"Wikipedia: Tarim, Hadhramaut." Wikimedia Foundation. Last edited June 13, 2022, 01:30. en.wikipedia.org/wiki/Tarim,_Hadhramaut.
"Wikipedia: Upper Yafa." Wikimedia Foundation. Last edited June 21, 2022, 06:38. en.wikipedia.org/wiki/Upper_Yafa.

"Wikipedia: Wahhabism." Wikimedia Foundation. Last edited June 28, 2022, 15:31. en.wikipedia.org/wiki/Wahhabism.

"Wikipedia: Yafa." Wikimedia Foundation. Last edited June 21, 2022, 19:10. en.wikipedia.org/wiki/Yafa.

"Wikipedia: Zaydism." Wikimedia Foundation. Last edited June 30, 2022, 15:23. en.wikipedia.org/wiki/Zaydism.

Wikitravel: The Free Travel Guide. "Ta'izz." Last edited May 31, 2022, 6:09. wikitravel.org/en/Ta%27izz.

"Yemen: One of the Worst Places in the World to Be a Woman," *Amnesty International.* December 16, 2019. amnesty.org/en/latest/campaigns/2019/12/yemen-one-of-the-worst-places-in-the-world-to-be-a-woman/.

Zaufishan. "Why Muslims Don't Drink Alcohol." *Green Prophet.* November 28, 2011. greenprophet.com/2011/11/muslims-alcohol-haraam/.

Endnotes

Introduction

[1] Wikipedia; Wikipedia's "Sultan" entry; Wikipedia's entry on Sultans.
[2] Wikipedia; Wikipedia's "Zaydism" entry; Wikipedia's entry on Zaydism.
[3] In subsequent mentions, "peace be upon him" will be abbreviated (pbuh).
[4] Caliph: a successor of Muhammed [pbuh] as temporal and spiritual head of Islam —used as a title, Source: *Merriam-Webster.com Dictionary*, s.v. "caliph," accessed June 26, 2022, merriam-webster.com/dictionary/caliph.
[5] Wikipedia; Wikipedia's "Shia-Sunni relations" entry; Wikipedia's entry on the relationship between Shia and Sunni Muslims.
[6] "Khalifa … is a name or title which means 'successor', 'ruler' or 'leader'. It most commonly refers to the leader of a Caliphate, but is also used as a title among various Islamic religious groups and others. There were four khalifas after [the Prophet] Muhammed [pbuh] died, beginning with Abu Bakr." Source: Wikipedia; Wikipedia's "Khalifa" entry; Wikipedia's entry on the Khalifa.
[7] Wikipedia; Wikipedia's "Shia-Sunni relations" entry; Wikipedia's entry on the relationship between Shia and Sunni Muslims.
[8] Jeremy Jeffs and Gregory Doran, dirs., *In Search of Myths & Heroes*, Season 1 Episode 1, "The Queen of Sheba."
[9] I have four half sisters and one half brother on my father's side. I refer to them as my sisters and brother even though we have different mothers. To me, they are my siblings.
[10] Our Yemen Campaign and New Hadith Collection., "The Story Behind #IamYemeni."
[11] Ad is the nickname my father gave me; he named me Ade after this tribe, and when I started school, I added L to the end to make my name less offensive to Arabs.
[12] Qur'an 46:21.
[13] Our Yemen Campaign and New Hadith Collection, "The Story Behind #IamYemeni."

[14] Ayah: individual verses of the Qur'an.
[15] The Qur'an is made of the Hadith and the Sunna. The Sunna contains the words of the Prophet Muhammed (pbuh) and therefore provides the theology of Islam. The Hadith contains writings about the life of the Prophet Muhammed (pbuh): his actions, habits, and practices as reported by those who knew him.
[16] Our Yemen Campaign and New Hadith Collection, "The Story Behind #IamYemeni."

Major Life Events

[1] Volumes Two (Yemen) and Three (the US and Canada) are both divided into two parts, as I lived in the US between the two periods I lived in North Yemen, and then I moved to Canada.

I

[1] Qat is a shrub that is grown on the mountains of Yemen, as well as in various parts of the Horn of Africa and East Africa, and possibly as far south as Mozambique. Addicts stuff their mouths with the leaves for long hours and steadily chew on them. It gives a certain feeling of relaxation and ease, which is why many people use it. Qat is chewed in groups. People get together inside large rooms and close off all windows and doors, thus minimizing ventilation, and chew for endless hours, usually in the afternoon.
[2] At the time, North Yemen and South Yemen were two separate countries, much like East and West Germany were before the Berlin Wall came down and the two countries united. North and South Yemen united in 1990, when I was living in the US.
[3] Kinship through close social or business connections is considered to be as close as blood relations in Arab culture.
[4] YR: Yemeni Rial, the currency of Yemen.
[5] Shemalin is a term for North Yemeni, like saying "Northerners."

II

[1] Allahu Akbar means "God is great."

Endnotes

III

1. Wikipedia; Wikipedia's "Governorates of Yemen" entry; Wikipedia's entry on the Governorates of Yemen.
2. Wikitravel: The Free Travel Guide, "Ta'izz."
3. Wikipedia; Wikipedia's "Taiz" entry; Wikipedia's entry on the city of Ta'izz.

IV

1. Wikipedia; Wikipedia's "Ibb" entry; Wikipedia's entry on the city of Ibb.
2. Wikipedia.
3. Homes and hotels in Yemen don't typically have backyards or courtyards, but maybe 20 percent of them have rooftops that are used as entertainment areas. Children play and adults socialize on the rooftops.

V

1. Wikipedia; Wikipedia's "Mocha, Yemen" entry; Wikipedia's entry on the city of Mocha.
2. FTD Facts, "10 Surprising Facts About Yemen," 3:39.
3. Wikipedia; Wikipedia's "Mocha, Yemen" entry; Wikipedia's entry on the city of Mocha.
4. Wikipedia.

VI

1. "The GCE is a subject-specific family of academic qualifications that awarding bodies in England, Wales, Northern Ireland, Crown dependencies and a few Commonwealth countries, notably Cyprus, Sri Lanka, Pakistan, Malaysia, Singapore, and Yemen, confer on students." Source: Wikipedia; Wikipedia's "General Certificate of Education" entry on the GCE.
2. Wikipedia; Wikipedia's "Al Hudayah" entry; Wikipedia's entry on the city of Al Hudayah.
3. Wikipedia; Wikipedia's "Mocha, Yemen" entry; Wikipedia's entry on the city of Mocha.
4. Wikipedia; Wikipedia's "Al Hudayah" entry; Wikipedia's entry on the city of Al Hudayah.
5. Wikipedia.
6. The Yom Kippur War, also called the October War, the Ramadan War, the Arab Israeli war of October 1973, or the Fourth Arab-Israeli War—fourth of the Arab-Israeli wars—was initiated by Egypt and Syria on October 6,

1973, on the Jewish holy day of Yom Kippur. For more information: wikipedia.org/wiki/Yom_Kippur_War.

VII

[1] Wikipedia; Wikipedia's "Muladi" entry; Wikipedia's entry on the term Muladi.
[2] Sophia Pandya, "Yemenis and Muwalladīn in Addis Ababa: Blood Purity and the Opportunities of Hybridity."

VIII

[1] For more information: wikipedia.org/wiki/Wollo_Province.
[2] For more information: wikipedia.org/wiki/Al-Jumu%27ah.

IX

[1] "One Thousand and One Nights (Arabic: Alf Laylah wa-Laylah) is a collection of Middle Eastern folk tales compiled in Arabic during the Islamic Golden Age. It is often known in English as the *Arabian Nights*, from the first English-language edition (c. 1706-1721), which rendered the title as *The Arabian Nights' Entertainment*." Source: Wikipedia; Wikipedia's "*One Thousand and One Nights*" entry on the literary text known as *Arabian Nights*.

XI

[1] Wikipedia; Wikipedia's "Law Enforcement in Yemen" entry; Wikipedia's entry on law enforcement in Yemen.

XII

[1] Wikipedia; Wikipedia's "Marib" entry; Wikipedia's entry on the city of Marib.
[1] Wikipedia; Wikipedia's "Lower Yafa" entry; Wikipedia's entry on the Lower Yafa area.
[2] Wikipedia.
[3] Wikipedia; Wikipedia's "Hadhramaut" entry; Wikipedia's entry on the Hadhramaut area.

Endnotes

4 "Sheik or Sheikh, literally 'elder' in Arabic, is the honorific title for the ruler of a tribe." Source: Wikipedia; Wikipedia's "Sheik" entry; Wikipedia's entry on Sheiks.
5 "Originally, it [sultan] was an Arabic abstract noun meaning 'strength', 'authority', 'rulership', derived from the verbal noun *sultah*, meaning 'authority' or 'power'. Later, it came to be used as the title of certain rulers who claimed almost full sovereignty in practical terms ... The use of 'sultan' is restricted to Muslim countries, where the title carries religious significance." Source: Wikipedia; Wikipedia's "Sultan" entry; Wikipedia's entry on Sultans.
6 Wikipedia; Wikipedia's "Sheikhdom" entry; Wikipedia's entry on Sheikhdoms.
7 Wikipedia.
8 Wikipedia; Wikipedia's "Haile Selassie" entry; Wikipedia's entry on King Haile Selassie.

XIII

1 Ahmed Bansser was a good friend of my father's and was my father figure in the last six years that I lived in Ethiopia. His influence on me is covered in-depth in Volume One.
2 Unlike in the Western world, Hadhrami husbands were known to be away from home for extended periods of time, as they worked abroad. They would be absent for months or even years. Often, women had only three or four children at most, as the men were away up to five years on the road. Out of those four children, due to child mortality, a family was lucky to have one or two to grow to adulthood.
3 The Ras Hotel was where most expats (British, American, French, and other Europeans) used to socialize.
4 Umm Kulthum: an Egyptian singer, songwriter, and actress popular from the 1920s to 1970s.
5 The more detailed version of the story is in Volume One.
6 This event, too, is presented in more detail in Volume One.

XIV

1 My last name is Harhara. In Arabic, "bin" and "ben" mean "son of." As in Sweden, where the last name "Anderson" means "the son of Ander/Andrew," I use "Ben-Harhara" to indicate that I am the son of Harhara. I hyphenate the two words because without the hyphen, people in Canada and the US assume that Ben is my middle name.

² Wikipedia; Wikipedia's "Tarim, Hadhramaut" entry; Wikipedia's entry on Tarim in Hadhramaut.
³ Wikipedia.
⁴ FTD Facts, "10 Surprising Facts About Yemen," 3:15.
⁵ Wikipedia; Wikipedia's "Seiyun" entry; Wikipedia's entry on the city of Seiyun.

XVI

¹ FTD "Facts, 10 Surprising Facts About Yemen," 5:44.
² ExecutedToday.com, *1978: Salim Rubai Ali, President of South Yemen.*
³ Pegah Malek-Ahmadi, "The Himyarites."
⁴ Wikipedia; Wikipedia's "Abraha" entry; Wikipedia's entry on Abraha.
⁵ Al-Qalis is a city in Yemen twenty-seven kilometers or seventeen miles southwest of Sana'a.
⁶ Wikipedia; Wikipedia's "Al-Qalis Church, Sanaa" entry; Wikipedia's entry on the Al-Qalis Church near Sanaa.

XVII

¹ Moment Magnitude (Mw) "is a measure of an earthquake's magnitude based on its seismic moment. ... [Small earthquakes measured using the Richter scale] have approximately the same magnitude on both scales." Source: Wikipedia; Wikipedia's "Moment magnitude scale" entry on moment magnitude.
² For more information on the earthquake:
csmonitor.com/1982/1216/121654.html
- and -
Wikipedia; Wikipedia's "1982 North Yemen earthquake" entry; Wikipedia's entry on the 1982 earthquake in North Yemen.
³ North Yemen didn't have car insurance of any kind.
⁴ The word "habeshi" is a racial insult used to refer to Ethiopians. The nuance is "you are dirty; you are a criminal." "Habeshi is a word used to refer to both Eritreans and Ethiopians, or, more specifically, to the Semitic-speaking inhabitants of those countries." Source: *Urban Dictionary*, s.v., "habesha," accessed July 4, 2022,
urbandictionary.com/author.php?author=Ge%27ez.

Endnotes

XVIII

[1] Sanford International School, "The History of Sanford International School."
[2] Sanford International School.
[3] Safa and Marwa are two small hills in Mecca, adjacent to the Kaaba.

XIX

[1] "Amharas are a Semitic-speaking ethnic group which is indigenous to Ethiopia, traditionally inhabiting parts of the northwest Highlands of Ethiopia." Source: Wikipedia; Wikipedia's "Amhara people" entry; Wikipedia's entry on the Amhara people.
[2] Wikipedia; Wikipedia's "Marriage in Islam" entry; Wikipedia's entry on Marriage in Islam.
[3] Wikipedia.
[4] Qur'an 24:32-33.
[5] Qu'ran 4:34.
[6] Qu'ran 4:4.
[7] Tirmidhi Hadith 3096.
[8] Halal: sanctioned by Islamic law. Source: *Merriam-Webster.com Dictionary*, s.v. "halal," accessed January 30, 2022, merriam-webster.com/dictionary/halal.
[9] Qu'ran 4:19.
[10] Qu'ran 4:128.
[11] Qu'ran 4:35.
[12] Endogamy: marriage within a specific group as required by custom or law. Source: *Merriam-Webster.com Dictionary*, s.v. "endogamy," accessed June 26, 2022, merriam-webster.com/dictionary/endogamy.
[13] Countries and Their Cultures, "Yemen.".
[14] Sharia law: "Islamic law based on the Koran," Source: *Merriam-Webster.com Dictionary*, s.v. "sharia," accessed January 30, 2022, merriam-webster.com/dictionary/sharia.
[15] Countries and Their Cultures, "Yemen."
[16] Countries and Their Cultures.

XX

[1] John F. Kennedy Presidential Library and Museum, *Historic Speeches*, "Televised Address to the Nation on Civil Rights."

XXI

[1] TOEFL is the Test of English as a Foreign Language—an internationally-recognized standardized test used to measure the English language proficiency of those whose first language is not English. It is mainly used by universities. Most US and Canadian universities require students whose first language is not English to have a TOEFL score of at least 550 or 600. A score above 600 is considered excellent.
[2] 1 Kings 11:3.
[3] Mohammad Golam Sarwar, "What Does the Quran Say Regarding Polygamy?"
[4] "Is Polygamy Allowed in Islam?" *Al Islam*.
[5] "Is Polygamy Allowed in Islam?"
[6] Qur'an 4:3.
[7] "Is Polygamy Allowed in Islam?" *Al Islam*.
[8] Nasim Rehmatullah, "Significance of Number Four."

XXII

[1] My time in the US, including a detailed account of why I had to return to Yemen, is found in Volume Three.
[2] Unification took place in 1990.
[3] The Immigration and Naturalization Service—a former agency of the US Department of Justice. "The INS administered federal immigration laws and regulations …. Its officers inspected foreigners arriving at an official Port of Entry (POE), detecting and deterring illegal entry between the ports (with the assistance of the Border Patrol, a component of the INS) and by sea, and conducting investigations of criminal and administrative violations…. The INS also adjudicated applications for permanent residency ("green cards"), change of status, naturalization (the process by which an alien [foreign-born person] becomes a citizen), and similar matters." Source: Wikipedia; Wikipedia's "Immigration and Naturalization Service" entry; Wikipedia's entry on the US Immigration and Naturalization Service.

XXIII

[1] Wikipedia; Wikipedia's "Wahhabism" entry; Wikipedia's entry on Wahhabism.
[2] Norma was the woman who took me under her wing immediately upon my arrival in the US and treated me as her adopted son the eight years that I

Endnotes

lived in the US. Rich (Richard) was one of my managers at the last job I had before I left the US.

XXIV

[1] Qur'an, 4:43.
[2] Qur'an, 5:90.
[3] Qur'an, 2:219.
[4] Zaufishan, "Why Muslims Don't Drink Alcohol."
[5] Wikipedia; Wikipedia's "Khamr" entry; Wikipedia's entry on Khamr.

XXVI

[1] Wikipedia; Wikipedia's "Socotra" entry; Wikipedia's entry on Socotra.
[2] Wikipedia.
[3] Wikipedia.
[4] Speleology: the scientific study or exploration of caves. Source: *Merriam-Webster.com Dictionary*, s.v. "speleology," accessed June 26, 2022, merriam-webster.com/dictionary/speleology.
[5] Wikipedia; Wikipedia's "Socotra" entry; Wikipedia's entry on Socotra.
[6] Wikipedia.
[7] Wikipedia.
[8] Summerland Hotel, "Socotra History (Socotra Island)."
[9] Wikipedia; Wikipedia's "Socotra" entry; Wikipedia's entry on Socotra.

XXVII

[1] Jihad: a holy war waged on behalf of Islam as a religious duty. Source: *Merriam-Webster.com Dictionary*, s.v. "jihad," accessed June 26, 2022, merriam-webster.com/dictionary/jihad.
[2] "Yemen: One of the Worst Places in the World to Be a Woman," *Amnesty International*.

XXVIII

[1] For more information: wikipedia.org/wiki/Yemen_Times.
[2] For more information: wikipedia.org/wiki/Abdulaziz_Al-Saqqaf.
[3] This article can be found in Appendix One.
[1] Adel Ben-Harhara, "Qat is a Drug and Most Yemenis are Addicted to It!"
[2] Wikipedia; Wikipedia's "Abdulaziz Al-Saqqaf" entry; Wikipedia's entry on Abdulaziz Al-Saqqaf.

XXX

[1] IMF—the International Monetary Fund: "The International Monetary Fund (IMF) is an organization of 190 countries, working to foster global monetary cooperation, secure financial stability, facilitate international trade, promote high employment and sustainable economic growth, and reduce poverty around the world." Source: "About the IMF," *International Monetary Fund*.

XXIII

[2] David Steinman, "Ethiopia's Cruel Con Game."
[1] "How Express Entry Works," Government of Canada.

Glossary

[1] Wikipedia; Wikipedia's "Ād" entry; Wikipedia's entry on the Ād tribe.
[2] Wikipedia; Wikipedia's "Gushl" entry; Wikipedia's entry on Gushl.

Appendix One

[1] When I was working in the US, my colleagues used to call me Pascal because computer programming language was something I was good at.

Appendix Two

[1] Wikipedia; Wikipedia's "South Arabia" entry; Wikipedia's entry on South Arabia.
[2] Wikipedia; Wikipedia's "Himyarite Kingdom" entry; Wikipedia's entry on the Himyarite_Kingdom.
[3] Wikipedia.
[4] Wikipedia.
[5] Wikipedia.
[6] Wikipedia.
[7] Wikipedia.
[8] "Southern Arabia," Nabataea.net, 2020.

Endnotes

Appendix Three

1. Yoel Natan, *Moon-o-theism: Religion of a War and Moon God Prophet, Volume I of II.*

Appendix Four

1. Wikipedia; Wikipedia's "Yafa" entry; Wikipedia's entry on Yafa.
2. Wikipedia; Wikipedia's "Upper Yafa" entry; Wikipedia's entry on Upper Yafa.
3. Wikipedia; Wikipedia's "Qu'aiti" entry; Wikipedia's entry on Qu'aiti.
4. Passage to Yafa' (1891-1967), Vol 15, 2007, The British-Yemeni Society.
5. The translation for this was done by Nesma Abdalaziz.
6. Hood was located in the same general area as Marib.
7. Al-Muhajiba: a port town on the southeast coast of Yemen.
8. Dhul-Q'adah is the eleventh month of the Islamic or Hijri calendar, which is a lunar calendar. Source: "AskIslampedia: Dhul-Quadah."
9. The year 1113 in the Hijri calendar equates to 1702 in the Gregorian calendar. For more information: habibur.com/hijri/1113/.
10. Al-Bayda: a town 130 miles or 210 kilometers southeast of Sana'a.
11. Al-Awlaq: a land east of Yafa.
12. Bahran village: twenty-four kilometers (fifteen miles) east of Sana'a.
13. Dhofar: a mountain range in the southeastern Arabian Peninsula.
14. Qibla: in the direction of Mecca.
15. Muharram: the first month of the Islamic calendar, one of the four sacred months when war is forbidden. Source: Wikipedia; Wikipedia's "Muharram" entry; Wikipedia's entry on Muharram.

Appendix Five

1. Qur'an 27:23.
2. 1 Kings 10:10.
3. TFF, "In Islam and the Qur'an: The Queen of Sheba."
4. Wikipedia; Wikipedia's "Marib" entry; Wikipedia's entry on Marib.
5. TFF, "In Islam and the Qur'an: The Queen of Sheba."
6. "Ma'rib—Capital of the Kingdom of Saba," *Heritage Daily.*
7. Kaushik Patowary, "The Collapse of the Marib Dam and the Fall of an Empire."
8. Wikipedia; Wikipedia's "Marib" entry; Wikipedia's entry on Marib.
9. Kaushik Patowary, "The Collapse of the Marib Dam and the Fall of an Empire."

www.ingramcontent.com/pod-product-compliance
Lightning Source LLC
Chambersburg PA
CBHW021838110526
R18278500001B/R182785PG44590CBX00001B/1